# Addiction

## What I Wish I Could Tell My Father

by

Denver J. Hamilton

Published by
Brain Bucket Publishing
brainbucketpublishing@gmail.com
denverjhamilton@yahoo.com

This is a conceivable work of non-fiction. Names, characters, places, and incidents are the product of the author's imagination or his recollections. Any resemblance to actual persons, living or dead, events, or locales is possible.

ISBN: 979-8-9875136-0-6 (print)
ISBN: 979-8-9875136-1-3 (ebook)

# Table of Contents

# Acknowledgments

Thank you, Gene, Betty, and Shannon. While I hope you never read this book, I want you to know how much it has helped me to write it. You have all given me a great life. I'm sorry that this book only explores the worst aspects of our life together. I look forward to applying what I've learned during this process to improve our relationships.

Thank you, Pepper and Jade. You both have already taught me more than I'll ever teach you. Life is full of exciting opportunities, but it is also filled with distractions. To be successful, you must find a way to tell them apart. I will never be angry with you for making mistakes. I expect you to make many. I will only ever be disappointed if you fail to learn from them.

Daphne, I owe you everything. You not only breathed new life into me, but you brought our children into this world and raised them to be shockingly creative, extraordinarily intelligent, and fiercely independent. I love you all more than anything in the world. This book wouldn't exist without you for so many reasons. I am dedicated to taking advantage of every opportunity your love has granted me. I am excited to live the next chapters of our life together.

Thank you, Will and Ruby, for your guidance, acceptance, and unwavering support.

Thank you, Ronnie and Margy Thrash, for your friendship and for providing feedback on this book.

Finally, thank you to anyone taking the time to read this story. I hope it opens the door to exploring your own perceptions and helps you find the peace I found in writing it.

# Introduction: Chapter 1

I have wanted to talk to you about my addiction and recovery for years, but I've never known how to do it. I've written music, painted, drawn comics, and even requested to sit down and talk in person. It's never worked out for one reason or another, but it hasn't stopped me from having the conversation in my head almost every day for the past four years.

When I have these conversations, it's mostly me talking to you and explaining myself. I have an expectation of what I think you'll say and how you'll react. I have this romantic idea that you'll understand me better after we talk, and our relationship will improve. The conversation in my head always goes well. When we meet in person, I try to share my story with you, but the scenario never goes how I've played it out in my head, and then I stop sharing. When I return home, I go back to telling my story in my head to my "expectation-you," but I change how I say certain things hoping for a better outcome.

In this new conversation scenario, I avoid the things that offended you. Maybe if I make it funnier, you'll be less guarded. You won't become defensive so quickly, and I can tell you how I feel. Again, the mental play goes unrealistically well, and I get excited about having the conversation with you next time. We get together, and I start cracking some jokes, but you don't laugh. You're preoccupied with traffic. You're stressed out about the guy at the Airport Passenger Pickup Station who keeps motioning you to move on. We've been together only five minutes, and you've already snapped at me. I consider how you would react if I were my older brother. I think to myself, "He never talks to my brother like this. Does he have more patience for him? This is not how our conversation went in my head; I'm not talking to him about it this time either."

A week later, I'm commuting to work and having the conversation in my head again. This time, I know humor won't work. Maybe I should write this down in a long letter. You can read it or not read it.

You'll have whatever reaction you're going to have, but it doesn't have to ruin a family vacation. I don't have to be the downer. If you get angry, it doesn't have to be weird. I don't have to try and separate you from my stepmom so I can talk to you privately. I won't get annoyed with her not picking up on social cues. She won't get her feelings hurt that I'm obviously trying to exclude her. Maybe I can write it down, publish it, and never tell you about it. Then I can leave it up to the universe, and perhaps someday, you'll come across it.

There exists the possibility that you do want to talk to me about all of this. For all I know, you could be searching bookstores for advice on approaching your alcoholic son who seems distant. You're finding new ways to reach out to a son that seems to shut down every time you get together and is rude to your wife for some reason. Every time you get together with him and you've planned to have that conversation, you get frustrated with how he seems "checked out," and it's just not a great time to have the conversation. Not now, not during a family vacation. Maybe you'll come across this book and read it, and our relationship will improve. Perhaps, like all my internal conversations, this will go really well.

# Dad: Chapter 2

## Part 1: Arm of the Chair

As an artist, I'm always searching for two things. First and foremost, I want to express myself. Secondly, I strive for that expression to be enjoyed. Now, "enjoyed" might not be the correct term. If I create something to express my sadness and make you feel sad, it's fair to assume there wouldn't be much enjoyment in that experience. The purpose of art is to give rise to emotion. The process can still be appreciated even when subjected to difficult emotions. If the art gives rise to the emotion I intended for you to feel, then I will have successfully expressed myself. The hope is that you will also find some value in that. In my experience, it is frustratingly difficult to express yourself *and* have it be something people like.

I've considered using my art to tell you everything I wish I could say. I could put it all down into a song I know you would like; it would be easy to make. I could create your personalized formula by just taking a collection of songs you enjoy and then mash them against the clichés of your favorite genres. That also happens to be my issue with pop music. With all these streaming services using algorithms to collect data on what we like and monitor our listening habits, the industry has the formula for what is the most common denominator, musically. You plug the formula into the big, bloated music machine, and it spits out a pop song. You give that song to a pretty person, and then radio stations everywhere play it to death without anyone expressing anything.

For your song, I would start with a simple drumbeat, "a boom tet, boom tet." A rhythmically nauseating beat like a country ballad or an alternative pop-type drum with a chord progression made of all majors. Then the lyrics would have to be narratively clever. Each verse leads you in a specific direction, but their meaning is relatively vague. Once the chorus comes in, it catches you off guard as it gives new subtext to the song as a whole—a clever Shyamalanian twist with the right mix of whimsical and cheeky.

The process, at some point, begins to feel almost manipulative. I could trick you into liking what I have to say. Really, I've only managed to trick myself into thinking you liked what I had to say when you just appreciated the song. I've essentially wrapped my trauma in a pretty package that I'm giving to you as a gift. At the end of the day, there's nothing enjoyable about the process of unwrapping one's trauma and likely nothing worse than reducing one's trauma into a catchy little tune.

This insatiable desire to be understood and liked isn't confined to just my art. Unfortunately, every aspect of my life is dictated by the premise that I must be understood and liked. My art is to my emotional insecurity as the chicken is to the egg. I do not do well without constant reassurance of this understanding and general knowledge of my level of likability. I am also fully aware that this character flaw is sometimes hard to understand and incredibly unlikeable.

This is all to say that I may never be ready to share my story with you because I'm too afraid you won't understand. I'm piss-scared of sharing my journey with you because of all my failures and lies of omission. I would like to maintain a certain level of your trust and acceptance. Our relationship, as it is currently, feels without understanding. I struggle with the concern that you don't enjoy my company. I am plagued by the idea that I cannot reach self-actualization unless you fully understand me. In this paradigm, with your understanding of me comes your enjoyment of whom I have become as a man on the other side of addiction.

As the years have passed, I've come to understand that *how* I share my story does not matter. I'm never going to be wholly understood, and irrespective of the medium I choose to share it in, you're not going to like it. I've now begun to ask myself why I want to share this story with you so badly. Why am I so obsessed with talking to you about this if I know I'm not going to get what I so desperately need out of it? For one, sharing this story with you will provide a sense of closure for me. I have moved through my addiction, processed the fallout, and am now looking for an end-cap to that chapter of my life. I can only get that from someone who was there for it all, or at a minimum, I'll feel like I've made some progress once I can talk about it openly with my father. Secondly, there's always this romantic idea that if I explain it all, you will stop thinking of me as having been a failure. Instead, you'll see that I achieved great success after overcoming significant hardship. To know I am the author of a success story, not a tragedy.

When thinking of where to begin, your divorce from my mother is where the timeline always starts for me. This was a drastic change in our lives, but I underestimated how much things would change. Initially, the divorce wasn't that big of a deal for me. My parents just lived on different sides of town, and you were both overly nice about everything. I was too young to understand what was happening, and nobody would tell me, but I knew it wasn't good. When you finally divorced, I had seen it coming, so I was understandably indifferent to it all. As I got older, my brother would tell me what he thought had happened and how bad the rumors around town were getting. Had I known then what I know now, I wouldn't have been so blindsided about why you would want to move 1,400 miles away to Texas.

Moving to Texas was very exciting. I knew they had football, tornados, a high cowboy-to-not cowboy ratio, and people would recklessly shoot pistols in the air to add emphasis during a conversation. I didn't want to leave Montana, but there was a level of mystery and excitement associated with going somewhere with a potential future, whereas Montana did not. I hadn't yet calculated how much I would miss my mom, brother, cousins, and all my friends. You were the only person I had when we moved because we didn't know anyone there. You were not only busy at work, but you were also a newly single man on the opposite side of an ugly divorce. You rarely seemed fully engaged with me at home. It felt like I had lost everyone, and I was alone.

All the people in my life had filled specific roles, so I had everything I needed. When it was just us, you had to fill every one of those roles. I don't blame you for not being able to do it; I'm not sure it was even possible. One of those unfilled roles was my mother's emotional and affectional role, which is often traditionally difficult for an old-school father to fulfill.

We had a sectional couch facing the TV, where we would sit and eat practically every meal. You sat on the right side of the couch, and to your left was a hideaway table with built-in cup holders that would fold down. Every night we would sit down on opposite sides of that table and watch Jerry Springer. I wanted to sit next to you, like physically up against you. I wasn't looking to cuddle or sit in your lap or anything, but sitting next to you made me feel more connected to you. I remember the last time I attempted to sit up against you. It was dinnertime, and you were beginning your nightly routine after getting home from work.

You had that tired look on your face, one I now recognize as the face one dawns after a long, stressful day at work. You made yourself a bowl of cereal, sat on the couch, and turned on the TV. I don't know if I was as stressed as you were, but I was certainly going through it too. I had made friends, but I had also established myself as a weird kid at school and wasn't exactly fitting in. I was a skateboarder that listened to punk rock and dressed like an 80-year-old golfer in a town full of good ol' boys who wore Wranglers with dirty boots. I needed to sit with you; I knew it would make me feel better. To feel that connection with someone in a world where it felt like I had no one. I couldn't fold up the hideaway table because you were using it, so I decided I would just sit on the arm of the couch on your right side. I walked over to you and leaned against the arm in an awkward attempt to be with you. I wanted to put my arm around you, make some small talk, and get your attention away from the TV. I hadn't planned anything, but I knew what I was after. As soon as I got close to you, you jabbed your elbow into my hip and pushed me off the arm of the chair. Without looking away from the TV, you said, "Don't sit on the couch like that."

I don't know if it was the coldness of how you said it or that you didn't look up to see the pain in my face, but my kid brain started to fit some things together. This felt like the last straw to me. I began having thoughts like, "He cares more about this couch than he does me," and, "Fine, I'll never try it again." As I entered a sort of survival mode, my perception of the world and my expectations of you changed. I decided at that moment that I was alone, and everything I needed, I would have to get for myself. I was getting to and from school, preparing my own meals, and following all your rules. Now it felt like you had broken some unwritten contract with me. I wasn't going to listen to you anymore. I wasn't going to ask for permission to go anywhere, I was going to sneak out at night, and I wasn't going to help around the house anymore.

Our first fights revolved around the laundry. You would wash my clothes, fold them for me, and then leave them on the sofa in the living room. All I had to do was bring it to my room and put it away, but I would leave it on the couch for weeks, only grabbing the things I wanted to wear that day. We would fight about it constantly. You'd come home from work with that tired look on your face and go into an immediate rage at the sight of my clothes, once neatly stacked, now disheveled on the couch where you had left them.

You thought I was so disrespectful because I wouldn't do what you said. I was expected to obey because you were the father, but I decided you couldn't be my dad and not be my dad at the times of your choosing. You assumed my abrupt change in attitude was due to me becoming a teenager, a convenient excuse most parents use when they stop understanding their kids. By not checking in with me, the first branch of the multiverse was created, and we headed down the difficult path that has led us here. The contract had been broken, and my behavior would only get more extreme. Like the flip of a switch, I was only ever going to do defiant asshole-type shit.

This is also around the time when my mom was going through her phase of trying to rectify her behavior that led to divorce and the subsequent loss of her children. She was spreading rumors about your role in it and making my brother and me out to be ungrateful pricks that abandoned her. I was struggling at school academically but also socially. I embraced the aspects of my personality that made me different and strived for uniqueness. While I found my clique in high school, I also found the shit-kickers and jocks who quickly became our sworn enemies. While I may not have had as many responsibilities as you or even some of my peers, I wasn't exactly living a stress-free life, and I definitely wasn't happy.

I found that happiness one weekend when my friend Grimy invited me to his party. Well, it wasn't his party; it was his brother's. Okay, it wasn't exactly a party. His brother was coming home from college, and some of his friends were coming over to drink beer. To us, at thirteen years old, it was a party, and we were invited.

# Part 2: Corndogs

You dropped me off at Grimy's, and the night started like any other. We played NBA Jam in his room with the door closed. Had it not been offered, I'm not sure either of us would have mustered the courage to get the beer for ourselves, but his brother eventually brought us four Budweisers hanging connected to a six-pack ring. He tossed it onto the bed behind us while standing in the doorway. He closed the door and left Grimy and me holding the Super Nintendo controllers representing our childhood, only 6 feet away from the beers that would make us men.

The taste was awful; bubbly like a soda, but it wasn't sweet. It was hard to imagine that beer was supposed to taste like that or that we hadn't been given ones that had gone bad. I took another large gulp of the fizzy bitterness and felt rebellious. I knew I was doing something other kids my age wouldn't dare, and I felt like I was conquering some life peak. We would be the first in our grade to plant the flag on Mount Beer. At thirteen, there is no subtle transition from talkative buzz to lovey-dovey drunk. If we were drunk halfway through the first beer, we were annihilated by the end of the second. We were not only suddenly hungry for food but also brave enough and, in our minds at least, now cool enough to hang out with his brother and his friends.

At first, Grimy's brother was amused by our attempts to play it cool. My world was already beginning to spin, and I suddenly had to pee. The drunken brain tends to regress to simpler times, and tasks like peeing become acceptable in public areas. I made my way to the corner of the backyard and unzipped my pants with great effort. I adopted a wide stance and pushed my hips as far forward as I could while getting my eyes close enough to my work so that I could figure out the zipper. Once I had freed myself, I supported my weight with one arm against the tall wooden fence and began to relax. I peed like I hadn't peed in days, and a shiver ran up my spine just as Grimy's dog ran in front of my stream to investigate the splashing sounds I was making in the grass. My urine splashed violently against the back of his dog's head, for my reaction time had been slowed by the barely two beers I drank. We were quickly escorted back to Grimy's room and given the most glorious tasting corndogs I have ever tasted. I may never be entirely sure, but I believe they may have been sausage corndogs wrapped in pancake batter. My gut tells me they were probably just regular corndogs.

You picked me up the next day around mid-morning, and I wasn't worried in the least that you'd know what happened. I jumped up from the couch as soon as I heard you honk the horn out front, and then I high-fived Grimy after promising to drink again as soon as possible. I climbed into the truck, and you asked me how it went. "Fine," I said vaguely.

"What did you guys do?" you asked as we pulled away from the curb.

I noticed you were looking at me with intent. It wasn't a look of being genuinely curious about the video games we played. It looked like you knew something was up. "Nothing. Just played games." I looked out the passenger window, hoping we could stop talking about it.

"Did you guys drink?"

*What the fuck?! This is insane. How?! There's no way. This is a test, but why would he test me? It was just Grimy and me; why would he suspect we would drink? How could we even get it? This is definitely a test.*

I semi-confidently straightened up in the chair and said, "No."
"You smell like beer."

*No way. Is that a thing?! Can you smell beer on people after they drink? This has got to be a test; he's just trying to see how I react to it. I must overreact and seem offended that he would even question me.*

"Dad! Why would you even think that? It was just Grimy and me. How would we even get beers? Do you think we were at some crazy party last night or something? I didn't do anything wrong!"

That was it. You stopped asking, and we went to the grocery store. I tried to find sausage corndogs in pancake batter, which of course, did not exist, and life went on. I did learn a few things that day, though. For one, you must have a tremendous sense of smell to detect two beers in my sweat over the stench of an innumerable amount of corndogs. You would routinely ignore this extraordinarily acute sense of smell as I got older and continued to experiment with other things. I also learned that I was an exceptional liar. It would be nearly 15 years before I realized you were just avoiding having these uncomfortable conversations with me and that I was a terrible liar.

I sometimes wonder what would be different if we would have had a different conversation. I wouldn't have responded well if you had come down harder on me. I would have served my time and then rebelled even harder. If the conversation had focused on *why* I was starting to drink rather than just that I had drunk and broken your rules, you would have known how sad I was. You would have known I was running from my emotions and acting out for attention. Maybe we would have spent more time together, and I would have never found peace in being drunk. I would never have realized that I didn't think about my mom while drinking. I wouldn't learn that drinking meant the shit-kickers would never cross my mind, and an enormous swelling of confidence and fearlessness would replace all my self-doubts. I would never have had to learn the hard way that no matter how much you drink or for how long, it doesn't make your problems disappear. The issues always remain, but now you have to deal with them in an inebriated mental state that is poorly equipped for such things. There's no way of knowing what would be different now. All I knew after my first night of drinking was that I had gotten away with it, and from that point on, I just needed to be more careful.

My drinking was innocent enough; we would only drink when we could get it, and we rarely ever got it. I knew a few older people at the skate park that would let us have a few here and there as long as we were cool about it. As I got better on my board, these people started taking me places and feeding me more beer. It was relatively safe because we were usually at someone's house, skating a backyard ramp. When other kids my age started to drink, they were going to big keg parties and running from the police. My drinking was always associated with skating, playing music, or some form of art. This made it seem less criminal, and I learned to be a highly functional drunk.

Alcohol provides a brief window where your anxiety melts away, and you feel genuinely happy. As you develop a tolerance, it takes more alcohol to reach this level, but you can stay in that window longer. If you take the right amount, alcohol becomes the perfect medication for the depression and anxiety you have. Inevitably, you take too much of the drug and miss that window. You always miss that window as a young man out to impress his friends. The drug that once eased your pain begins to drag that pain to the surface. Those emotions you intend to hide from now come bubbling up in a confusing mess of regret, anger, and sadness. You cry in front of strangers and scream at those you love.

Imagine a dam holding back years of repressed anger finally giving way in an instant, and then imagine trying to express yourself rationally while it happens. Now you're miserable, and you've made even more mistakes. You've embarrassed yourself in front of people you care about and love. The thought of what they must think of you haunts your waking life, and the only thing that can shut it up is that small window granted to you by alcohol. "Just one drink, and then I'll feel better. I won't care about any of this, and I can feel like myself again." The self that is more social at gatherings. The self that makes people laugh, not this self. Not this miserable failure that doesn't know what he wants to do with his life while everyone around him seems so sure of themselves. You drink to silence it all, but it doesn't seem to work. You've passed the window again, this time without any enjoyment. Now the only cure is to drink until the next window, the one that blacks out.

I would go back and forth between episodes of anger for not being celebrated for my uniqueness and then bouts of depression for being too different. It wasn't until I met my wife many years later that I started to feel good about who I was and where I was in life. As a fellow artist, she loved my quirkiness. Soon the shame I felt about my desire to create rather than just be a cog in a great machine melted away, and I was again inspired. Instead of hoping to forget and feel numb, I strived to remember every detail of our nights together in raw sobriety. It made me wonder what could have been different if I didn't have so much self-doubt. Would I be more successful if I hadn't questioned who I was and what I was doing? How far would I have gone if you had been more supportive? Then, after much thought, I realized you had supported me a great deal. You let me do anything I wanted, almost to a fault. You certainly had a vague path set for me: go to college and get a job. There wasn't any real guidance on how I could pull that off in a way that would lead to my hopes and dreams. Just college, in the general sense. You made a deal with me; if I went to college, you would pay my rent. I took the deal and signed up for a random assortment of classes toward nowhere at a junior college, but my rent was paid. Even when I failed those classes, my rent was paid. I just had to go to college; nobody said I needed to do well. I could have done anything I set my mind to, and you would have let me do it. The only reason I didn't take full advantage of that opportunity was that I had low self-esteem. The success I did enjoy along the path I had set for myself felt like a failure compared to the path of expectations that were set before me. If my only criticism is that you had set vague goals for me, but I felt unconditionally supported, then whose path of expectations was I obsessed about?

I realized I needed to chew on this for a bit longer. Perhaps alcoholism is more complicated than one instance of trying to sit on the arm of a chair 25 years ago. What other factors could be at play in my alcoholism? Why did I feel so bad about myself? Why was my inner voice always so confident in the inevitability of my downfall? It finally occurred to me when I graduated with my bachelor's degree, and my brother came to watch me walk the stage.

# Brother: Chapter 3

## Part 1: Cap and Gown

I got an email from my school that my cap and gown were ready to be picked up in the main building on campus. The semester was almost over, but grades wouldn't be posted until just before or after graduation. At my current standing, I was going to pass all my classes with an A. Some of the class credits counting toward my degree were transfer courses from over eight years earlier. They were the few random courses I managed to pass but barely remember taking. I had no idea if they would use the many Fs I had accumulated toward my final grade point average. Adding that abysmal record to my grades would mean I would barely get my degree. If they only used the grades I earned recently, I'd be graduating with honors. The only part that mattered in the grand scheme was that I would graduate. These last few years had felt like two separate lifetimes, and I wanted to be recognized for whom I had become, not held back by whom I had been. Graduating with honors would be tangible proof of the distance I had created, separating my past mistakes from my future success. As I walked across campus toward graduation registration, I thought about how much it would mean if those golden ropes, designating me as summa cum laude, were sitting in the bag when I arrived.

I walked into the main hall and saw a long line weaving its way from booth to booth. There were neatly sorted piles of alumni swag like pens and license plate decals. It all seemed rather silly, but if this is what tuition was paying for, I would use those pens until they ran dry. As we circled the room, I could see the rack of caps and gowns toward the end of the line, looming like a dark cloud about to rain on everything I had worked so hard to accomplish. If my cap and gown didn't have honors ropes, I might as well walk with a giant dunce cap. A feeling I'd later learn was the people-pleasing mentality that I had previously coped with by drinking excessively. Now that I was sober, I had merely replaced one addiction for another and was now attempting to cope with my insecurities through perfectionism. I continued to accept each congratulatory swag bag with a smile. Still, my anxiety was increasing with each step closer to the last booth and the final decision that would determine my honorary status or not.

"Name?" a short brunette woman asked without looking up from her clipboard. She was chewing gum that I imagined had also lost its flavor several years ago. I began picturing her in the candy aisle of the Qwik-N-Go, scanning the wall of different gum flavors before ultimately deciding on the Arctic Mountain Blast. She would take her new prize to the counter, pay, and then put the same piece she was now chewing in her mouth before she could even hit the door to leave.

The cool mint flavor was refreshing, and the texture was soft and chewy. She liked it so much that she would chew on it until lunch. She would take it out of her mouth and fold it into the original wrapper. After lunch, she would continue munching on the piece she had started with. It still had some flavor left, but the texture was becoming less chewy, replaced with a bit of tough resistance. By the time dinner rolled around, she would be relieved to take it out of her mouth; after all, she had been chewing the same piece all day. She would finish her meal, brush her teeth, and go to sleep.

The following day she would wake up and start getting ready for work, but then inexplicably, she would put that same piece of gum back in her mouth. It now tasted more like her own spit than it did an ice-capped mountain, and the blue coloring of the gum wrapper was beginning to flake off. She would place her gum in a small plastic container. It wouldn't do anything for the flavor or the texture, but she would feel like she had done something nice for herself. As days passed, chewing the gum would become routine. She had completely forgotten what it initially tasted like, chewing only to chew as the experience had become devoid of all joy. A shiver ran up my spine as I wondered how long I would have until my new career would start to feel the same way.

I shook my head and blinked several times, bringing myself out of thought and back to her question. "Denver Hamilton," I said, and then I spelled my last name for her slowly, "H.A.M.I.L.T.O.N." She started thumbing through her clipboard of names, and my mind began to wander again. I was weeks away from you and my brother watching me walk across the stage to accept my bachelor's degree, and I would finally be welcomed as being like you both. I would no longer be just the little brother or the baby of the family; I would be a successful man. That's why I couldn't graduate in a dunce cap; I had to have a 4.0. I had to remove all doubt about the validity of my degree and prove that I hadn't just slipped through the cracks here. I had to be at the top of my class. This was atonement for years of drug abuse and spiritual wandering. Without those damned ropes, I would still be tied to my past and feel like a failure by some measure. I would achieve this great honor, and through it, I would grow out of the shadow cast by my brother and all of his success.

As the gum lady continued slowly tracing the names on the clipboard with her finger looking for my name, a brief memory crossed my mind of something my brother said to me when I was younger. We were playing H.O.R.S.E. in the driveway of our childhood home. We were standing under the basketball hoop, the one he had painted the words "Shannon's House of Pain" across the backboard in blue spray paint. He had just beaten me by shooting the ball over the back of the backboard from the yard. He caught my errant shot before it could bounce down the hill, and then he tucked the ball under his right arm and stood over me. At the time, he was 18 years old, so beating a nine-year-old so soundly shouldn't have come as much of a surprise. He routinely enjoyed reminding me, "You will never be as good as me at anything you ever do." Perhaps this was just the kind of shit-talking that went down at Shannon's House of Pain, but those words burrowed their way deep into my medial prefrontal cortex and began defecating on all the neurons that lived there. Those words would sometimes act as a motivating force, but more often than not, they would encourage me to give up when it looked like I might fail.

I idolized my brother. Since he was so much older than I was, he was, in some ways, more of a second father figure than a traditional brother closer in age might have been. I copied everything about him, down to how he would alternate black low-cut Nike socks over white mid-calf Nike socks. Even to this day, if you look at our handwriting, it looks nearly identical. I'm sure it was annoying from his perspective that I had become a tiny carbon copy of him and wanted to follow in every footstep he would ever take.

My brother was a surprisingly decent artist who liked to doodle little cartoon characters. I would take his doodles and redraw them thousands of times. Eventually, you couldn't tell the difference between his drawings and mine. I branched out and started looking for my own things to draw. I bought all the *How to Draw* books at every book fair the school ever held. I also drew every character from every *MAD* magazine we had boxed in the basement. I remember Shannon was furious when he found out I was using the magazines because they were a part of a collection handed down to him by our family friend, and I had folded the back covers and stressed the spines. After finishing all of the magazines, I had essentially taken a master's class in how to draw.

I had incorporated hundreds of styles across different media and was making original creations. My brother didn't share the same enthusiasm for my newly acquired talent. As it became apparent that I was getting better than he was, he stopped drawing. He would tell me that drawing was a waste of time and that I was stupid for spending so much time on it. He stopped drawing altogether, and if you asked him today, he would tell you he couldn't even draw a stick figure. He would rather never lift another pencil in his life than admit I had gotten good at something. To be clear, it wasn't just that I had gotten good at it; I was better at it than he was. He rationalized that I was only better at it because he didn't draw anymore.

Mind you, this was coming from someone I viewed as the most extraordinary person alive. His opinion of me meant everything, and I was now torn between the thing I had learned to love and the validation I sought from my brother. I was confused about how something he had taught me to love had become a stupid waste of time. I started to feel highly conflicted as I went through stages of feeling proud that I could do something he couldn't, but then back to a sense of shame for having wasted my time getting good at something nobody cared about.

I remember dealing with these feelings while we were still adjusting to life in Texas. I went into my art supplies and noticed all my drawings were gone. On a poster-sized piece of paper, I had drawn the entire city of Springfield with every character I could remember from the Simpsons. I had stacks of celebrity caricatures and weird mashups of cartoon characters drawn in the style of different production companies, like Bugs Bunny, if drawn by Hanna-Barbera. Several years of my favorite drawings were all missing. I later discovered that you had thrown them away and didn't even realize what they were. You likely thought of them as a mess I hadn't cleaned up. Between my brother telling me drawing was a waste of time and you confirming my art was just trash, I stopped drawing every day.

My search for meaning quickly dissolved into an existential crisis as I bong-ripped my way through high school. I hated school so much that I graduated a year early. I was immediately confronted with navigating the complexities of adulthood, freedom versus responsibility. I would continually struggle to find the correct balance between the two. I would slip further into addiction as more time passed between finishing high school and achieving the vagueness of successful adulthood. I signed up for business administration classes, thinking they would teach me how to own a skate shop, but nothing I was learning seemed applicable. I stopped going and failed every class that semester.

I had a friend, Rose, who was vacationing to Costa Rica for a few weeks and was paying for the trip herself. She bought a condominium, fixed it up, and sold it. She made thousands of dollars in profit, which she put into her next property. Any amount remaining she would pay toward her vacations. I decided then and there that I would go to school for real estate. I knew nothing about it, didn't look like a professional, and couldn't imagine anyone buying a home from me, but I did like the idea of making lots of money and going to Costa Rica.

That upcoming semester I signed up for a full helping of real estate classes and started mentally spending all the money I hadn't yet made. That dream lasted less than a week. Those classes were full of the driest, most repellently boring material I'd ever read. It was academic torture. I considered dropping all my courses, but you'd stop paying my rent if I did. If I just failed them, on the other hand, it would buy me the semester to formulate a plan. There was, however, one class in particular that I continued attending. I had sat next to a pretty girl who was into rock-n-roll, and she dressed the part.

# PART 2: STORAGE SHEDS AND WHISKEY

Her name was Megan, and she lived with her brother and a couple of their friends nearby. She referred to their home as the band house because they had a band, and the living room was where they jammed. They were in need of a vocalist, and she invited me over to audition. Now, I'm as much of a vocalist as anyone who can blow air out of their mouth is a harmonica player. I can make noises, but the verdict is out on whether or not it can be considered singing. At the time, I prided myself on my ability to play guitar, but I had a few songs with lyrics, so I figured I'd give the audition a shot.

Megan introduced me to my future best friend Dean, she introduced me to the band Muse, and she showed me what a night of cocaine was like. Walking out of a strip club after a night of binge snorting and being surprised by the mid-morning sun will always remind me of Megan. I had amassed a grade point average of 0.25 and was officially on academic probation by the end of the semester. I couldn't possibly care any less because the band was doing well. We called ourselves Scoundrel Pop and played a sort of jazz-funk fusion. It was fueled by psychoactives, and it remains one of the greatest bands I've ever played in. The scales had tipped entirely to the side of adulthood freedom as I continually ignored all my responsibilities.

Unfortunately, I was the only one in the band who was ignoring their responsibilities. Our guitar player earned his bachelor's and was headed to graduate school out of state. He was dating our drummer, so she left with him. A few weeks later, our bassist and my best friend, Dean, invited me to a night of depravity at the Renaissance Faire. We showed up just as the Faire was closing. All the characters and patrons were building their camps for the night, and we found a spot for our tent near a group of seasoned veterans.

We mixed hard drugs with home-brewed bathtub mead and walked around in the dark. It's easier to distinguish reality from hallucination when you're in the safety of your own home, but we were surrounded by fat minotaurs and sparkly river fairies. Luckily, I was with my closest friend at the time, so coming face to face with a demon in the flickering light of a bonfire can still be fun. Dean seemed distant the entire night, and it wasn't until the mead ran out that he decided to tell me he was moving to Iowa in the morning. He didn't want to sour what would be our last night together by telling me, but his mind kept returning to a feeling that his current chapter here was going to end that night.

His relationship with his girlfriend had fallen apart, and he cried about her every time something reminded him of her. She was a crystal-gripping hippie, and every pixie that walked by us made him start sobbing. I eventually broke away from our camp and tried to get lost in the night. My increasingly sour attitude made the overstimulating barrage of renaissance creatures impossible to deal with. By some miracle, I found the parking lot and slept in my car. I didn't even look for Dean in the morning. He was supposed to catch the Greyhound early, and I wasn't interested in extending our awkward goodbye.

My relationship with Megan had already soured as I spent more and more of the day intoxicated, pretending to be Jim Morrison. Before I knew it, the band house was empty, and I was alone. The drugs and alcohol that fueled creative nights behind an instrument were now just lonely nights curled around a cold porcelain toilet, wondering where I'd go next.

This is the risk one takes when adulthood freedom and responsibility are unbalanced. That was why you and my brother wanted me to do something else. It was a more guaranteed long-term success if I followed a more realistic career path. My depression roared back as I became overburdened with the weight of my ignored responsibility and the realization that both of you were right. I was depressed that I had ignored your advice, done it my way, and failed exactly as predicted. To make matters worse, I was also now addicted to drugs.

You had moved to the corporate offices in Texas, and I moved back with you to get clean. You didn't know any of this, of course. All you knew was that I was failing my classes, and you were pissed that I had no direction. I started playing open mic nights in the city, trying to meet other musicians and get another band started. My performances garnered local attention, and I managed to headline a concert as a solo performer. A few popular bands were opening for me, and I was enjoying the company of everyone that had come out to support us. I had an open tab at the venue's bar, and I drank straight whiskey for three hours, waiting for my turn to take the stage. The bartender had cut me off by the time my set started, and I blacked out halfway through the first song. I don't remember the rest of the night, but I'm told it did not go well. I stopped getting gigs after that and had to go back to the open mic circuit.

After embarrassing myself on the whiskey night, I took the music more seriously. I put together a solid thirty-minute set of interesting compositions. I was pushing my limits of technicality and creative writing. I worked hard on the set and was looking forward to sharing it with people. I don't invite anyone to open mics, the entire event is somewhat embarrassing, but this particular evening I had invited loads of people. I wanted to showcase the new stuff, win back some support from the community, and get on to playing real shows again.

The night before the open mic, you asked me to pick you up from the airport at 8 p.m., right in the middle of the set I had planned. I told you I couldn't do it and explained I would be playing a show I had worked on obsessively for weeks. I was relatively certain we had clarified that I would, most definitely, not be picking you up.

The show was terrific, I was sober, and I nailed every little trick I planned. There were guitar loops that required precise timing, or the rhythms would quickly break down into nonsensical noise, but they all hit right on cue. I had bent the circuits in a few small toys, manipulating the sounds they could make, and had them running through the pickups of my guitar. Those who didn't like the music I played that night were still intrigued by the artistic performance. Curious people swarmed me for the rest of the night, and I felt like I was in heaven. I also noted that I had several missed calls from you.

I finally broke away from the crowd and checked my phone. Your voicemails started with, "Hey D, just landed. Where are you?" The messages got angrier and the attacks more personal as you waited longer, "You ungrateful little shit. All I asked of you was to pick me up..." etcetera, etcetera. The high I was riding quickly faded, and I coped with it the only way I knew. I went to the venue's bar and ordered a glass of whiskey on ice. Seeing the drink in my hand disappointed everyone who came out that night to support me in turning a new leaf.

I decided I'd be out of your house before you even woke up the next day. I left a note apologizing for not being there. I attempted to clarify that I thought you were aware of my plans and knew I wouldn't be there. I packed my things and left. I didn't have much money, but I had enough to rent a storage shed. As Scoundrel Pop was dissolving and the members were moving out of the house, we had a short stint in one of these storage sheds. I asked the manager if that unit was still available, and, as luck would have it, it was. It was almost poetic, coming back to this place like it held some energy from the life I longed for, but all that was left was the faded Scoundrel Pop chalk art we had drawn on the back of the wall. I sat in my new home, looking at the faded rainbow of remaining art. It was cold, and everything smelled like dirt. I had a mattress in one corner, a T.V. with built-in VHS, an empty bottle of tequila rose, and a bunch of random instruments. The scale was no longer tilted, finally balanced, with no freedom or responsibility.

I got a respiratory infection by the second night, and as I slowly died, I wondered how long it would take management to check my unit. Maybe it would take a month when the rent was due, and they were coming to throw away the things I had abandoned. How appropriate it would be that I'd be found amongst all those forgotten things.

The storage shed wasn't all that bad, if I'm being honest. There were plenty of times we had not gotten along and I sought shelter elsewhere. Usually, I had a friend's couch or a nice lady I could stay with, but the stress of intruding on people led me to find more creative places to sleep while only needing to borrow a quick shower. The most reliable spot I found was the Chemical Engineering Building on campus. There was an unlocked entrance in the basement that would lead to the upper floors. The third floor was the darkest, and it had flat upholstered couches. I would take just a pillow and blanket with me. I'd leave all my valuables in the car, but getting robbed seemed unlikely. Most people didn't know how to get to the basement entrance, and anyone who saw me inside would assume I was a stressed-out, hardworking engineering major. The storage shed seemed comfortably luxurious in comparison.

I had been in the shed for a few weeks when I ran into Jesse at the Revolution bar. Jesse, you'll remember as one of my friends in high school, the one that we recorded a skit of us kidnapping him in his underwear, only for him to escape from the trunk of my car and run half-naked across Main Street toward the high school. He and his girlfriend had just lost their roommate and offered me the extra room. Jesse was also working with Chuck cleaning out vacant apartments and maintaining the lawns until a new tenant would move in. His roommate leaving also created a vacancy on Chuck's crew.

The apartment was nice and clean; it was much more than I needed to survive. The job was quite interesting too. I learned a lot on that job as Chuck had us doing all sorts of random home maintenance tasks. My life had suddenly improved drastically. When I was home, I mostly kept to myself in my room, and Jesse stayed in his room with his girl.

They started bringing their private lives into the shared living space more often as we grew more comfortable. They were doing drugs, which I was sure of, but I didn't know what they were taking and honestly didn't care. Chuck would pick us up from the apartment at 6 a.m., and Jesse was getting harder to wake up each day. I told Chuck what was going on, and he told me not to worry about it; we'd go without him. Chuck didn't talk much; we'd either sit in silence or listen to talk radio as we drove from location to location. I'd try to comment on the world events they were covering, but he'd often only reply with the occasional grunt or nod. The only times he spoke were to tell me what to do or to offer some sage-like advice that I'd never be prepared for or appreciate until much later.

Jesse hadn't been to work in two weeks, so I knew he wouldn't have the money to pay rent. When the time to pay rent came, he mysteriously had the money, but he seemed stressed. I recognized the look, he was selling drugs, and those drugs were running out. If he continued to miss work, he would have to increase his sales. More strangers were coming around our apartment, a random dude had been asleep on our couch going on three days straight, and Jesse was no longer keeping any of his actions private. They were selling methamphetamines and were planning their next cook.

Considering I was on the lease, they were thoughtful enough to ensure I was cool with them cooking meth in our kitchen. They told me the story of where they had stayed before their current apartment and even took me to the blackened burnt-out hole where their last cook had gone horribly wrong. They wanted me to be fully aware of the risks involved and promised not to do it if I wasn't okay with it. For the record, I was unequivocally and undeniably, against it. Unfortunately, that considerate attitude was for show. They were going to do whatever they wanted anyway. Now they would have to figure out how to pull it off without me knowing or just kick me out. Ultimately, they chose to try to get me addicted to meth, figuring the rest would fall into place naturally.

One night, I was writing music in my room when I heard a knock at the front door. I had the apartment to myself, and I wasn't expecting anyone. I figured they had come to see Jesse and would eventually leave when I didn't answer. Then the doorbell rang, and I heard someone call my name. Reluctantly, I put my guitar on its stand and pulled on a dirty t-shirt. I opened the door, and a shifty-eyed dude who looked to be my age quickly asked, "Hey, you're Jesse's friend, right?"

"Yeah, what's up?" I asked as my position in the doorway felt increasingly less safe.

"Yo, dude, I need a ride. Can you help me out?" he asked.

I looked over my shoulder and nodded toward nothing, "Aww, man, I'm right in the middle of something. I can't, dude, sorry."

"Listen, man, I just need a ride there. You don't even have to wait around. It's just down to the highway. I can give you some gas money; it'll take two minutes." He pressed his hands together as if praying to the Gods of mooching.

I begrudgingly accepted his offer, but I didn't invite him in. I told him to wait outside, and I'd be right out. We talked about our mutual friend and other random small talk as we drove toward the highway. I also noticed he was staying clear of saying anything about what I was about to be an accomplice in. We made our destination under the overpass of the highway, but nobody was there. I suddenly got the awful gut feeling that I was about to be mugged, and he would steal my car and leave my body on the side of the road. I tried to suppress my flinch as he suddenly turned to me.

"Dude, thank you so much. I seriously appreciate it." He opened the door and got halfway out of the car before turning around and handing me three dollars for gas and a tiny sealed plastic bag. I took what he handed me without giving it much thought as I was still waiting for him to surprise me with what would be the murder weapon, and I didn't want to seem ungrateful that he was letting me live.

I sped away with my life as I watched his baggy clothes slowly fade away in my rearview mirror. I was still waiting for the trap to spring, but nothing happened. I just drove away, strictly obeying all traffic laws. I eventually found myself safely back home with three dollars and what turned out to be a small bag of meth. I ran to my room, locked the door behind me, and emptied my pockets onto the bed. I laughed at the small bag. Who gives someone meth as a thank you for a ride without asking if you'd like to have that meth? There was no way I would use it. I didn't even know how to use it. I couldn't sell it because I had no idea if this meth was any good or even real, for that matter. I also didn't know how much this amount of meth would cost. I would have to ask Jesse.

It was later that evening when I finally heard him come home. I grabbed the bag and ran out to the living room. This silly bag had now become a major interest of mine the longer I spent with it. "Hey, yo," I said as I came out of my room, "I have a question for you." I handed him the bag. "What do you think of this?"

"I think it's cute!" he said, examining the bag. "Where'd you get it?"

"Some dude came by looking for you and asked for a ride. I took him, and he gave me that," I said.

"Oh, yeah, yeah, yeah, I told him you might be home. He just made this stuff and is trying to get rid of it as soon as possible. I've been wanting to try it!" he said, as he headed to his room and loudly yelled from behind his door, "You ever tried this stuff before?"

"No, never," I said truthfully. I had grown a sense of ownership over this bag and wanted something for it. "How much do you think I could sell it for?"

The rummaging ended briefly in his room, and he stuck his head through the doorway, "HA, for this? Five bucks? There's enough in here for a couple of hits." He dipped back into his room for a few more seconds and then returned with a long, thin glass pipe with a round bulb at the end. "You might as well just smoke it. Do you mind if I try it out?"

Realizing my new meth business wouldn't be as profitable as I had imagined, I just let him have my once highly valued treasure. I watched him pass the flame under the bulb, rocking it back and forth slowly until my hard-earned prize began to smoke. He cleared the smoke and then handed it to me. At that moment, I was confronted with the very real possibility of smoking meth. I was safe at home, everything had been prepared for me, and now all I had to do was breathe in. In that split second, I decided to just go for it and see what all the fuss was about, and I smoked meth for the first time.

# PART 3: METHAMPHETAMINES

Meth was and is the most fantastic drug in the world. That night I played my guitar until my fingers bled. I had tried cocaine before, but coke wears off quickly. When compared with meth, it wears off immediately. Off one suspiciously cheap hit of meth, I was wired for nearly eight hours. My first thought when it did start to wear off the next day was that I needed to get more. I started thinking about all the things I could accomplish on meth. The commoners drink their coffee in the morning, giving them a small pick-me-up, but mostly just making them all need to poop. The highly successful in society, I imagined, probably did meth.

Ironically, the greatest blessing in my life at that time was that I wasn't surrounded by the highly successful in society. Instead, I was around a bunch of super sketchy meth-heads. I saw where that life was likely to lead, and I was in no way interested. I can see how people get caught up chasing that high. I was the perfect candidate for getting addicted to meth. I could picture myself sleeping on a stranger's couch for three days straight and realized, as productive as it might make you in the short term, it evens out when your body suddenly shuts down for days at a time.

That was the first time drugs scared me. The first time I realized I was heading down a dark path, I was playing with fire continuing to walk that line. Jesse purchased himself some of the cook from the mysterious meth man, and he stopped coming to work altogether. Chuck and I continued mowing the lawns ourselves, and I started considering moving out as the likelihood of Jesse making rent became increasingly less likely.

A few weeks later, Chuck and I were finishing up for the day when he told me he was letting me go. He was moving to the coast in a few weeks and would have to give all his clients to someone else. He told me to get a small business license and then gave me a list of all the equipment I should buy. He promised to give all those clients to me if I wanted them. Thus, the Here Comes the Sun Lawn Care Company was born, and I was the boss.

By the first of the month, rent was due, and Jesse was nowhere to be found. He had gotten irreversibly deep into the binge and was barely lucid when he was around. I called you and told you I was in a bad situation. I said I needed to get out of the apartment but never said why exactly. You were there just a few hours later with a truck and didn't ask any questions. I could always count on you for that. While I think it would have been better to talk about why I lived in a meth house, it was nice knowing I could always turn to you for help whenever I needed it. I didn't have to worry about getting in trouble or being threatened with rehab.

We drove to Century 21 to see if we could get me off the lease, and it turned out Jesse had never officially signed off for me to be added to the lease in the first place. I was free to leave without any repercussions. I paid half that month's rent anyway, and then we bounced. You helped me get situated in a new apartment across town, and then you went back home. Again, no questions asked.

I went from a dirty old storage shed to my very own apartment and the owner of a small business. My life continued to improve, and I felt like a contributing member of society. I could hire my friends to work, and I had enough money for plenty of booze. My depression was pretty well managed as things were going relatively well, but my depression was predictably cyclical, and I'd soon be on the downside again. I remember getting the opportunity to paint an entire apartment complex. I had no idea how long the job would take to complete or what to charge them. The quote I gave was probably lower than any other bid they heard, so they were happy to offer me the contract. Every time I took a job where I was likely to eat the cost of my mistakes, I'd justify it as an opportunity to gain experience, which I figured had value. I picked up several gallons of light blue paint and rented a paint sprayer, something I'd never used before.

I made quick work of the buildings despite my frustration with the paint sprayer not being as easy to use as I thought it would be. I was exhausted by the end of the day, but I had quoted them appropriately, and it looked like I would make a good amount of money on the job. I packed my things and headed home to crash into my bed for an early night. I was still covered in dry paint, but my back and shoulders were aching too much to lift a bar of soap. The next morning I got a call from the furious landlord who wanted to talk to the owner of my company. I silently wished I employed more people than just myself.

Apparently, I was supposed to use a shield between the wood I painted and the brick accents that should have been left untouched.

When I returned to look at what he was describing over the phone, I saw the light mist of blue that had created an ombre effect on every single unit of the complex. An attention to detail I hadn't yet developed. I could hear my brother's voice laughing at me as I spent another two days, unpaid, brushing paint thinner on the bricks, building by building. I felt stupid for not knowing how to do things the right way instead of being proud of myself for having a willingness to try anyway. There is no better way to learn something than to screw it up so publicly, but I missed the upside of it and fell back into the old patterns of shame and disappointment. That's about the time that psychedelic mushrooms came in.

I had started taking field mushrooms several years prior when I was still in high school. They were easy to get since we lived near so many cow pastures. You could head out to the fields early before the sun came up and look for cow patties with shrooms growing out of them. You would flick the cap with your finger, causing the spores to fall onto the patty. Then you could take your shroom, and a new one was likely to grow in its place in a few days. We'd take a shopping bag full of those things home, clean them off, and then boil them in water with enough sugar to hide the strong shit flavor. After boiling for a while, we would drink the "tea" and wait.

Nothing happens for about thirty minutes, and then you're suddenly overwhelmed by a wave of nausea. It feels like you've been poisoned, but it only lasts five minutes. Another ten minutes pass, and you get another wave of five-minute nausea. This time, when you come out of the queasiness, the room's colors have taken on a new quality. They're not brighter or more saturated; it's hard to explain as it's beyond everyday experience. For example, the solid color of a painted wall will have taken on a subtle raised texture, but when you feel the wall, it still feels perfectly smooth. Another cycle of nausea, and you return to find the surface is now gently swaying like wheat in a field. You're thoroughly poisoned about an hour after drinking the tea and have cycled through several rounds of nausea. Everything in the room is gently bending and twisting, just enough to be noticeable, but not so much that the movement seems unbelievable.

When the movements remain believable, it's hard to know what's really happening and what is simply a hallucination. One example that comes to mind is a trip I had back when Hurricane Katrina made landfall in Louisiana. Cities all across the Texas coast were shutting down as it was predicted the hurricane would start heading west. The highways were clogged with people trying to evacuate, and gas stations ran out of gas. The only place open in town was Wal-Mart. My friends and I all decided to take psychedelics and hang out in the toy section during what felt like a pre-apocalyptic event. Those subtle, believable movements made all the toys on the shelf appear battery-operated. It seemed unlikely that all the toys would be moving and playing by themselves, but it still existed in the realm of possibility. That's a fair example of the feeling you get when the first actual phase of the trip kicks in. It's arguably the most fun phase, and it's often why people take shrooms in the first place, but not for me. I was hooked on shrooms for the second phase.

The second phase is different for everyone, but it was very introspective for me. The waves of cyclical nausea continue throughout your trip. Each time you start to feel sick, there's a minor panic attack as you question if your brain can handle hallucinating more than you currently are. Somewhere around the midway point of the second phase, you have to start bracing yourself for the increasing peaks of the high. With every wave of nausea, I would close my eyes and breathe slowly until I could adapt to the new level of high. The high plateaus, and then I could open my eyes again and carry on with the night. Inevitably, as you're judging your mind's capacity for such things, you start to feel self-conscious about how you must look to others. Once you begin thinking about yourself, the shrooms completely take over.

For me, it was always ugly at first. I'd think of my mom and wonder why she didn't want anything to do with me. I would think of my brother and how he always seemed so ashamed of me. He would brag about "writing off" the people he didn't like. I'd realize he hadn't spoken to me in a long time. Had he written me off? I probably deserve it. I'd think of you and about how you were always there to help me, but I would worry that you were disappointed in me for not having a life plan. I'd feel guilty that you always needed to bail me out of stupid situations, but you never had to do that with my brother. Shrooms hyper-focus your thoughts, causing you to delve deeply into any topic that crosses your mind. They grab a thick handful of hair from the back of your head and rub your face in every thought you've tried desperately to ignore.

That's the worst part of phase two, but toward the end of phase two, you start to have little epiphanies about yourself. Things become more apparent as you begin to deal with your emotions. It feels like months of therapy ripping through your mind, and as long as you can survive each wave of nausea, you might learn something about yourself. Phase three is when you start to come down and feel like you've had a psychological breakthrough. Like you've touched the hand of god, she has shown you the way toward living a better life, and you feel reborn with a second chance to get it right. Putting that meth pipe away for good and getting out of Jesse's apartment was a phase two epiphany. Shrooms were now an every three-month self-medicating therapy I consistently used to keep my depression at bay. I was in my new apartment for almost a year when my mushroom therapy abruptly stopped working.

# Part 4: Emo Girls

I had been dating a girl named Samantha since I had moved back to town. That should give you an idea of how much she liked me back because she was willing to overlook that I was living in a storage shed. She had been there through all the Jesse drama and was now living with me in the new apartment. She'd even mow a couple of lawns with me here and there. We would do mushrooms together too, and she was cool with doing them at my preferred frequency of every three months. We had graduated from field shroom tea to a higher potency hydroponic mushroom that had been folded into a warm chocolate brownie. The high was cleaner, and the epiphanies were more profound. We were becoming better people together, and we would talk about our big plans of getting real careers and potentially starting a family someday. My friend Hammy was a teacher in Idaho, so Samantha and I started kicking around the idea of moving there. I wanted to get my teaching credential to teach grade school kids, and she wanted to work with animals. I felt like we were headed down a positive path.

Samantha was working at a small coffee shop on the north side of campus when she met a new guy friend. I wasn't jealous of him at first. I had more time to skate and play music when she was with him. Before long, she spent more time with him than with me. His name was Devon, and after several months of working together, he invited her to go with him when he moved back to Colorado at the end of the semester. She accepted his offer and brought it up to me one night after dinner. I was spiritually devastated. It solidified the idea that they were screwing around, but it also occurred to me that she would be out of my life entirely. It would be bad enough that she was leaving me for another man, but the thought that we couldn't even remain "friends" after our split broke my heart.

She saw how much her leaving hurt me as I begged her not to go. I'm not entirely sure if that was what she was looking for or if the guilt made her stay, but she didn't leave with him when he left for Colorado. For her, she had seen how much I loved her when I cried for her that night. Alcoholics can be distant and guarded, not always showing their true emotions. Maybe she just wanted to see if I did love her, and this had proven it to her. For me, everything had changed between us, and the spiritual bond had been broken. She had all but packed her bags to leave me for someone else. Although she always denied it, I assumed she had cheated on me at some point before he left. She stayed to work on our relationship, but I never fully recovered from her threat to leave.

I had issues getting close to women after everything I had gone through with my mom. I wasn't trusting of them and was scared to get close. When I did open myself to them, I became utterly vulnerable. When this happened with Samantha, I immediately started looking for a new woman to blunt the pain with a rebound. I found that in a disastrous emo girl named Wren, who could be the perfect distraction. I never cheated on Samantha, but I wasn't there for her emotionally anymore. I had grown cold, and she rarely saw me sober. Eventually, she had had enough and left me. I called Wren the same day, and Samantha had been replaced by the next morning.

I hid my feelings for Samantha and drowned out how much I missed her and how much guilt I felt for letting her go with copious amounts of alcohol and cocaine-fueled nights with Wren. My relationship with Wren was doomed from the start. Still, I fought harder to keep that relationship alive than I did with Samantha because if my relationship with Wren didn't work out, it would mean I had made a mistake by letting Samantha go.

Wren was a nightmare; her personality reminded me a lot of my mom. Maybe my fighting so hard for Wren also had some weird Freudian aspect that meant I was secretly fighting for my mom; I don't know. Wren's mother died from cancer when Wren was ten years old. She saw how much love and care her mother had been given by her family and friends during her treatment. Wren began to associate pain and sickness with being loved. By the time we were dating, she had become a hypochondriac that would fake illness for attention. Early in our relationship, she had been diagnosed with an inoperable brain tumor. We cried together as she described how she didn't want to die alone, and then she asked me to marry her. I told you about it, and we called her father to express our condolences. We also asked him how he felt about me marrying his daughter. He was not only surprised to hear of this inoperable brain tumor but also furious that I would lie about something like that. Wren was seriously a total nightmare, but my mother had also lied about having cancer, and damn it all to Freud; I was going to fix this girl.

Wren was also a cutter. Her way of dealing with depression was to make light, superficial scratches on her hips with a knife. The cuts were deep enough to draw blood but wouldn't need medical treatment. They were conveniently hidden under her clothes, and the wound would heal within a few days. Evidently, the cutting released endorphins that gave her a high that helped her cope with depression, not unlike the high I got from a good slam on a skateboard. Maybe I loved skating so much because it hurt so badly. I became interested in cutting and wondered if it would work for me, but I was much too scared to try it.

One particularly drama-filled evening with Wren led to her locking herself in the bathroom while I was drunk and alone in the kitchen. She would always hide in the bathroom. I found it infuriating. We would start to argue, and then she'd lock the door and threaten to hurt herself. The first few times, it legitimately scared me because I thought she'd actually try something. Once I learned it was just an act, I stopped checking on her, and I'd give her some space to cool down.

As I drunkenly waited for her, the sharp knife on the kitchen counter caught my eye. My depression was at an all-time high, and I had been having thoughts of suicide relatively often. It wasn't the first time I had felt this way. I remember the first time I had suicidal thoughts. It was within the first year of living in Texas. I knew I couldn't talk to you about it, but I thought I might be able to open up to my brother when he came home from school for winter break.

I waited until Shannon and I were alone in the car on our way to grab something to eat. I told him I had been thinking about suicide lately, and he was instantaneously furious with me. He told me I was selfish and stupid for even thinking about it, and he promised he'd never forgive me if I ever even tried. I was hurt and scared by his reaction; it wasn't what I expected to hear, and I didn't think he'd be mad at me. It's not as if I was asking him for advice on how to do it or asking for his permission. I just wanted to tell someone I was having those thoughts, and I didn't know what to do about it. That I was scared and that I was depressed. I was maybe fishing for attention. I wanted to hear him tell me he loved me and that I'd be missed if I weren't around. I was having thoughts of suicide because I felt stupid and selfish. Telling me I was stupid and selfish for having those thoughts didn't help. I was now there again, having the same feelings in an emo girl's kitchen. Only this time, I was too drunk to think straight, and the knife had somehow gotten into my hands.

# PART 5: DENTAL FLOSS

I recklessly took three quick swipes. They landed a third of the way up my arm, just above the wrist. It wasn't a suicide attempt, but what I was attempting isn't exactly clear. Blood gushed from my arm as the third slash opened to an inch-wide crevice. I panicked and dropped the knife, I tried holding my arm closed, but it did nothing to stop the bleeding as it trickled through my fingers. Wren was the last person I wanted to talk to about it, but I figured Miho was probably home. He lived on the other side of the same apartment complex. I grabbed my jacket and ran there as fast as I could. I was worried I had accidentally just killed myself.

Wren heard the door slam, but she waited for ten more minutes in the bathroom, just in case I came back. She eventually peered out the cracked door to see if I had truly left. The room was quiet, so she stepped out of the bathroom that led into her bedroom. She could see the kitchen through the hallway and noticed I had spilled something on the floor. Irritated, she stormed through the house, assuming I had intentionally flooded the kitchen with a drink of some kind. Slowly, as she got closer, she realized that it was my blood and a lot of it. Her fears were confirmed when she saw the unnecessarily sharp knife sitting in a puddle of blood on the floor. There was blood on the cabinets, splattered against the wall, dripping down the front of her refrigerator, and bloody shoe prints creating a long red path through the living room and out her front door. She ran to the door and swung it open, only to find the trail leading down the stairs, across the walkway, and then it disappeared into the grass.

I got to Miho's apartment in less than two minutes, and I knocked loudly on his door. His roommate Bryan answered and looked pleased when he recognized me. "Hey, what's up, D?" he asked as the look of happy surprise slowly melted from his face.

Noticing his gaze fall to my legs, I too realized for the first time since it had happened that my shirt and pants were soaked in blood, only partially concealed by the blue Members Only jacket I was now wearing. My left arm wasn't in the sleeve, and I was holding my wrist inside the jacket with my other hand. "Hey, man, I had a little accident. Is Miho here?"

"Yeah, man, he's right here. Miho! Come here quick." He looked shocked and worried as he stepped aside to let me in. I could tell a part of him didn't want me there.

"What's wrong?" Miho asked as he came to the door. He quickly ushered me into the house and brought me to the back bathroom when he saw me. "What the fuck happened to you!"

"I don't know, dude, I was just fucking around, and I cut my arm pretty bad. I think you'll have to sew it back together, man," I said as I took my hand off the wound and showed him the full extent of the injury. A fresh oozing of blood coated the older blood that had already begun to dry.

"The fuck you mean sew it?! You need to go to the hospital," he said with one hand on his head.

"Everything Okay?" Bryan asked from just outside the bathroom. Miho slammed the door without answering him.

"Won't it get infected? I don't know what I'm doing!" Miho looked stressed.

"It's fine. Just get a sewing needle and some thread. We will boil the needle in water to kill anything left on it. We have to do something, dude. I'm losing a lot of blood. If we go to the E.R., they will admit me for suicide watch or something." I was drunk enough to withstand the pain of him sewing my arm, and there was nobody I would trust it to more than Miho.

"Fuck, man, fuck. Okay." Miho left and started heating some water on the stove. He returned a few minutes later, "Dude, we don't have a thread. All I have is dental floss."

We argued for a few minutes about whether or not dental floss was a good idea, and I was just about to suggest we also boil the floss when a knock came at the door. It was Wren; I could hear her crying, screaming between sobs, asking Bryan if I was there. Miho reassured me he would handle it.

I could hear the commotion outside, but I couldn't quite make out what they were saying. Miho eventually calmed her down and sent her back home. He grabbed the needle and floss and met me back in the bathroom. "You ready?" he asked, looking uncertain but willing to go through with it.

I took my hand off the paper towels we had bunched up on the wound and slowly peeled the layers back. The gash was disgusting, but the bleeding had mostly stopped. Only a small trickle of blood ran down my forearm, so we decided to glue it together, and then Miho taped a massive wad of gauze to the site.

The laceration bled for three weeks, sometimes just a yellow-orange oozing of semi-clear liquid. You saw my home bandaging in the first week I had it. "What happened there?" you asked.

I was leaning into the window of your truck from the driveway as you were leaving for work. "Oh, nothing," I playfully chuckled as I quickly pulled my arm away. You didn't question me any further and just said your goodbyes as you drove away. I sometimes wonder what would have happened if you had pressed the issue. Would I have admitted my depression then? I felt like I had gotten off the hook more than anything. I wasn't in the mood to talk about it anyway, but you had to notice the shame in my eyes as I pulled my arm back.

Now with the world crumbling around me, I needed my shroom therapy more than ever. I contacted my street pharmacist who prepared my antidepressants in that warm chocolate brownie and made home deliveries. I wanted to improve my relationship with you. I wanted to be a better brother. I also welcomed any insight into my relationship with my mom. Psychoanalyzing those relationships and my role in them was something I valued in the experience. I didn't want to think about Samantha or Wren, and I didn't want to think about suicide. Unfortunately, shrooms hyper-focus your thoughts, and I couldn't think about anything else.

As I rocketed through the first two phases of the trip, I started thinking about every prior shroom session I had and each eye-opening epiphany that resulted. The shrooms reminded me that I hadn't done anything I promised myself. Each major life-altering walk back down the mountain had been treated as a splendid idea that would never be enacted, and the euphoria of hope would fade in a few months. I'd again be back on the living room floor with my eyes closed, bracing for the next epiphany, just as I was now. My brother's voice echoed through the psilocybic loudspeakers, demoralizing me further for being such an epic failure. Then came the guilt for the relationships I had ruined with two innocent women. I had discarded one relationship out of fear of rejection, and the other I had used as a tool to ignore the pain that I was only postponing until this exact moment. I closed my eyes and braced myself as another wave of nausea made my stomach flip. I began the exponential climb toward enlightenment, but the epiphany never came. I just sat with the stark realization that there was nothing left for me to do. There was no bright idea, nothing I could change about myself. I was a terrible person, and because of that, there would be no touching the hand of God today. Then something in my mind snapped.

That anxiety of passing through the threshold for being able to handle hallucinogens, and the gradual adaptation to the new high, never broke. The feeling lingered uneasily. I kept my eyes closed, shutting them tighter and tighter. I felt like the guy in the Maxell cassette tape commercials, being blown away while trying to maintain my seat on the couch, only it wasn't worth it. I imagined my mind as a reservoir, filled to the brim, about to spill over to the other side. That other side, I could tell, was psychosis. I had done the exact amount of drugs one must do to walk up to the line of losing your mind and was now peering over the edge. I knew, for a fact, that if I ever did shrooms again, the floodgates would open, and I'd lose control of self and rational thought. I would abruptly dissociate from my current identity and lose the ability to recognize who the real me was.

Several hours later, when even the worst bad trips should have worn off, I was still teetering on the edge of crisis. I became terrified of all mind-altering substances. I stopped smoking weed; I felt even the slightest puff could send me toppling over the edge. The only thing that made it feel better was alcohol. Being drunk was my normal; it felt like my baseline. Staying drunk helped me feel in control, easing my newfound anxiety. I was still terrified of any other substances, and I was well aware that mixing any of those with alcohol would only do the job of breaking my brain that much quicker and more thorough.

I became socially awkward and started to overanalyze everything I would say. I started stumbling over my words as I struggled to find the right ones. Each time it happened, I feared my reservoir had finally spilled over. The internal panic it would cause made finding the words I was searching for nearly impossible, and I would lose my train of thought. This would eventually become another aspect of my social anxiety that I would attempt to quell with more alcohol.

My fear of finally losing it got so bad that I couldn't even be around people who were in an altered mental state. I feared they'd say something strange, and my mind would trick itself into thinking I was on a hallucinogen. Via an associative high, I'd shatter the delicate barrier holding my mind on the right side of reality. I had to get away from everyone and everything; I again came running home to you.

Getting off drugs was easy because I was terrified of them.

Moving away from everyone who was using also helped to eliminate temptation. Unfortunately, I had just turned 21, and I could now buy alcohol anytime I wanted. I started getting alcohol every time I left the house and found my go-to in a fifth of Bacardi that would accompany me to every outing. I was again living under your roof, which meant I had to go back to school, so I began my second attempt at college, now free from drugs.

# Part 6: Snot Rockets in Vegas

I wasn't honest in this second attempt at school. The plan was to take as many music classes as they offered while looking for a new band. When the time came to apply and build my class schedule, I was rejected on the grounds of academic probation. I went and spoke with admissions and was allowed to take classes with the caveat that I'd maintain a 3.0 GPA and I'd have to work with a counselor, so I made an appointment the same day.

I told the counselor what I was interested in, and he built a path toward an associate of arts degree with an emphasis on music. He also showed me how those courses could transfer to a four-year bachelor's degree in music at a university. My interest in teaching and my love of music could be combined into one exciting career as a music teacher. I couldn't believe I hadn't known about this option before. The idea still seemed so foreign and unachievable. I dismissed the idea and decided to focus on one semester at a time. The first thing I had to do was audition for the music program.

This wasn't music school; this was an associate of arts degree with all music electives. The audition was relatively mild, but I stressed about it regardless. I looked up the basics of reading sheet music, memorized the lines on a clef, and prepared as best I could by doing a crash course in scales on the internet. I was good with my instrument but used my ear, not theory. I didn't even know the names of the chords I was playing. I barely tested high enough to be accepted, so I wasn't able to skip any prerequisites. My next semester was going to be the counselor-suggested English 101 and Geology plus Music Appreciation and Jazz Ensemble.

I immediately had a sense of pride in the school. Up to this point, school was a given. It was something I *had* to do. To go, all you had to do was pay for it, but now I was in a special program you had to test into, and it felt exceptional. The idea of riding this thing to a music school at an actual university started to take root, and I got excited about school for the first time in my life. I was going to keep that 3.0 GPA, and I was going to accomplish the vague college experience you required of me. The first person I wanted to tell was my brother.

I remember the night in Vegas, the day of your second wedding. My brother and I went out to gamble, a short-lived experience when he convinced me to bet everything we had on black. The "what if" surge overwhelmed me, and I did as instructed. The ball bounced around quickly and then cut our evening short as it came to rest on red. We made our way to the bar before heading back to the room. Shannon wasn't a drinker, he often warned me how alcoholism ran in our family, and then he'd name off the list of aunts and uncles he now refused to talk to because they were so worthless. I agreed with the list mostly, but his hatred for Uncle Wighty always hurt my feelings.

Wighty was gentle and loved Marylyn Monroe. I remember every holiday we spent in Georgia visiting family, and Wighty would be in his small room off the garage of Grandma's house. I would run down to see him, and he'd be listening to music or playing his guitar. One Christmas, I ran to his room, and he seemed genuinely surprised to see me. I could tell he didn't know we were coming that year. He gave me my unwrapped present, a cassette tape that he plucked from the table next to where we were sitting. I couldn't name anything from the band off the top of my head, but I knew I had heard the name Pink Floyd before. He popped it in and fast-forwarded it to *Money*. It would be years before I knew just how cool that song is or that it's in 7/8 time, but I could tell immediately that it would be my favorite Christmas gift that year.

Wighty didn't know the names of his chords either, but he loved to hear me play the same songs every year that we visited him. I had written the first couple bars to a new song and was stuck creatively on where to go next. We sat in his room for hours as I would play the first few notes of what I had written and then insert something new. He'd say yes or no to the few note run and then suggest I go higher or lower. We wrote the song this way, note by note, hour by hour. By the time we left that year, the piece was almost finished; I just had to get my fingers to do what we had written down in basic tablature.

# Listen: Track 1

# "Wighty"

https://denverjhamilton.bandcamp.com/track/wighty

When we returned home, I kept working on that song and finally mastered it, added a bridge, and was anxious to show Wighty the final product. Wighty had battled alcoholism for years, and his unhealthy lifestyle would lead to a heart attack that same year. I played the song we had written together for him, in his empty room alone, on the day of his funeral. Losing the chance to share that song with him caused my blood to curdle every time Shannon would use him as the example of where alcoholism gets you. Maybe if my brother ever shared a genuine moment with someone, he'd feel the pain of loss and not just boil everyone down to their mistakes.

As the night in Vegas was nearing its end, Shannon had barely drunk, but I was thoroughly intoxicated. We got to the bar, which was too loud and dark. We pushed through dozens of people half-dancing, leaning in close to each other's ears trying to hold conversations over the bombardment of repetitive thumping bass. Everything in the bar was a shade of dark purple or black with occasional bright blue lights. The bar was in the center of the room and made a ring around the center stage. We found seats just as the male bartender climbed onto the stage and began pouring shots directly from the bottle into women's open mouths, like baby birds awaiting regurgitated worms. Ready to party and eager to make my brother laugh, I elbowed my way past the first baby bird and received a proper splashing of vodka. He wasn't laughing when I turned around, he looked embarrassed, and I had that familiar feeling of thinking we were bonding when, in reality, I was just making a fool of myself.

Sensing his discomfort and mild annoyance, we left soon after and headed to the room. We hadn't been out long, but I could tell he had enough excitement. I had created the expectation in my mind that we would have bonded throughout the night, and I would have brought up music school during breakfast, but the opportunity for that was quickly fading, and I would need to tell him now.

We had gotten comfortable in our beds, and the T.V. was on, mainly to provide light in the darkened room. I told him I had gotten into the music program and was genuinely excited about school for the first time. I recited the path to bachelor's my counselor had described and explained how I wanted to be a music teacher. I had held this information in secrecy, waiting for the perfect opportunity to tell him. It felt like a gift you get someone when you know it's exactly what they wanted. I told him everything, and then I waited as I watched him unwrap the perfect gift I had worked so hard to prepare.

"That's stupid," he said, discarding the wrapper of my metaphorical gift and tossing it into the proverbial trash, then "you should be an accountant instead."

I nervously laughed it off. This was a cruel joke, but it was probably just a joke. I mean, why would *I* ever be an *accountant*? Is there anything about my personality that screams, "Accountant?" The longer the joke went on, the angrier I grew as he continued to describe the benefits of accounting in further detail. It wasn't pure anger, though. I wanted to be angry. I wanted to be pissed off, and I wanted to punch him in his stupid face, but what I felt wasn't just anger. I was furious, sure, but I was far more disappointed than angry. I was frustrated with myself for having come up with such a stupid plan that wasn't good enough. The excitement I felt for the upcoming school year turned into a familiar shame, and my anger morphed into embarrassment. I was irritated with myself, but I was also discouraged that he didn't get it. I didn't know what to do, but I was far too drunk to let his slight go.

I started hysterically crying and laughing as I struggled to attach the correct response to emotion. Accounting didn't fit who I was as a person. I had grown up in a generation that had been lied to. We were told we could grow up to be anything we wanted, only to grow up and be told we had to be accountants. Accounting also represented the fact that I would never be happy. If I succeeded as a music teacher, I would have failed my family, but if I succeeded as an accountant, I'd be failing myself. Music school wouldn't be good enough, but it was my only plan and felt attainable. I was completely taken off guard; I couldn't fathom the prospect of my teaching children as being anything other than admirable. The vagueness of "just go to college" became "and then become an accountant." The bar had moved radically, and it didn't feel fair.

We wrestled onto his bed as I yelled at him. I continued laughing through the tears, trying to keep a playfulness to my outburst while also attempting to separate myself from the reality that this was even happening. I could see in his eyes that he was overwhelmed by my overly dramatic response, and I knew he wrote it off as me just being drunk. He wasn't wrong. My inability to control how I reacted was mainly because I was drunk, but the pain I felt was genuine. He shouldn't have written me off, but I was admittedly irrational. He tried to get me to stop and calm down, but I was blinded by drunken rage, and my nose began to run as I continued to cry. He kept me at arm's length, and a long strand of snot began falling from my nose. I blew a snot rocket onto his chest, and he finally pushed me aside and left the hotel room, leaving me alone with my thoughts again.

I was in such a dark place at that time, but the idea of being a trained musician became a lifesaving rope at the edge of the pit. I would use that rope to climb out of my depression and end my alcoholism for good. That night I had given my brother the other end of that rope and had every expectation that he would help pull me out. I wasn't sure what it would look like, but I anticipated it would be congratulatory and encouraging. Instead, it felt like he looked me straight in the eyes and tossed that rope back into the pit. I again felt misunderstood and alone.

First, I considered dropping out of school again. I was sure as shit not inspired to change my major to accounting. I'd rather suffer through real estate classes again before I stepped foot into an accounting class. Music school had now ceased to be the missing puzzle piece of scholastic compromise I was searching so desperately to find that would make you and Shannon proud. Then I considered going for it and proving him wrong.

I assume his intention wasn't to hurt me. I bet he genuinely thought I should be an accountant. The career seemed more guaranteed to provide a reasonable income and job security. Like you, he's worked in jobs he hates his entire life, but they paid well. Favoring stability over happiness seems like a wasted life to me. You arrive at your funeral in a hearse, not a U-Haul. I imagine that whenever he told me something I wanted was stupid, he sincerely felt it was unwise. Likely, he legitimately wanted me to be better. This was his way of trying to help me achieve something great. In some ways, he succeeded. I started to think everything I wanted was stupid, and I wanted to improve, but every time I tried, it still wasn't good enough for him. His attempts to motivate me this way would work temporarily, but unfortunately, the motivational force of shame never lasts very long.

Putting me down every chance he got would sometimes put a chip on my shoulder and get me to try harder, but when things got tough,

I'd give up. When he told me I couldn't do something, my pride would light the fire to try hard. I heard my voice when trying new things. I'd tell myself I could do it, and I excelled at finding creative solutions. His words were never the motivation to work hard. His words didn't come to mind until the going got tough. If I weren't catching on quickly, I'd hear his voice reminding me I'd never be as good as he was at anything. That chip on my shoulder would be replaced with a heavy heart, and I'd remember I was wasting everyone's time again. Music school ended up being extraordinarily more difficult than I imagined. As I struggled to keep up with people far more prepared than I was, it was Shannon's voice from the hotel in Vegas that would remind me why I should give up. It became just another thing to silence with alcohol.

Fifteen years later, his daughter is preparing to finish High School and will be majoring in accounting. I often wonder what her music school equivalent is. My niece and I don't have the relationship I wish we did. I felt like Shannon kept me from his kids. My wife and I once drove 18 hours out of state to visit him and the kids. He knew for months I was coming, and we had been in touch several times in the days leading up to my trip there, but as I was coming into town, he canceled on me. He said they were "busy." His kids had some "stuff" going on, and it "wasn't a good time." I essentially wouldn't take no for an answer, and we came anyway. He took us to the Noodle Company, told my wife a bunch of horrible things about our mom (whom she had never met), and then we left. I stopped calling as much after that because I felt like I was intruding on his life, and I didn't feel welcome.

I was starting to realize that my cold relationship with my niece was likely due to me being her version of Uncle Wighty. I had become the example Shannon would use to show his kids what happens when alcohol ruins your life. Without the opportunity to bond over something we both loved, like Pink Floyd, I became a tragic family member that made her feel uncomfortable.

I eventually fell asleep back at the hotel in Vegas, but I had made the commitment to myself that I would go to school the following semester as I had planned. I had lost the excitement I brought with me to Vegas, but I was ready to start taking things more seriously. The idea of being a schoolteacher seemed silly now, but figuring out my instrument more fully felt like a welcomed distraction. I also knew you'd be happy I was just going to college. I knew school would be a challenge, but I welcomed it and started mentally preparing myself for the commitment I knew it would take. I didn't think I would hit the limits of my ability in music within the first day of class.

# Music School: Chapter 4

## PART 1: THE HICK FROM FRENCH LICK

I had signed up for Jazz Ensemble as a guitarist and figured I could play anything if I were able to play jazz. I wasn't deeply familiar with the genre, but it represented the highest level attainable for musical skill and improvisation. On the first day of class, I walked into a large room where someone had pushed chairs into a large semi-circle around a black grand piano. I was grinning ear to ear as I imagined the music I would learn to play in that room. There were horn players, wind instruments, a drummer, and a pianist, all milling about, talking, or warming up. I waited by the yellow lacquered tweed guitar amplifier left out for me, wondering how many guitarists would be in the class.

Our professor walked into the room at the scheduled start of class and handed out sheet music as he introduced himself. He then had us all introduce ourselves, starting from the far left side of the semi-circle. My new band had fifteen people, and everyone seemed eager to play. After the introductions, our professor quickly counted off, "a one, two, three, four." The horns blared to life as the piano started chopping away at the keys, stringing together a complex chord progression. It was unlike anything I had ever heard. The drums were fast but subtle as the brushes lightly scratched across the snare. I stared vacantly at the sheet music in front of me, not knowing what to do or where we were in the song. My page didn't even have notes written on it, just the name of the song and a suggested chord progression that sat above the lines of the staff. With horror, I slowly realized they must have been meant as a placeholder for each bar and left blank for taking notes. I had the full freedom of musical expression and creativity, but without the knowledge or skill to do anything with it. As the song ended, I realized we wouldn't be learning how to play jazz in this class; we were supposed to know already.

The class ended, and my professor stopped by to ask why I hadn't played during class. I confessed that I had no idea what was going on, couldn't read sheet music, rarely ever listened to jazz, and didn't know the names of my chords. He didn't seem very empathetic to my situation. He told me that as a saxophone player, he wouldn't be able to help me with guitar. He reminded me of the deadline to drop the class and wished me luck as he walked out of the room. Being on the extremely thin ice of academic probation, I couldn't drop any classes. Whether I dropped or failed, I would have been kicked out of school either way.

I went home and tried to find the old jazz standard we had played. I figured I could find tablature somewhere or learn it on my own. I found a black and white video of it on the internet. There wasn't even a guitar in the song. I pulled out the blank sheet music with the chord names written above each measure. There were a few chord names I recognized. I knew some of the fundamental open chord majors and minors, but this song was full of chords that also had 6, 7, 9, or 13 written after the name. It meant nothing to me. I had music books for Neil Young and The Beatles that I started flipping through, hoping to find a description of the more complicated chords. Out of the complete Beatles anthology, I found less than half of the chords from just one jazz standard. I wrote down every chord I could find in my notebook.

I started by drawing a box with five columns and four rows. The lines represented the strings on my guitar as they intersected each fret. On each of the six vertical lines, I would place a number representing the finger I would use to make each chord and then wrote its name below it. I had to find a chord book to learn the more complicated jazz chords, but soon each of the songs we were assigned had a mess of chord boxes written all over it.

I didn't know what codas were, so I would draw arrows showing where the song was going and when to go back to previous sections. Two days later, I showed up at the next class, and my professor ignored me. I didn't even sit with the group. I sat on the side of the room and tried to see if I could follow along, not on guitar, just visually, as I scanned the charts with my eyes. I made more notes and went back home to practice the chords more. I had been playing guitar for years, so my fingers could make the jumps to each chord, even those that felt unfamiliar and awkward. It wasn't easy to memorize them all, but the chord boxes helped. I struggled to keep up with the band because the songs jumped through each chord change so quickly, and I was strumming them like a folk song, not jazz.

By the third week, I had rejoined the group but kept my volume low. It was terrible, but I was technically playing along. After the first couple of songs, my professor walked by and looked at my sheet music. A pit in my stomach grew as I assumed I had been playing so poorly that he was looking to see if I had been playing the wrong song. When he saw I covered the sheet entirely in written notes, arrows, and boxes, he frowned with his eyebrows raised and nodded his approval. Then he told me to stop playing along. He gave me a song to listen to, finally one with guitar. He told me to focus on chopping the chords to the beat instead of strumming. The silence between chords would allow more room for the other instruments and would likely be easier to follow. He seemed warily impressed, especially since the official drop deadline had passed.

He worked with me more and more over the coming months, but he kept me out of every concert they played. I was progressing faster than he expected, but I was still light-years away from anything anyone could call "jazz." We had a major concert coming up, our second to last of the semester, and one that would follow an all-professors band from other schools led by a guest musician. I was definitely not allowed to play in this one either, but my instructor invited me to the all-professors band rehearsal the night before the show.

I sat in the audience a few rows back, eye-level with the stage. I was the only person in the audience, and I got a private concert with some of the best jazz professors in the area. The music was complex, and each member confidently placed every note with nothing going to waste. They didn't sound anything like our class. I thought the men and women in my ensemble were otherworldly; these people were masters. It was startlingly impressive to see some people that had never played together gathering at the center of the stage and playing a perfect thirty-minute set as though they had been playing together for years. When they finished, a tall man who vaguely looked like Larry Bird stood and clapped as he walked to the front of center stage. I could barely hear him, but he appeared to be giving notes to each professor. The professor he spoke with would play back to him, he'd say something else, and then you'd see recognition cross their face as they nodded and wrote something down on the sheet in front of them. I assumed their notes looked much cleaner and were far fewer than mine were.

Larry then counted out the beat, and the band jumped back to life. He made minor corrections with hand gestures to specific people as the band continued playing. Then, as the song wrapped around on a theme that I recognized as the likely chorus, Larry Legend entered a blazingly fast and complex trombone solo. I realized my knowledge of jazz proficiency and the limits of ability had increased from the young people in my class, to the professors' band, and then to whoever this was.

When they finished, my professor motioned me onstage and handed me a C.D. with Larry on the cover. He then told me to talk to him. I don't know if my professor arranged this for me or if Larry recognized me as the youngest and only non-instrumented person in the room, but he pulled me aside and had me sit next to him on the piano.

He played the piano beautifully and strung together chord combinations in ways I couldn't understand. Instead of resolving back to the chord he had started, he'd play a large two-handed chord full of complex emotion that would modulate the key, providing him space to continue building the story. Instead of a repetitive 12-bar blues, he just kept expanding the progression ever longer until it finally did resolve, excruciatingly beautiful yet full of sorrow. I recognized my mouth had been hanging open, so I closed it.

"What's your instrument?" he asked, as he half turned to look me in the eyes.

"I'm a guitar player, but I'm new to jazz. I also love to play piano, bass, and drums, and I want to learn to play everything." I could hear the awkwardness of newly brewing fandom in my voice.

"I see," he said, his voice sounding exactly like Woody Allen. "I love the piano; in some ways, it's my favorite instrument."

"You're very good at playing it," I interrupted.

"Thank you, but I could never do what I did tonight with this band on the piano; I'm nowhere good enough to be a piano player." I couldn't tell if he was being humble or if I was just in denial about how far away I was from ever being considered any good. He continued, "I had to decide if I wanted to be good at piano or great at trombone, so I picked trombone." He grabbed the C.D. that I had placed between us on the bench; he signed it, got up gingerly, and then squeezed my shoulder before walking away.

"Thank you!" I called after him. He had written his signature in the bottom right corner of the cover. Below his name, he wrote, "Keep Practicing." The longer I thought about his words, their meaning grew. On the way to the venue that night, my professor had given me the backstory of Larry and told me he was considered the greatest trombone player at the time and that he had been nominated for multiple Grammy awards. When Larry said he had to choose, he was choosing to be the best. He meant you could only be great at something if you focused all your attention on it. I needed to pick a single instrument and then dedicate myself to it. It was great advice, but music was never so granular to me. I could learn to be content with being mediocre on several instruments. It could also serve as a convenient excuse for why I wasn't a "great" guitar player. I started thinking of myself as a composer and left the technicality of playing to those with the gift.

I was surprised I could be so star-struck by someone I didn't know existed a week prior, but I was swimming in the knowledge that I had just been part of something special. It turned out that my professor had known Larry personally, and he was the one that had put this entire gig together. I patiently waited as he said his goodbyes to everyone and then thanked him profusely for allowing me to come. As I shared my thoughts on everything I had seen that night, Larry walked up to us and asked if we were ready to go. Puzzled, I looked at my professor; he had given me a ride there. "Want to have dinner with us?" my professor asked me with a big smile on his face.

We went out to a fancy Italian restaurant downtown. My palpable lameness mortified me. I in no way belonged in the same restaurant as these two men, let alone at the same table. I know I worked harder than anyone who had ever taken his class, if only to overcome my musical ignorance. Allowing me to sit in on the professors' rehearsal was a very cool thing to do. To take me out to dinner, one on one with someone regarded as the greatest of anything in jazz, was far too much. I didn't speak unless spoken to because I knew any burning questions about music would only embarrass my professor. I kept my mouth full of table bread and listened intently as they both reminisced about jazz clubs on the east coast.

Larry cut his jazz teeth on the streets of New York and had played every night during the era the mob controlled the clubs. He told us stories of doing coke in the bathroom of Frank Sinatra's tour bus and being thrown out by one of his guards, afraid for their lives. That night, I realized jazz was far more rock and roll than it looked from the old black and white videos I'd seen of the jazz standards we were playing in class. My failures and battles with drug addiction now felt less shameful and more like I was a part of this culture. Suddenly, I felt like I belonged at their table.

# Part 2: Tone Deaf

By the end of the semester, I had improved enough to play in the final concert. I was terrified and calmed my nerves with another fifth of Bacardi. I smelled of alcohol, and I regretted it when I saw the look on my professor's face. In his eyes, I had thrown away the opportunity, but he didn't know that I was a highly functional drunk and that I had come more prepared for the occasion than if I had been sober. We were given our set list, and I saw my name on the last song, followed by the words "Guitar Solo." I had not prepared a solo or even considered *how* to play a jazz guitar solo. I was too concerned with just chopping out new chords to music that was too fast. Playing those chords felt like a solo to me! When the time came, I threw down my best pentatonic scale and walked away feeling like someone after their first night of fight club who managed to avoid getting their ass beat too severely.

I was doing well in my required classes too. I was enjoying the music classes and was well aware that passing my required courses meant I could keep learning more about music. Ironically, music theory was the most challenging class I had in my second semester. We were given a recorded melody at the end of each class, and we were supposed to come back with it written as sheet music. Other students in my class had perfect pitch; they could hear a note and tell you what it was. One of my friends had bought the new Zelda video game and then played the opening theme on the piano the next day in class after hearing it just once the night before. I must have the opposite of whatever it is that allows people to do that. I called my Zelda friend for help with the homework that night.

I didn't ask her for the answers. Instead, I had her show me how she did it. Unfortunately, it wasn't like a math problem. There was nothing to study or memorize as I had through Jazz Ensemble. Transcribing sound into written music was something she could do without thinking about it. Once you get the first few notes, music theory gives you all the most likely next steps, but I couldn't even get off the ground with my ears as bad as they were. I was undoubtedly working harder for school than I had my entire life. I practiced with notecards, had books full of notes, and called other students for tutoring, but I was still struggling to keep up.

It took her a couple of hours to walk me through the homework that took her sixty seconds to finish on her own, but I had done it. After class that day, the teacher asked us to stay behind as everyone was filtering out of the room. He was failing us both for having cheated. He knew it was her because she was the only one to get every note right in the class, but he was unsurprised; she was truly gifted. There was, however, absolutely no way in hell that I had also been the only other one to get it right. I panicked; I was finished if I got caught cheating or failed any classes while on academic probation. For her, she'd be fine if I let her take the fall.

She was a great friend, and I instantly felt ashamed for even considering bringing her down with me. I told our professor that I was struggling with the assignment and that I had reached out to my friend for help. I explained how she hadn't just given me the answers but did her best to show me how to figure it out on my own. I also reminded him that he hadn't said anything about us not being allowed to work together. He agreed to let her go unpunished, but he gave me an F for having not done my own work. He also promised to work with me one-on-one and forbade me from working with her in the future.

The following week, I met this professor in one of the practice rooms. They were small soundproof rooms, just big enough for a large chalkboard, two shiny-blue plastic chairs, and a piano. We sat on the piano bench together, and he played a recording, not unlike the homework he had failed me on, and then told me to recite the notes. Obviously, I couldn't; that was why we were there, so he told me to play it on piano. My process for playing it on piano was blindly hitting keys until I found the one that sounded most similar. Being tone deaf, "sounding most similar" includes many notes that, in this case, would be considered incorrect. I could hear when a note was in the wrong key, but I struggled with distinguishing the right ones from being the same or just harmonizing. I could barely match the tones of another piano, but this recording was a trumpet, so even the right notes sounded different to me because of the contrast in timbre. Even playing the same note at different volumes would make me think it was not only louder but also higher in pitch.

With the pressure of him watching, I had lost the first note in my mind and was getting nowhere, fast. He eventually stopped me and then asked me to sing the melody back to him. An electric jolt of anxiety ripped through me; this just kept getting worse. I hummed rather than sang and seemingly hummed the wrong notes. That was the full extent of our one-on-one training as he declared me tone deaf and beyond his help. This man had once described reading sheet music as being similar to hearing the voices of people talking when you read a conversation. He could listen to an orchestra and visualize the sheet music scrolling across his eyes for each member. My inability to perform the basic task of reciting a simple melody labeled me as unteachable.

I might have trained my ear to recognize tones better with more time and patience. With more experience, I'd surely progress, but it was times like these that the voice inside your head gets louder. That voice is your own, but those around you influence what it says. For some children, the inner voice is a combination of both parents. For me, the voice I always heard was Shannon. When I needed encouragement, I heard, "I told you so."

This pitch issue felt unconquerable. I overcame my shortcomings in the Jazz Ensemble by memorization and hard work, but this felt like a minor disability that I'd never be able to compensate for with sheer willpower. I had the same issues in art. While I loved to paint and create, I struggled with color because I am colorblind. I can make my own paintings, and those creations may look beautiful to other people. If asked to replicate another painting, the color would be off. While I could play music beautifully, I could never perfectly reproduce what I heard, and like my color vision, there would be no way to correct it. I could be a musician, but I would never make it in a music school where replication is how one is tested for comprehension of the material.

To make matters worse, I was still dating Wren. I left town after cutting my arm, but we tried to work things out in a long-distance relationship. I heard from other friends that she was spending much of her time with my childhood friend, Toad. I was delighted to hear that news because I knew Toad would keep her safe, and he'd tell me if anything unsavory happened when she was out on the town. I was so trusting of Toad that I didn't find it strange when he started spending the night at her house. I remember the day I finally confronted him about how much time they were spending together.

# Part 3: Dear Old Friend

I felt so awful accusing him of messing around with my girlfriend. I knew he wasn't doing anything with her, but I couldn't deny that they had been spending a lot of time together. My trust withered as our mutual friends kept telling me they were screwing around. My friend Perry sent me a picture of her sitting in his lap at the bar, and even I had to admit that it seemed a little too cozy.

"Big D, what's happenin', brother?" he answered when I called.

"Toad, my dude, good to hear your voice. Listen, man, I have to ask you a question, and I feel so bad even asking." I had my eyes closed, this was going to be like ripping off a Band-Aid, but I knew he would make me feel better when he explained that nothing was happening. I just wanted to hear it from him. "I've been hearing rumors around town, and I'd rather just ask you straight, are you messing around with my girlfriend?"

There was silence on the other end for about five long seconds, and I immediately feared I had pissed him off for not trusting him. "Yeah, dude, I'm sorry. When it happened, I didn't know how to tell you."

"What?!" I yelled into the phone. "I admire your honesty, but what the fuck, man?!"

"I know. I'm sorry," he said. The brief window of opportunity for him to declare his admission a sick prank came and went in silence.

"I mean, Jesus, dude. Were you drunk or something?" I was hoping he would attempt to justify it somehow, and I was trying to give him an out.

"I was the first time."

"The first time?! How many times? No, don't answer that. You're done now, right?" My heart was beating so fast, and I felt like throwing up. I had not only been betrayed by a girl who didn't deserve the slightest fraction of effort I put into our relationship, but I had also been stabbed in the back by a good friend. Toad was one of the first people I had met when we moved to Texas, and he'd even lived with us for a few months when his parents were fighting a bunch. Toad was like a brother to me, so this had completely taken me by surprise. We talked for another few minutes. He told me he was in love with her and then declined to stop seeing her. I hung up the phone and called Wren.

"Hey, baby," she answered, with a pleasant tone in her voice.

"Hey, babe…" I tried my best to sound normal, but the smoke was pouring out of my ears. "Are you cheating on me with Toad?"

"No! I would never do that to you." She sounded so honest about it that I almost believed her. She was very good.

I strung together a long list of terrible insults as I struggled to hang up on her, and then I immediately grabbed my keyboard and recorder. I placed the keyboard on top of our upright piano and started recording. I set the keyboard to a drumbeat with an accompanying chord progression that I could change by playing the chords on the bass half of the keys. With my right hand, I played lead on the upright and sang the first things that came to mind. In one take, I recorded the following song immediately after getting off the phone with Wren and Toad; this is the one and only time I ever played this song.

# Listen: Track 2
# "No More"

https://denverjhamilton.bandcamp.com/track/no-more-explicit

## Lyrics

You took my heart
Right out of my body,
And you gave it away.
Oh, and how could you do it?
Cause I'm just sittin' here,
And I'm thinkin' about you
I'm thinkin' 'bout what you've done to me.
Oh, and how could you do it?!
Couldn't you just keep it for a second?
Keep it in your back pocket
And think of me, just once today?

## Meaning

*I felt like my heart had been ripped out, but I struggled to identify who had hurt me more: my girlfriend or best friend. I believed them when they said they loved me, so I imagined they could have only done this by not thinking about me. If they had thought about me, even once, they wouldn't have gone through with it.*

> She's a killa. She'll do it to you.
> She did it to me without a warning
> And she'll do it again.
> So I hope she makes you happy,
> Happy, my friend.

> I don't wish any harm onto you,
> I just wish you didn't do it to me.
> I'd like to take my revenge.
> I'd like to put you both in your place,
> But what would that do for me?
> 'Cause you both have my heart
> And I've got somethin' to give you.

*Saying she was a killer is a metaphor for a cheater. She had cheated on me and would likely cheat on him too. This verse was a warning to my friend. I hope she makes you happy now because she will break your heart. I was starting to get angry by this point in the song, and I was beginning to think of revenge.*

> She opened up my chest,
> She ripped it from the sternum
> And she pulled it apart.
> Whoa, and the blood it flew,
> It flowed right out my body
> like something I would regret.
> Oh, and baby let me tell you,
> I regret everything.
> I regret you
> I regret him
> I regret this
> I regret you the most.
> Oh, and they told me if this is how I want it,
> Well this is exactly how it would be.
> Oh, I wish I would have listened to them now.

*Wren had built herself quite the reputation before we started dating, but I didn't listen to those people who had warned me that this was exactly how it would be. The blood flowing from my chest was graphic imagery representing that my heart had been ripped out, but it also foreshadowed the following lines as my anger grew.*

Oh, wait a minute,
Wait just one time,
Did you tell me what I think I heard?
Cause I will kill ya,
I'll rip ya in half,
I may just give you
What you gave to me.
Oh, and I can't wait to move on.
And I'm gonna,
I'm gonna move on,
And it's goin' to feel so good.

And you can tell me that you think I'm wrong,
And I can tell you,
Well, you started it
And I'll just end it here.
I'm gonna end it,
I'm gonna watch you bleed,
Out yo chest,
Like you done to me.

*I was now thinking of moving on with someone else, just like I had done to Samantha, starting my relationship with Wren. Ripping them in half wasn't a threat of actual violence but a metaphor for turning into a killer like her. My revenge would take the shape of me moving on quickly like I didn't care about her. Watching me move on quickly would rip her heart out too, and I wouldn't be wrong for it. She started it, but I would be the one to end it, and I'd watch her bleed out of her chest when I ripped her heart out. In the end, I didn't do any of that. I became depressed and was too scared to date anyone again.*

And as for you,
My dear old friend,
I hope you burn in hell for this shit.

I'm so glad you're gone,
I'm so glad I'm gone from that town,
I'm movin' up, I'm movin' on out

*This last verse did the most damage and remains the most cringe-worthy. Toad was hurt when he heard this line. We had been through so much together, and now we had let a nasty emo girl wreck our friendship. I didn't wish any ill will on my friend for this, but I recorded this immediately after I learned about their months-long fling, and I was in a musically induced hypnotic state. The words chose themselves, and this is what came out.*

I was understandably distraught and moved quickly from sadness to anger and then to intoxicated. Since I knew both people so well, my brain kept picturing them together, and I'd go through all the emotions again. The only thing that helped me forget how I was feeling, the thing I always turned to in times like these, again, was my rum. Luckily, I also had my classes that I could focus on, and I could lock myself in a soundproof practice room with a piano and my fifth. In the back of my mind, I prepared for the inevitability of failing at least one class.

# PART 4: CONVENIENT EXCUSE

The semester ended, and I had done well, aside from failing music theory. I was now officially suspended from school. I went and spoke with my counselor; I told him everything that had happened and pleaded my case that it wasn't my fault. I had honestly tried so hard, but the limitations of my ear meant I couldn't physically do it. Thankfully, they lifted my suspension based on my performance in my other classes and allowed me to continue. He also showed me that I was one semester away from graduation.

Being so close to completion shocked me; I hadn't been trying to graduate. I had plenty of elective credits that didn't count toward any specific degree, so now I just needed the right combination to graduate. I would be finished with school after taking math, creative writing, and speech. I didn't know what to do with myself. A swelling of pride came over me. I felt like I had done the impossible; I "just went to college," and I accidentally graduated.

I'm not sure I could have survived the heartbreak of realizing I had failed out of music school. Graduation would be the perfect way to save face, and it wouldn't be about my inability to finish but my successful completion and graduation. When I did graduate, I didn't let on that I was incapable of completing the music track and that I had graduated with a concentration in random electives. The plan was to finish music school at the University of North Texas. I could get to town and delay registration for a little while, find my niche in a new community, and figure out a new plan at some point.

You were leaving Texas at the same time, work had you relocating to Colorado, and we hit the road together. The plan was to leave me in North Texas, and you would continue to Colorado. I took a campus tour, and they took me to the music hall where I'd be training. If the students at the community college I had just been to were intimidating, the students here were utterly demoralizing. At the community college, I was the only jazz guitarist, but there were classrooms full of them at the University. I walked into one particular class where at least thirty guitarists sat around preparing for class to start. Hearing them tune their guitars and warm up their fingers was enough to show me that I didn't belong there, and again that depressing internal dialogue kicked back in.

I stayed with an old friend that night and told her about my plans to attend music school and what I wanted to do with my career. She was excited to have me in town and promised to take me to all the coolest places she liked. By the next morning, I had instead packed my things and followed you on to Colorado, leaving North Texas behind for good. I auditioned for music school in Colorado. The program seemed more manageable than what I had seen in Texas, and there were fewer guitarists. My audition consisted of this song that I had written with guitar loops and neat tricks.

# Listen: Track 3

# "School of Jazz"

https://denverjhamilton.bandcamp.com/track/school-of-jazz

The interview panel seemed to be impressed, but I was also required to play something with sheet music. I had a Django Reinhardt book that I purchased for this exact situation. I hated playing other people's music. I didn't have the patience for it and was always more interested in creating original compositions. I knew the intros to several songs, but I could never stay motivated long enough to learn an entire piece. My Django audition was no exception to that rule.

I pulled out my sheet music and told them what I'd be playing; they again looked impressed. I played the intro and part of the first verse before stopping. I was going to make it look as though I was giving them a sampling, but they interrupted me and asked why I had stopped. They asked me to finish the first song. I tried my damnedest to pull it off, but the audition fell apart pitifully. I told them I had only recently learned to read sheet music and couldn't translate quickly. I slowly picked through the song, but they cut me off. In the end, I was accepted into the University, but I never returned.

I was living in your basement, and my life felt devoid of purpose again. I drank alone every night at a stale-smelling Chili's off the highway close to the house. One night I was flipping through your community association pamphlet to find something to do. Residence in your neighborhood granted you access to the gym, the pool, and all the classes they offered to the community. I found a section for music classes.

I had once heard that Randy Rhoads would take guitar lessons from a local guitar player in every city he toured. He'd usually end up teaching the instructor a few things, but he'd always come away with some little technique or trick that person had figured out. I thought it might be fun to check it out and hoped to meet some other musicians in the area.

The next day I called and attempted to sign up, but they informed me the advertisement in the pamphlet was just a placeholder because they hadn't yet found a teacher. I told them I had just finished music school, technically a lie but built with some semblance of truth. They offered me an interview for the following morning. I gathered my textbooks from school, chord progression books, and gimmicky scale books. I brought everything I could think of, including some synthesizers and weird pedals to play through.

I completely steamrolled through them at the interview. I dropped my stuff on the table and outlined the curriculum I would teach. It wouldn't be anything like the classes I had struggled with in school. There would be nothing about learning by ear. It would be about music theory and learning to create original compositions. My classes would feature the tricks and shortcuts I had figured out that had gotten me up to the doorstep of music school. It would be more than enough to expect from a free community association guitar class.

They loved it so much, and since they had zero knowledge of music, they offered me the position of Music Director for the Association. The role would see me teaching the classes, hiring more teachers, and developing the curriculum those future teachers would use. In ten minutes, my music career had gone from a tone-deaf music school dropout to a music director.

As the director, I was making five times as much money as I ever had in my entire life. I loved teaching, and I loved all the people I met. My students were inspiring, and I became close to the families in the community. My students ranged from age six to seventy years old. I had achieved my end goal, and despite the plan falling apart, I was a music teacher. I had a classroom with an office, and the company had purchased instruments for me. I should have been happy, but I wasn't.

I felt like a fraud. It also felt like settling, I wasn't a real teacher, and I panicked at the thought of what I would do when my students had learned everything I could show them or someone truly talented walked through the door and expected me to be an actual professional. I feared that someone would figure me out, that I'd lose everything I had built, and that it probably wouldn't take very long.

Because of this, I started drinking until I blacked out almost every night. Not intentionally, but I would drink after work and wouldn't stop until I woke up the next morning. I had moved closer to the mayhem of downtown, and I now lived across the street from a cool bar. I was making more money than I knew what to do with, so I just drank more expensive alcohol. I would sometimes play shows downtown and drive home drunk or wake up, confused, in my truck frantically checking my pockets to ensure I hadn't been robbed.

I felt like this was around the time when Shannon didn't want me around him and his family the most. He was never so outward with it but canceled plans and avoided phone calls started around this time. In hindsight, I can't blame him. I was a mess and losing my ability to hide it. It was also around this time that I started experiencing a lot of unexplained joint pain.

I had been skateboarding for most of my life, but I almost completely stopped when I lived in Colorado. My knees hurt all the time, and skating was nearly unbearable. I was in my early 20s, but I assumed years of hard slams and big gaps had just blown my knees out. When it got to my wrists, I again wrote the pain off as old skater problems. I had broken and sprained my wrists more times than I could count. I started to panic when my wrists got so bad that I couldn't play music.

Music was my life, and now it was also my career. It was the only thing keeping me alive, and I knew I wouldn't survive without it. I would try to play through the pain, but my hands were slowing down, and I couldn't play anything faster than 120 beats per minute. I would drink heavily to try to mask the pain, but the pain would only get worse. I would black out, teach the class the next day, and then head to the bar to numb the physical and emotional pain. I played that on repeat for a long time.

It wasn't until I started shitting my pants that I knew it was time to draw the line. I sat on my couch with a warm bowl of ramen noodle soup and hit play on the DVD player. It was my fourth time watching season 3 of *House M.D.*, and I was on the episode "The Jerk." I set my beer on the coffee table and began to swirl my first bite of noodles around my fork when the urge to fart overcame my body. I leaned to one side and lifted my leg slightly. I was mid-bite when I felt the undeniable ooze of diarrhea instead of the comforting reduction in abdominal pressure one would expect from a good fart.

I don't know what the acceptable amount of grown adult pants shitting is normal, but it has to be a relatively low number of times. My movie night was ruined, along with my futon, and I had to admit skateboarding couldn't be to blame for the latest development in symptoms. I called and made an appointment with my doctor and gave her my list of symptoms; joint pain, heart palpitations, itchy palms, and a host of others that I couldn't necessarily differentiate from being drunk all the time. When asked how much I drank, I lied and said I only drank a few times a month. I was still in denial about my problem and didn't think it was related.

She performed some testing and found my iron levels were elevated, along with my heart and liver enzymes, suggesting something was wrong with the two organs. I was given a Holter monitor, a small device that I'd wear for a week that would allow me to record my heart rhythm whenever I experienced any palpitations. The recorded data would then be forwarded automatically to my cardiologist. My primary care doctor also scheduled a liver biopsy a few weeks later.

One night I went out drinking with some friends, wearing my Holter under my shirt. It was small enough that you couldn't see it, but I could hit a button on the top of the box to begin the recording easily from my pocket. The recording box also had a volume setting, which would beep with every recorded heartbeat. I generally kept the volume off or very low. I was a little embarrassed by the ordeal and didn't want anyone to know I was wearing it.

Ever since I started getting sick, my tolerance for alcohol began to drop. It made drinking with friends hard to navigate, and I often got more drunk than anticipated. When we finished eating, and everyone went their separate ways, I realized I was bordering on being too drunk to drive. I figured I felt drunk, but I was probably fine. Considering I had driven in much worse condition, I hopped in the truck and got on the freeway.

# Part 5: A 1, 2, 3

I learned the hard way that you should wear gloves when you change your taillights, or the oils from your fingers will cause the bulb to burn out more quickly. The left taillight I had recently changed had done that exact thing, and the flickering of red and blue lights set my palpitations a flutter.

It wasn't the first time I had been pulled over drunk, and I found that as long as you remained calm and had your paperwork in order, you were most likely to get to stay in your car and go home. Besides, I told myself, I only had four beers. They're not going to smell it on my breath, and I'll probably pass a breathalyzer test. I popped a mint in my mouth anyway.

The officer walked up to my window, and I had my hands firmly placed at ten and two. Like a true professional alcoholic, my window was already down, and my license and registration were ready. "Good evening," he said, as he shined a flashlight in my face and around the truck's cab.

"Hello, sir," I said with the friendliest smile I could muster.

"Do you know why I pulled you over?" He was now looking through the back window.

"Actually, no, sir. I don't think I was speeding."

"You weren't, but your tail lights are out."

I was genuinely surprised but added some sauce to my frustration, "Dang it!" I said, "I just replaced them. There must be something wrong with them, electrical maybe?"

"Maybe," he said, as his eyes narrowed. He stepped closer to my window. "Have you had anything to drink tonight?"

"Fuck," I thought. Your best option when dealing with the police is honesty. Even when you've broken the law, admitting your mistake will sometimes let you off with a warning, but that rarely applies to drunk driving. "Yes," I said and then mentally damned myself. I tried to recover, "I was just studying with some friends, and we had a couple of beers, but it's been several hours, and I feel fine."

"I'm going to need you to step out of the truck, please," he said, as he backed away, walking back toward his car.

I got out and started following the path that his flashlight was illuminating. We were on the side of the freeway, and I noticed his backup had already arrived. I imagined what people thought as they drove by us, and I wondered if it looked as bad as it was starting to feel. I muttered a silent prayer, wishing you or Shannon weren't in any of the hundreds of cars zooming past, witnessing my inevitable arrest.

The police officer told me to hold my arms wide and touch my nose, only bending at the elbow. Then he had me stand on one leg and recite the alphabet, counting to three between each letter. Standing on one leg was no problem; I had spent the last several years skating drunk and had done much harder tricks than this while intoxicated. The alphabet was a bit more difficult, but I nailed it with phonetic ease. "A 1, 2, 3, B 1, 2, 3, C 1, 2, 3, D..." I counted off as I balanced and again thought about how this must look to the people driving past. As I counted to three repeatedly, the echo of my voice made me laugh, and I struggled more with the task. He had seen enough and asked me to stop. I felt like I was killing it, but my stomach dropped when I saw him pull out the breathalyzer. The balance and counting I could do, but I couldn't fake a breathalyzer.

An idea occurred to me as he started walking back over to where I was standing. I slowly slipped my hand into my pocket, increased the volume on my Holter monitor to the max, and then pushed the record button. My heart was thumping in my chest, and the beeps from the monitor were fast and loud. The officer lifted the breathalyzer to my mouth but stopped just short of my lips. He looked down at my waist as the monitor squawked in my pocket. I took the momentary hesitation as an opportunity to feign lightheadedness.

I put my hand on my head and rocked slowly from side to side. "Oh no, do you mind if I sit down?" I asked him as I headed to the curb. "I have a heart condition," I lied as I pulled my shirt up to show the wires connected to my chest. "Every time my heart has an episode, this monitor goes off."

The officer motioned to his partner with a nod, and they walked to his car. I sat alone, behind my truck on the side of the freeway, wondering if I had done myself any favors or if I had just bought myself a little time before getting arrested.

The officer came back over to me and asked how I was feeling. He helped me to my feet and told me to be safe. As I gingerly made my way back into my truck, he asked me if I needed anything, and I assured him I was already feeling better, pointing to my now silenced

Holter. I was still driving home when the cardiologist's technician called my cell phone, afraid I must have been having a heart attack based on the recording they had just received. I told them the increased heart rate was because I had been exercising. They reminded me not to record any events unless I had chest pain or palpitations and that an increased heart rate during exercise was normal.

A few weeks later, my liver biopsy results showed a considerable amount of scarring. Coupled with the more legitimate results from the Holter monitor and my other symptoms, my doctor diagnosed me with hereditary hemochromatosis. She explained that I had inherited a genetic condition that causes the body to absorb excess iron from my diet. This iron then moves throughout the body, causing injury to the joints, heart, and liver, causing all my symptoms. She didn't bother performing genetic testing to confirm because the only possible alternative was that I was a major alcoholic, and I had still not let on about the amount of alcohol I consumed daily.

Hemochromatosis gave me an excuse to pretend I didn't have a problem, and unfortunately, it gave you and Shannon a reason to do the same. It was easier to believe I had a rare genetic condition than a drinking problem. Hemochromatosis, also known as iron overload, comes in a few different flavors, and you have two options for acquiring the mutation. One is autosomal recessive, meaning I'd have to get one mutated gene from you and Mom. The other is autosomal dominant, meaning only one of you has the mutation, but it is strong enough to give me the condition. Shannon was the first to be tested.

Shannon was negative for the mutated gene, which hadn't ruled anything out, but it made the math a bit more complicated. When you tested negative, it whittled down our chances of continuing to have this excuse. The only other option was that my mother could have it, but I hadn't spoken to her in years, and there was no way to find out. The disease is rarer in women, and the effects of iron overload disease are typically masked by menstruation. We were unlikely to glean any helpful information from her or the small-town gossip we could likely hear from anyone.

All signs pointed to this not being hereditary but rather a form of iron overload brought on by alcoholism, and I was now starting to develop cirrhosis. Shannon was always looking for opportunities to create separation between us being brothers or to put our mother

66

down. This was his chance to do both. He told me the mutation was likely because our mom had an affair and that you weren't my biological father. I had a problem and needed help, but Shannon made me feel more alone than ever. He spent more time trying to think of potential suitors with hemochromatosis in the town where I was born than he did in seeing if I was okay. I was torn between admitting I had a problem or that you were potentially not my birth father. While Shannon continued his attempt to poke fun at my situation, I continued living in denial about my alcoholism.

Hemochromatosis causes the blood to retain iron, so if you remove the blood, you remove the iron. Thousands of years ago, in ancient Greece, they would use leeches to remove the blood from patients thinking it would prevent or cure disease. In my case, it actually would have helped. Instead of leeches, I had a prescription to donate a pint of blood every week. My doctor was supposed to monitor me through the process, but my case must have slipped through the cracks. I went from having an iron overload disorder to becoming severely anemic with iron deficiency.

I wanted to learn more about my condition and started researching. This diagnosis of a rare genetic disorder masking a patient's lie of alcoholism felt like it was torn directly from an episode of *House MD*. I loved that show so much, and I was now living in one of the episodes. The longer I spent in and around the hospital, the more interested I became in medicine and the closer I came to admitting I had a problem. Almost on a whim, I decided to enroll in nursing school the following semester.

Due to the anemia, I would get instantly intoxicated when drinking. A few beers were enough to knock me over, and my depression had become unbearable, but I would get lost in my study of human anatomy and physiology. I applied the same techniques I had picked up in music school and maintained a 4.0 GPA. I was also teaching music classes and nurturing a high level of alcoholism. To perform well under that level of stress, one must live a healthy lifestyle. The pressure was mounting quickly as my health declined.

The depression made me feel like I had to leave Colorado and start over somewhere. Austin had the allure of live music, and the University of Texas had a great nursing program. I saved what I could and left for Austin at the end of my first nursing school semester. I was surprised you'd help me move a block away from the chaos of 6th street after being diagnosed with an old man's alcoholism disease, but you never tried to talk me out of it.

After you left me in Austin, I immediately started contemplating creative ways to commit suicide. I started taking iron supplements to trash my liver or heart. I figured that when I died, everyone would blame it on the disease, and no one had to know I had done it intentionally. Ironically, since I had donated far too much blood, the iron supplements helped reverse my anemia and made me feel better. I had gone from one extreme to the other and was now getting back to a moderate iron level. That's when I met Creek View Antonio.

## Part 6: Bag of Unused Organs

Antonio was a very gay man who lived in the same apartment complex as me. He was the unspoken leader of a group of older men and women who played water volleyball in the apartment pool daily. I was painting on my balcony overlooking the pool when Antonio saw me and flagged me over. He invited me to play volleyball and introduced me to everyone.

All the people gathered around the pool daily in Antonio's group lived in the Creek View apartment complex. I met my neighbors, and they showed me where they lived. We gathered every day after work to play volleyball, barbecue, and drink beers. We all moved freely in and out of each other's apartments, and they fully welcomed me as part of their community. My depression was easier to manage, but it never went away. I think that's what most people don't understand about depression.

I had everything someone would need to be happy. I was pursuing things I was passionate about and was surrounded by good friends. I had enough money to pay my rent and keep myself entertained. I laughed hard every day, but I always went home at the end of the day and fell back into a dark hole. I had screwed up; I had fallen into the life pattern I'd seen you and Shannon inhabit my entire life and considered it normal. I had become a victim of the idea that life success was measured by earning potential and stability. I had always been more interested in the present moment. I would rather enjoy the company I held than sacrifice relationships to move up some empty corporate ladder. I had a community of people who cared about me, encouraged me to drink in moderation, came to my art shows, and supported my music. A large group of people I saw every day cheered when I got home and showered me with love. I couldn't enjoy any of it because I was crippled by the idea that I was somehow failing at life. Happiness was staring me in the face, and I was too worried about my future to cherish it. The depression never faded, and I continued searching for the courage to end my life.

Everything changed the night I rented Seven Pounds. In it, Will Smith struggles to live with himself after causing the deaths of six people and his fiancé. Wracked with survivor's guilt, he kicks off this elaborate plot to identify seven people he could help by donating his organs to them. He kills himself, and his organs go to all the people he picked, and then they show up at his funeral, and they're like, "Oh my god, you have his eyes," it's this whole thing. The concept, while a bit unbelievable, was such a great idea. I wasn't encouraged to buy any jellyfish (that's ultimately how he did it), but I did realize I could be helpful to someone, even if I were just a bag of unused organs. I was at such a low point in my life that a bag of organs seemed like an improvement. It took a drama by the Fresh Prince to help me realize I was an able-bodied young man, capable of building homes for the poor, serving soup to the homeless, or working dangerous jobs for the people who would rather live. I felt selfish that I was taking iron pills and staring at my ceiling, trying to control my double vision when I could be out there making a difference to someone less fortunate than I am. Being sad was no excuse for being selfish.

I decided I would dedicate my life to helping others, and I started first by working in a soup kitchen. I met good people and found other ways to help, but I felt I could do more. I tried to quit drinking during this time, but it was nearly impossible. I went to a salon to get a haircut, and they had free beer in the waiting area. It was hard to escape the temptation. Even when I could avoid the scene, I'd still think about drinking every few minutes. The amount I drank decreased, and my friends at Creek View were there to help me. I'd usually only be successful at quitting for two to three days, and then I'd break, but I'd feel successful if I just drank less each time.

My goals for the new job were simple; it had to help people while also being so dangerous that the likelihood of death was high. The first and most obvious choice was at the Austin Fire Department. Saving someone from a burning building worked two-fold, you saved the person in the fire, but you also prevented someone else from having to run in. If I died doing it, win-win.

I talked to a tall, noticeably unenthusiastic man at the front desk. "Hi, I'd like to apply for a position."

"For what?" he asked, looking puzzled.

"For... for a firefighter, please." I was starting to realize this might not be how you applied to be a firefighter.

"We're not hiring." My shoulders dropped at how quickly my great idea had fallen apart. My perfect plans for dying were unraveling, but then he added, "We do have a point system, though.

If you have a college degree, you get a point. If you know Spanish, a point. Military service is another point. They hire a lot of Military guys."

I already had a point! I had an associate's degree, which meant I was well on my way to fighting some fires, maybe, someday when they're hiring. My brief moment of hope was squashed by the urge to die more quickly than that. I thanked him for his time and went back to the drawing board. Applying to be a police officer briefly crossed my mind, but I imagined I'd end up ruining people's day more often than I'd save anyone. The ratio of giving out traffic tickets to saving lives was too high for my plans. I was surprised to realize that getting a job where you die is harder to find than I thought it would be. I started filling out the application for an offshore oil rig technician. You would don scuba gear, sink to the bottom of the Gulf of Mexico with an underwater cutting torch, and then most likely die in the effort to repair the rig. I realized it only checked one of the boxes, and without helping others, it didn't feel worth it.

Every time I move to a new city, I like to drive around aimlessly and build my mental map. The next day I'll retrace my steps, but then take a left instead of a right and see where that takes me. It's an excellent way to find unique shops, good food, and new skate spots. One afternoon, I made my way into a small strip mall and decided to drive around the parking lot. It was just a dollar store, a Mexican restaurant, a tax place, and then three separate storefronts dedicated to the different branches of the military. I realized they were recruiting centers. The same butterflies you get when you drive through a speed trap caused my stomach to flip. Under the control of fate, something in my mind told me to pull into a parking spot.

I pulled in front of the Navy building only because it was in the middle, and I stared at the life-size troop decals on each of the windows. Serious-faced men and women were running through a collaged battle scene with eagles, flags, and random military vehicles in the background. I realized I could help people as a medic in the military and the chances of dying were respectably high. Check and check. The scary part was that I knew they would hire me if I walked into that building. Then it occurred to me that they'd probably pull up my records in some overly detailed post-9/11 mass surveillance database and immediately throw me in jail. That didn't check any of my boxes. Why would I willingly walk myself into prison? I threw my car in reverse and went home.

On my next mental map-building joy ride, I didn't change course and found myself back in the strip mall parking lot, staring at the photoshopped masterpiece. Again, I talked myself out of it and drove away. The fourth time I pulled into the same parking lot, I had almost worked up enough courage to walk in, but instead, I called my brother for advice.

"Hey, what's going on?" I asked when he finally answered.

"Nothin' much, what's goin' on with you?" He always had a tone that sounded partially playful but mostly annoyed.

"Well," I began, "I'm thinking of joining the military." I didn't know what he'd say, but I would have bet money he was going to tell me it was a stupid idea. In some ways, I was kind of hoping he would. I mean, it *was* a stupid idea. I heard they could test drugs in your hair years after use. If they tested mine, it would break their machine.

"Yeah? Which branch?" He sounded amused but unbelieving. He didn't know I was sitting in a parking spot outside the recruiting office.

"I don't know, Air Force, I guess." I was basing my decision mainly on the art in the windows and which one I could see myself in most. The Army window looked too much like a *Call of Duty* poster, and I had no interest in living on a boat in the Navy.

"Yeah, you should do it." His sincerity took me off guard. This phone call was the first time I had gotten support from him for something I had come up with on my own; I didn't know how to respond. Then I realized he might not have known what I knew.

"There's a problem, though. I…" I trailed off momentarily as I considered how much to admit. He had found pot plants growing in my closet in high school and had once temporarily disowned me after realizing I had a gram of bud in the console of my car while driving him around, so I knew he knew about me smoking weed. He didn't know the full extent of my criminal record. For example, I never told him about the time I smuggled weed across the Mexican border when I was eighteen.

# PART 7: MASS SURVEILLANCE DATABASE

My friend Jack had invited me to South Padre Island with his family. His mom, dad, and younger sister were in their van, and we followed behind in my car. Jack and I went to Mexico, bought a half-pound of shwag, and then did our best to smoke it all in a week. We didn't even get close, and now we were confronted with leaving it all in Mexico or trying to get it back home. We duct-taped our bag into a ball and then buried that ball in a larger bag of beach sand. We had heard drug dogs couldn't smell weed through coffee grounds, and I guess we just assumed sand was fundamentally the same. We hid the massive bag of sand under my spare tire in the trunk of my car and followed his parents to the border crossing.

We had gone back and forth across the border for an entire week, and every time it was super mellow, but this final time across, there was a long line of vehicles. As we got closer, we realized the police were walking a dog around the outside of each one. We argued about whether we should turn around, but we would have had to head back down the wrong way, which would look incriminatingly obvious. It was too late; we would be arrested in front of his parents. His family went through the checkpoint relatively quickly, and we were motioned forward. They checked my license and asked if we had any drugs in the car. My stuttering response was probably grounds enough for an arrest, but he handed me my license back anyway. The dog walked around the car and barked at my trunk once. I let my body go limp, and I stared at the ceiling. I tried to enjoy the feeling of freedom for as long as I could. Again, the police officer should have arrested us on our expressions alone because we were clearly stunned when he told us to have a good day and motioned us forward. At the first gas station we hit, we pulled out our bag and rolled a giant blunt of freedom weed. His parents were furious, knowing we had just smuggled weed across the border and tainted their family vacation forever.

Shannon didn't know that when you went to Africa for work, leaving me home alone for a month with a bunch of money to get by, I had attempted to double my money by selling Xanax. My girlfriend and I decided to see what they were like and took one each. I remember swallowing one with a beer, and then I immediately woke up the following day as if walking through a wormhole. I thought we had been robbed initially, but friends helped us piece the night together. Apparently, we thought the pills weren't working and took them all, finished a 30-pack of keystone, and then crashed my car. He also didn't know that we used to add lighter fluid to cough syrup to isolate the dextromethorphan and walk around town like zombies. He didn't know about the acid, the cocaine, any of it. How much did I want to share? I eventually settled on, "I've smoked weed before."

"Have you ever been arrested before?" he asked.

"No. I don't have any criminal record, but can't they find that stuff out some other way? And if they do, what happens? Do they just kill you? I don't even know." Every bad thing I had ever done had been racing through my brain the past few days while sitting in this parking lot. I made the crime of the month on crime stoppers once for wrecking our school in junior high, but we had never been caught. On multiple occasions, after skateboarding around the University's campus, we would break into the football stadium. A crime that was likely considered sacrilegious at such a storied franchise in a city overly crazy about football. You could walk up the ramp toward the field, between the parking garage entrance and the concession stands. Before the locked gates, you could climb the railing and get on top of the concession stands. From there, you could climb up and walk across a one-foot wide beam connected to the second-story parking garage. The first floor was the only area of the entire stadium with locked doors, so once you got onto the second floor, you had full access to everywhere else. We did a lot of drugs and broke many things in that stadium, including in the coach's box overlooking the city. One night we found out how to get on the roof of the five-story School of Engineering building. We went and bought some beers, set off the fire alarms in the building next door, and then sprayed fire extinguishers down the hallways as we ran back out of the building. We then headed back up to the roof across the street, where we drank our beers and watched the fire department attempt to figure it out. My name had to be on somebody's list somewhere, and if anyone had access to that list, it was the military.

"If you don't have a record, then lie about it. They don't need to know." He was being oddly supportive about this, and I considered telling him how much stuff I had actually done when he added, "The military will lie to you if it serves the mission. Why can't you lie to them? As long as you don't smoke any weed while you're in and you serve your country well, there's no reason they need to know about your past."

He was making some excellent points. I had already scared myself away from drugs, so I had zero desire to play with that fire again. They only ask if you've done drugs to see if you're at risk of continuing to use them. I wasn't at risk, so I saw no problem with pretending to have always been on the straight and narrow. We got off the phone, and I stared at the window for another forty-five minutes before finally walking in. I had convinced myself it was safe to go in, ask a couple of questions, and then bail.

# Part 8: Ropes

"Ah, here we go, Hamilton." The gum lady had finally found my name on the cap and gown list for graduation. "Here's your stuff, and congratulations, you earned summa cum laude." She reached into a medium-sized bin behind her chair and pulled out a set of golden ropes. A rush of relief, pride, and exhaustion hit me all at once. Tears filled my eyes, and I instinctively looked away in embarrassment. I took the ropes and left the hall as quickly as I could. I needed to get away from everyone and finish analyzing what had just happened. I turned a corner near the bathrooms and found an empty hall with a few couches and a study table.

I threw my backpack and collection of grad swag on the couch. I laid my gown on the arm of the chair and placed my cap on top of it. Then I sat down and held the ropes in my hands, letting the tears roll off my cheeks. I knew you would be so proud of me, and my brother wouldn't be able to take anything away from the accomplishment. I did as well as one could do. I had received multiple scholarships for academic performance, joined and led numerous clubs on campus, maintained a 4.0 GPA, and was now a father to a beautiful six-month-old daughter. I had been living with a nagging voice in the back of my head telling me I wasn't smart enough or dedicated enough to do something like this. These ropes represented the fact that I had not only done it but that I had been perfect. There were no wisecracks to be made and no eye rolling. I did it, and I had left zero doubt about its validity. I had blown the monkey off my back.

Those ropes had lifted a heavy weight from my shoulders, and I knew everything would change. I would be accepted as my brother's equal, both in your eyes and in his. I was a scientist just like him now. I would soon have a meaningful career, and I would show you both that I could be a great father and provide for my family just as you wished. I had done it my way, and my way was better than anything you or Shannon had ever suggested. As a scientist, I was inspired by the work, I could use my creativity, and it paid respectably well. I would be able to take care of my family while working a job I could love doing for the rest of my long career. I wasn't doomed to crunch numbers as an accountant. I didn't feel I had to sacrifice anything while still satisfying the expectations you and Shannon had set before me.

As I sat staring at the yellow-colored ropes, I thought about all the nights I spent studying at school. I thought of the best teachers I had, and I thought of the worst teachers I had. I imagined how my past self would feel if we could meet each other now. Suppose I could go back to the Denver who was sitting in the parking lot of the recruiter's office trying to decide if the military was a good idea or not. I would lightly knock on the passenger's side window and wave. My past self would look out his window and stare in shock at my familiarity. His brain would struggle to recognize the face he had seen his entire life, but now on someone else. He would slowly unlock the door and let me in; too confused to ask how any of this was possible.

"Relax, dude," I would say to myself. "I'm you, but from the future. You're thinking about going in there, huh?" I laugh as I recognize the awful war collage plastered across the windows.

"Ugh, yeah. I gotta do something. Nothing is working out the way I want it to. I'm getting tired of trying. There are days where the only thing that gets me out of bed is the urge to drink at the bar." I look so young and thin, and I also look so sad. I put my hand on my past shoulder and give myself a firm squeeze.

"If you go in there, everything is going to change for you. You will work harder than you ever have in your entire life. You're going to end up in California and meet a woman that will enrich your life beyond your wildest dreams. I hope you take the time to try and enjoy it because it will fly by, bud." I'm just looking back at myself, not knowing what to say. "You might think that the alcohol helps you forget how you're feeling right now, but the only thing it has helped you forget is how special you are. I'm very proud of you. You're so close to figuring that out for yourself, don't give up." I watch the person I used to be break down and start sobbing. I can tell he desperately wanted to hear that from someone. I'm glad I got the opportunity to be the one to say it. I'd squeeze my past shoulder once more and give him a warm smile, and then I'd get out of the car. Before leaving, I would say, "Oh, and you should skate more." I'd close the door and walk away.

I'd get to a good vantage point on the other side of the parking lot and watch to see what my past self would do. He would just sit in the car for a while, unmoving. After a couple of minutes, he'd finally get out and walk into the Air Force recruiting building. I'd be so happy for him. I know how great everything will turn out, but I'd also feel a little bad for him. He's going to have a tough time getting through basic training.

# Military: Chapter 5
## PART 1: COLORBLIND

I walked in the front door of the recruiting center and froze; it was the first time I had seen people in uniform up close like this. One guy on the right side of the room was doing pull-ups on a portable chin-up bar and dropped down when I walked in. I looked behind myself, feeling like I must have walked in through the wrong door. A voice called out from the far end of the room, "Hey, welcome. How can I help you?"

I felt weird yelling across the room, so I quickly walked over to his desk. "I just have a few questions about joining," I said in a low voice while trying to ignore the pull-up dude who was now staring at me.

"Come sit down; let's chat!" my new recruiter said, motioning me over to sit in front of his desk. I sat down, noticing the squeakiness of the chair in the silent room. We talked about my experience and what I hoped to get from joining. I had already made up my mind that I would only work in something medical-related. If they didn't have that, I wasn't going to join. I knew little about the military, but I had heard that medics weren't allowed to carry guns. I was joining to help people, not shoot people.

"I'm only interested in medical jobs. I want to be a nurse someday, so I hope to learn in the military and get money for school." I tried to sound firm since I had heard recruiters try to talk you out of stuff or lie about things just to get you to join.

He pulled out a manual and started scanning the different jobs. He stopped on something he called a 4N Flight Medic. He described the job as an ambulance EMT but in a helicopter. You'd drop behind enemy lines and provide medical support, transportation, and evacuation. He might as well have just pointed to the advertisement on the door and said, "That." It was an insane idea, checking all my boxes and then some. All I had to do was score high enough on the ASVAB test and get through MEPS.

"Let's fill out some paperwork, and then we'll get you scheduled!" he said, as he rummaged through the drawers in his desk. He pulled out a folder and opened it to a stack of papers inside. "Before we get any further, I have to ask, have you ever been arrested for anything, and have you ever done any drugs at all."

My excitement over the prospect of my new journey had distracted me from seeing this question coming. The question I had rehearsed in the parking lot the previous four days hit me as if I hadn't ever considered it. I stuttered and stammered but quickly recovered with a sly laugh, "Ha ha, me do drugs? No, no, no, that stuff terrifies me. I've never been interested." We stared at each other a little while, and then I added, "And I've never been arrested. I've had a few traffic tickets, though."

"Those don't count. As long as they're paid, you should be good." He then reviewed the paperwork I needed to fill out and the references I would need to contact. We just moved right past the drug question, and I realized this would be much easier than I thought.

I bought an ASVAB study book and tried to remember how to do math. I had a few weeks to study for the exam, but it didn't feel like it would be enough time. I was 25 years old and hadn't seen some of this material in over eight years. I treated it like homework and forced myself to do math problems at the bar. It became fun. I felt like an old lady doing Sudoku puzzles, but with algebra. When the time came to test, I met my recruiter at his office. He gave another dude and me a ride to MEPS, which was located on base. We climbed into the back seat of his sedan, and the other future airman introduced himself to me. His name was Serling Stilver. Like sterling silver, but Serling Stilver. He talked to me the entire ride to MEPS, but I didn't hear a word he said. I just kept thinking about how stupid his name was. I kept thinking that Serling isn't a normal name, but neither is Stilver. Then I'd think about how stupid his parents must have been. The recruiter finally called back from the driver's seat, "We're here. Get your identification ready." I snapped out of my daydreaming and looked around at the base we were entering. My anxiety tripled when I saw the guards at the gate were all packing heat and looked overly serious. I hadn't noticed I was holding my breath until after my recruiter handed me back my license, and I relaxed again. We pulled up to a building with large letters that read "MEPS" above the door. Serling and I both climbed out of the car and went inside.

The exam was relatively easy until I got to the math portion. There were an unnecessary amount of physics questions, and I hadn't seen anything about any physics in my study guide. I did my best to answer them, but I was entirely out of my depth. I finished the exam before Stilver, but I didn't wait for him; I just headed to the next MEPS station alone, where things got less friendly quickly. I was suddenly in trouble with everyone I talked to; it was exactly like the DMV. I got in line behind other males I assumed were headed into the military too. New recruits usually have a distinctly uncomfortable look of fear and uncertainty on their faces. They had me walk back and forth on my heels from one side of the room to the other, lift a fifty-pound weight, and then tested my eyes and ears. They stripped us naked and examined our butts for some reason. I'm not sure exactly what they were looking for back there, but they looked very closely. When he saw the scars on my arm, he asked, "What are these?"

"Construction accident," I said, holding my wrist pronated to make the scars appear more on the side of my arm than over the wrist. His eyes narrowed, but he moved along on his checklist.

Toward the end of the ordeal, they asked me again, "Have you ever done any drugs?"

I confidently responded with a "No!" that was the right mixture of surprised and offended.

Then they'd ask again, "Not even once?"

"No, I haven't."

"This is your last chance. If you say no and they find out once you get to basic training, you can be tried for lying on your paperwork, and you *will* go to jail."

"Holy shit," I cursed in my mind. Thoughts of that mass surveillance database popped into my head again. I panicked a little and started drumming up my own conspiracy theories in my head. Can they do a lie detector test? *Will* they do a lie detector test? My brother's words echoed in my ears, "The military will lie to you if it serves the mission." I was here to serve my country and would lie to it if I had to. I considered admitting to some marijuana use, lies are easier to maintain when they contain some truth, but I fully committed, "No, not even once," I lied.

I left the MEPS building and headed to meet my recruiter in the parking lot. Serling was sitting in the front seat of the car, and he kept his head down when I got in. The ride home was strangely quiet, and we dropped Serling off at his house instead of going straight back to the recruiting office as planned. When the recruiter and I got back on the road, he told me Serling had failed the ASVAB, and they never sent him over to complete his physical. My stomach dropped; that meant I had at least passed, but what if I scored on the lower end? I had signed all that paperwork. I better not get put into some security forces job. Imagine the irony if I ended up being a police officer anyway.

"You scored a 95, Hamilton. Great job! Let's go back to the office now, and we'll get you situated for the 4N position." He looked genuinely proud of me, and I was stunned.

Once back to his office, I sat in the squeaky chair in front of his desk. I patiently waited as he went through the files I was given at MEPS. He would read something from my folder and then crosscheck with the manual on his desk. "Oh no," he said, his eyes narrowing as he put one finger on the file and another on the manual. He leaned closer and then repeated it, "Oh no."

"Sir?" I asked. One of those files must contain the mass surveillance data, I thought.

"Are you colorblind?" he asked.

I knew I was colorblind, but I hadn't ever been tested for it. When you and I first moved to Texas, we went out to buy stuff to decorate the house. I had my own bathroom with blue wallpaper, and I picked out a blue soap dish, blue towels, and a blue shower curtain. I threw it all in your shopping cart, and you asked me what I was doing with a look of shock and disappointment on your face. We argued about whether or not the bathroom was green while still in the store, then we argued in the truck on the way home, and then we argued about it in the bathroom when we got back home. I knew one of us was colorblind when we walked into the bathroom, and we both said, "See! I told you!"

"Yes, I think so." I laughed a little remembering the test I took at MEPS and how badly I had done. I was shown a circle of small, multicolored dots surrounding a number in the middle, also made of dots. Out of the ten images I was shown, only two of them had apparent numbers in the middle. The rest just seemed like dots, nothing else. I couldn't even guess anything on most of them.

"You can't be a flight medic if you're color blind."

"Oh," I said, dejected. I hadn't realized that this was what that meant, and it was suddenly less funny.

"You can't do anything medical. They all require color vision. I think it's because of the lights on the aircraft and the medical equipment. You have to be able to distinguish them based on color." He was cross-referencing his two manuals, my records, and sometimes typing something into his computer. "Are you sure you only want to do medical? You tested high enough to do any job in the Air Force."

"No." I flinched at the unintended harshness of my voice. "I'm only interested in medical jobs."

He continued looking for a few more minutes and said, "Wait a second, here's one." He turned the manual around and pushed it toward me, his finger pointing to a job labeled 4A0X1, Medical Admin. He explained that this one was more like a medical secretary, very different from a deployed helicopter nurse. I wanted to say no, but I had already come so far. I was so close to this new idea and had already bought into it. The recruiter did his best to spice up the medical secretary job, but it didn't sound like I'd be saving any lives or dying anytime soon.

I sat on it for a few minutes before deciding to go for it. Reluctantly, I said, "Yes, let's do it."

He tried to smile away a frown, but his lips just made a straight line as he nodded. "There's one more thing. That position isn't available in Austin. There's only one spot open, and it's in California."

# PART 2: OPEN CABINETS

California?! I was a kid from Montana who spent his teen years in Texas, but I looked and acted like the California kids I had seen in movies. I didn't know much about California except that skateboarding was born there, everyone surfed, and all the women were blonde. I knew a few people who had moved to California. They had all gone to L.A. and were trying to "make it." I had never once realistically considered moving there myself, but now the chance had fallen into my lap.

My recruiter pulled up a map of California and showed me where the base was located. Theoretically, you could swim in the ocean in the morning, snowboard in the afternoon, and then camp in the woods that night. On a map, the base looked like it was a hub in the middle of the most amazing places. The city where it was located was steeped in history as being one of the first gold rush towns, and I assumed it was full of skate parks. In reality, it was just a dirty armpit surrounded by nothing for an hour on every side, but I'd learn that truth much later. The admin job was a significant disappointment that I wasn't expecting. Still, the idea of heading to California, the place I was potentially always meant to be, had me excited again.

The other downside of losing my selected job was that the timeframe for getting to Basic would also change. Instead of shipping out immediately, I'd have to wait three months, and I only had a month left on my apartment lease. I spent my last month in Austin playing water volleyball, running a mile each morning, and I had cut back significantly on alcohol. It was the best I'd felt in a long time, and you and Shannon were proud of my choice to serve my country. My cyclical depression was on the up side since I was back on track and had a goal.

When my lease expired, I moved back in with you to wait for my spot in basic training to open up. You had moved from Colorado and were now living in some tiny podunk town in Utah. If the base I was moving to was an armpit, then the place you had just moved to was squarely between the butt cheeks of Utah. The boredom of Mormonism quickly smothered the healthy progress I made in Austin. You were highly stressed in your new role at work, and I recognized your tired demeanor that I hadn't seen since I left Colorado. Seeing you this way, I would always take it personally. I knew it was because of work, but I would subconsciously take offense if being around me didn't make you feel any better. Your snappy, stressed-out attitude was always a trigger for my depression, and I started spending more time at the Rusty Spur Saloon.

I overdrank one night and called you to pick me up from the bar. A trigger for drinking can be just about anything; it depends on what you think you get out of it. For some people, boredom can be the trigger. For me, things that triggered my depression also triggered my urge to drink. Drinking helped me feel less depressed and gave me a false sense of being happy. Being inebriated helps silence the trigger, but it can be disastrous if you are triggered while already drunk. There's no perception to change or feelings to numb. You can't alter your mental state any further, and now you're stuck dealing with the very thing you were attempting to avoid. On this night, I was triggered as soon as we entered the house.

It was late, and I had woken you up in the middle of the night to get me from a bar on the opposite side of town. You were doing your best to entertain me for a little while before going back to sleep. I was making myself a snack, so I grabbed a water glass and plate from the cabinet. As always, I left the cabinet doors open, and you followed behind me, shutting them with a frustrated vigor. You mentioned how much you hated it when I left them open and unintentionally pressed the trigger.

I wasn't a mean or angry drunk. I was a funny drunk that was often the life of the party. Had anyone else mentioned a weird quirk about me at that same moment, I would have laughed it off, or at worst, I would have become increasingly mischievous and opened all of the cabinets in the house when you went to bed. The point is, had anyone else mentioned the cabinets, it wouldn't have been a trigger for me. My depressed alcoholic brain made several unconnected linkages between the cabinets being open and how much you loved me. Believe me, I fully understand how crazy this sounds, but I'm just telling you how it works. I don't make the rules; I'm just crippled by them.

A trigger is something that gives an alcoholic the urge to drink. They are different for everyone and can be either positive or negative. One of my positive triggers was drinking beers with friends while skateboarding. Skating is scary, and alcohol is like liquid courage.

Having a few beers during the session makes you more willing to try new tricks and push the boundaries. Another example of a positive trigger is playing music with people. A little buzz can help get you into the groove and relax on stage. These are positive triggers because they enhance activities that bring about joy. They can also lead to alcoholism because you eventually get to a point where you have to have a few every time you skate or play music. Negative triggers are almost always more destructive.

Negative triggers, at least for me, are the ones that are associated with depression, lowered self-esteem, and insecurity. When my brother puts me down, that's a negative trigger that I cope with by drinking heavily. I can feel my trigger activate when you're stressed out and start getting snappy with me. I get immediately overwhelmed by the urge to drink and usually give in with little resistance. Negative triggers can also be more damaging because they're the ones that can activate when you're already drunk and unable to cope with them. When you brought up the cabinets, my brain went back to trying to sit on the arm of the chair many years ago. When you walk into the kitchen after a long day of work and see the cabinets open, your first thought is my laziness. I get it, we don't get to pick our pet peeves, but a part of me wishes that you'd see the cabinets open and be reminded that I'm home. In a perfect world, those cabinets would change your mood for the better. You'd walk through the door and throw your briefcase down. You'd untie your shoes and untuck your button-up shirt. When you walk into the kitchen and see those cabinets, you would think, "Denver is home! Fuck work, I'm a go fishin' with my boy!"

You also have to remember the headspace I was in at the time. I was awaiting the military with an enlisted death wish, which made me think about how things would be when I was gone. Would you miss those cabinets being open? Why do we have to wait until we lose someone to realize we miss the things that used to annoy us about them? When you are triggered while drunk, there is no option for coping. You can drink to silence a trigger, but not if you're already drunk. Instead, it's all you can focus on, and now you're too drunk to let things go. That's how a simple comment about a cabinet became about how they'd all be closed when I was dead. I was holding onto so many negative feelings, and those cabinets opened the floodgates. That's how we got into an argument about my stepbrother.

# Part 3: Old and Tired

Jeremy was different from us, and it was hard to understand him. We all pushed him to conform to our personalities, but he never fit in with us. He was more into video games and reading fantasy novels than he was into roughhousing and watching football. We mean-teased him into changing anything we found weird and gave him terrible nicknames. This stuff worked well on me growing up because I wanted to fit in and be like you and Shannon. I wouldn't realize how big of an impact that would have on my psyche until I was much older, and now I felt guilty for being so hard on him.

There was nothing wrong with Jeremy. He was a special kid with unique interests that we didn't appreciate. We couldn't understand why he would get so excited about dorky things, and we never tried to learn from him. Instead, we beat him down every time he'd get excited and forced him to like what we enjoyed. We relentlessly teased him until he stopped being different, even if he had only changed on the outside. The longer it continued, the more he felt ashamed of the things he found remarkable. He would feel uncomfortably out of his own skin trying to meet our expectations. A feeling I could relate to, and I now felt terrible for having done the same to him. This random assortment of complaints came out in a sloppy, drunken rant in the middle of the night as I tried to defend him. I accused you of being so tired from work that you were missing out on our lives. I told you that you were so critical of Jeremy, that you were failing him as a father figure, and that you were too preoccupied with work to notice how miserable he was. I was defending him, but I was speaking from my own experience with the emotions. I could tell the words I said to you that night hurt you. I regretted saying it all the next day; it wasn't how I wanted to say those things, but I was happy I got them off my chest. I started spending more time to myself after that to avoid the awkwardness.

One night, I was drinking in the basement, playing with a chord progression on the guitar and looping it through my Line 6 DL4. As the song started to come together, I thought about the career journey I was about to take. I knew it would be stressful, and I could see myself coming home drained each day. I'd take my shoes off at the door and then eat something cold. I would have skipped lunch that day because it was so busy, but stress would have killed my appetite for dinner anyway. I'd only be eating because I knew it would help relieve the headache I was trying to cure with a handful of Tylenol.

I closed my eyes and started singing to the chords that were repeating on their own through the loop pedal. It was, at first, just a melodic idea, and I sang pure gibberish. I kept singing, and lyrics began to form as I relaxed into the thought process. Writing music can be cathartic as you open yourself to thought and let the beat and tempo guide your words. Often, things come out you don't expect, or you say something that, in any other setting, you would have shied away from as you explore your embarrassment or shame. The following lyrics would eventually form:

# Listen: Track 4

# "Old and Tired"

https://denverjhamilton.bandcamp.com/track/old-and-tired

## Lyrics

And don't you know,
This world is meant to live on the ground?
So get your head out the clouds,
Get 'em out of the clouds, young man.
There comes a time,
We've all got to just sit back down.

## Meaning

*Written as being spoken by you, the idea is that I've had my head in the clouds, not taking anything seriously. Your advice is that to live a successful life, one must live on the ground, focused on the work at hand. We must get our heads out of the clouds at some point. Settling down was a prominent fear of mine. I thought getting my head out of the clouds meant I had to stop playing music, riding a skateboard, and painting.*

I wanna stay this young,
for the rest of my young life.

*This verse is spoken by me, expressing the fear that if I came down out of the clouds, I'd grow old. Like Rufio and the Lost Boys in Hook, I wanted to stay young and ride my skateboard forever.*

(Chorus)
But as we know,
Just like my dad,
I'm growing old and tired.
Just like my dad,
I'm growing old and tired.
I'm just like my dad,
And I'm growing old and tired.
I'm just like my dad,
I'm growing old and tired.

*This chorus came to me first, before any of the lyrics in the verses. It outlined my central concern while writing the song and influenced the direction the theme would ultimately take. I didn't want that look on my face, the one you always had when you came home. That face felt like the one you would make when you hated your job and family. If the purpose of working this hard was to provide for a family, what's the point in working so hard that it makes you unavailable for that family? I was now at a stage in this journey where I was beginning to submit to the idea that I was just wrong. That you cannot provide for a family with your head in the clouds, chasing selfish dreams. Adopting this face and working your fingers to the bone so that your kids could grow up without want was not only a typical expectation of a man, but it was the only honest means of being able to provide reliably.*

I love the view from here,
The city lights look beautiful down there.
They twinkle on,
And then they fade away at dawn.
If I could stay here,
I'd never grow old, for sure.
But I know at some point,
I'm gonna have to come back down.

*As the song came together, I decided to record it. I never write my lyrics down; I just sing nonsense until it starts to materialize like the force flowing through a Jedi. It's always an embarrassing process because I do it with headphones on. To the outside observer, all they hear is my tone-deaf, a cappella gibberish. I packed my equipment and headed up the mountain behind your house for privacy. I recorded the song in the driver's seat of my truck overlooking a tiny Mormon town at night below me. To describe the scene as beautiful is quite the stretch, so this part of the song refers to the city lights I was used to in much bigger cities where I had previously pursued my dreams. They twinkle on and then fade away at dawn. The transition from night to day represented that, at some point, imagination must die, and we all must come back down from having our heads in the clouds. The excitement of nightlife ends, and everyone heads to work in a single-file line. The final verse represents the idea that I'd never grow old if I could stay in the clouds, but I was submitting to the notion that the time had come for me to settle down.*

I was relieved when the date finally came for me to leave for basic. You and I headed to Salt Lake City, where I'd be flying out. We spent some time together, which was nice, but a feeling of impending doom hovered over me. I knew I'd soon have my face in the dirt being yelled at by a drill sergeant who I assumed would be similar to those I'd seen on television.

Several months before our night in Salt Lake City, a friend in Austin had gotten excited by the time on the clock. "It's 11:11," she squealed, "Make a wish!" I hadn't heard this before, but I played along. After that day, it seemed that I just so happened to look at the clock at 11:11 several times a week, day and night. My wishes would focus on the achievable and short-term goals that would help me become the person I wanted to be. My desires became daily affirmations, and I grew superstitious about them. When we checked into our hotel, and they gave us room 111, I took it as a sign from the universe that I was on the right track.

Time was passing faster the closer I got to leaving for basic. When you dropped me off at the airport, it felt like the past three months had fit inside a few weeks. The clock began to stretch as I transitioned to government time. We sat in the airport waiting area for several uneventful hours. We were eventually moved to the next holding area and waited for another several hours. I had assumed that by now, I'd have already been staring back at the bulging neck veins of an irate drill sergeant. Every step of the onboarding process was so long and monotonous that I had completely let my guard down when the drill sergeants did finally arrive.

We were on another bus, driving onto base, and everyone we had interacted with up to this point had been relatively pleasant. The bus came to a stop, and the internal lights turned on. It was 10 o'clock at night, and I stretched my arms wide and let a deep yawn close my eyes. When I opened them, an angry man in a forest ranger-looking hat had prowled his way onto the bus.

# PART 4: TRAINEE ELVIS

"Everyone off the bus, NOW!" the drill sergeant yelled. Everyone jumped up and started clambering for their things. It appeared there would be no introductions. The mad scramble made me feel a little better as it seemed I wasn't the only one caught off guard. We filed off the bus and collected our bags that the drill sergeants had thrown into a pile. We were ushered onto individual spots painted on the ground, five rows deep by four columns. Approximately four drill sergeants were walking around our formation, but I was too scared to move my head around to see what was happening. I stared straight ahead and wished I could disappear.

None of us knew what to do, but we learned by hearing others being yelled at for doing it wrong. We didn't know at the time, but this would be how we'd learn everything for the next eight weeks. Before I came, I had cut my long hair and shaved my beard. Relative to the way I looked before, I felt like I looked very respectable. Instead of long hair that hung past my shoulders, I had a shaggy haircut that sat mid-neck. My face was clean-shaven, but I had left sideburns that reached far below my jawline. Everything was happening so fast, but the sergeant who noticed me first sauntered up to my face with an expression as if he had seen something ridiculous. The thing he had seen was me.

He looked me up and down with pure disgust. I was wearing the Air Force shirt my recruiter had given me. It was screamed to me that you must "earn the right" to wear that kind of stuff, and I had yet to do anything. I was also wearing tight girl pants. In the early phase of emo, you couldn't find a good pair of trendy pants in Texas. You could maybe find something from a thrift store selling 70's clothes or pay a tailor if you were really serious. For simple dudes like me, you'd have to buy your pants from the girl's section. The key was finding ones without too many frills or sequins, just ordinary-looking pants, but for girls. To make matters worse, I held these "grape smugglers" up on my waist with a spiky white belt. Why I thought this look would grant me immunity from the drill sergeants is a mystery to me now, but hindsight is 20/20.

I had hoped to stay in the background for as long as possible. I didn't want to be yelled at, and I knew I wouldn't let someone bark in my face without giving some attitude back. My sideburns ruined that plan the second we got off the bus, and I was given the nickname "Trainee Elvis." As for being hardcore and not taking any shit from the drill sergeants, I promptly broke and fell in line. They split us up into flights and ushered us toward our new temporary homes.

We were taken to what looked like a classroom without any desks or chairs. We were allowed to call home on our cell phones while sitting on the floor, but the sergeant instructed us not to talk to the person who answered. If they didn't answer, we had to leave a message. We were given a script, and we couldn't deviate. You answered the phone, and I began to read:

*"I made it to Basic Military Training (BMT) safe. I am mailing you my new address and important contact information. If an Emergency arises while I am at BMT, you need to contact the local American Red Cross. They will contact my squadron and give me the message. Please do not attempt to contact my squadron directly. For additional information, please visit BMT's official website for family and friends."*

I hung up the phone and turned my belongings into the main hold. We wouldn't see any of our things until graduation. They had us shower, shave our faces, and then get into our bunks. I didn't think I'd sleep that night, but stress had wiped me out. I stared out into the dark and quietly questioned why I would put myself in this situation. I was already regretting my decision. The rest of the night was relatively quiet, aside from the lone straggler that would make it in from different parts of the country. I expected to be woken up at 5:00 a.m., but the time came and went. I woke myself up every thirty minutes until I fell asleep for good at 8:00 in the morning. I woke up naturally a few hours later to find daylight had completely filled the room. We were learning that the torture would be more effective if they kept us off guard.

We were marched everywhere on base in our civilian clothes for a week, and I hated myself for having dressed so stupidly. They shaved our heads and paraded us around for humiliation. We nervously completed our necessary paperwork, received our vaccinations, and then they measured us for uniforms. We weren't allowed to send any mail home yet, but I managed to write my first letter that night after lights out.

*Dad,*

*Holy Crap, this is nothing like Stripes. That movie lied. Basic <u>SUCKS.</u> It's so bad. I hate it. I wanna go home. Everyone is so rude. You could say they have bad people skills. They yell and don't wanna be my friend. My recruiter didn't tell me what to watch out for. Let me list a few things you should not do:*

*Don't wear an Air Force T-shirt.*

*Don't wear girl pants.*

*Don't wear a white or non-traditional belt.*

*And don't have sideburns.*

*If you remember what I looked like when I got on the plane, that's what Sergeant Taylor saw when I got here. "You look fucking stupid, Trainee Elvis!"*

*"Yes, sir!"*

*Zero Week sucked. I'm now in the first actual week of BMT, and it sucks, but with all the bad, I'm finding something really great in all of this. My wingman is a cool cat, and we get along really well. The rest of the men (48 total) are all pulling together, with a few exceptions. After a day of dragging my face through the dirt and being told I'm a "genius," I find myself bonding with total strangers.*

*I've been here… shoot… what day is it? Tuesday, damn! It's only Tuesday?! Anyway, I've been here a little while, and I'm beginning to figure out how to play the game. The game gets easier when you're not scared out of your mind and lonely. At the same time, the physical conditioning worsens every day, and the responsibility of memory work becomes more serious. The punishments for doing it wrong are more intense too. In any case, I can see the purpose now. When I'm in a hospital working, and a situation comes about that makes others nervous or timid, like water off a duck for me.*

*There is a large and angry man named Master Sergeant Bass. He scares the living CRAP out of me. This big ass dude will rush into your face, yell a deep terrible roar, and you must reply,*

*"Sir Trainee Hamilton reports as ordered, sir."*

*You then tell him what the correct answer is. Oh yeah, and there isn't one. So rule number one of an American Airman: integrity first. You take the blame, and you stand for your decisions. Hopefully, it is okay, but you can't move. You must stay at attention and do proper facing movements, or he'll kill you.*

*Our drill sergeant is Tech Sergeant Lewis. I tried to make a good impression, and I think I did, but I feel like he expects more of me. He selected me as captain of the laundry crew for our flight. If my element gets out of line or doesn't do its job, it's on me. He yells at everyone, but not me. He pulls me to the side, gets an inch from my face, and whispers in my ear how much he hates me. It's weird. I don't want to make mistakes because I can tell he's a really cool guy... outside of BMT. I hate letting him down, not just because of pushups, leg lifts, and other crap, but because he seems bummed when I screw up, not mad.*

*Mistakes cannot be avoided. They set you up to see how you'll react. They will have one training instructor (T.I.) tell you one thing, and the other T.I. will yell at you for doing it wrong to see how you'll react. You'll be okay if you play the game, relax, move quickly, and keep your military bearing. However, your wingmen are knuckle-draggers and get the entire flight in trouble. You will not survive in BMT if you try to go it alone. In seven short weeks, we should be lean, mean, well-oiled machines that work perfectly in unison, but until then, I wish I were playing the piano instead. We don't get to send letters or use phones, so I have to earn the chance to send these.*

*I hope they find you in good spirits,*
*Love Airman Hamilton*

The first couple of weeks were the hardest as we struggled to navigate all the changes and learned how to play the game. I was constantly getting in trouble for smiling, but I swear I wasn't smiling. Nothing about Basic made any of us happy. The problem was, every time we went outside, the Texas sun made me squint my eyes, and my damned teeth would show. By the time I left basic training, I could do 80 pushups in a minute, all because my teeth were too big to fit in my mouth.

I was put on the laundry crew because our sergeant liked me or because he didn't want me screwing up formation and had to hide me somewhere. I would gather everyone's laundry with two other dudes and clean it every morning while the rest of the flight practiced their marching drills. The laundry crew was the best. We were basically left alone for most of the day and could cautiously relax. The laundry room had three rows of stacked washers and driers. The laundry crew chief would stand near the entrance, and the other two trainees could goof off, sleep, write letters, or talk to the girls in our sister flight. Essentially the things we weren't allowed to do under normal circumstances. Sergeants from all over basic training would randomly peek their heads in to check on us. The laundry crew chief standing by the door would start counting pushups at first sight of anyone with any authority. You would drop and start doing pushups as soon as you heard someone begin counting. The person walking in wouldn't see you until they walked in far enough to see around the machines.

From the sergeant's perspective, it would look like the crew chief was leading the exercise while waiting for the machines to finish. The crew chief would pretend to recognize belatedly that the sergeant had walked in, and he would call the room to attention. As long as the laundry machines were running and everyone got down quickly enough, everything would be fine. If anything were out of place, that crew chief would lose his job and be back marching around with the rest of the flight all day. I was in the third position but had worked my way up to crew chief within the first week since the previous two chiefs were quickly cycled out before we had figured out a foolproof plan and dialed in the timing.

Meal times were the most stressful. I was not only sober for the first time in years, but I was also denied caffeine and sugar. I'm not sure which one I missed most. As you walked through the chow line, you could grab these little peanut butter packets with just enough in them to spread on one piece of toast. If you could smuggle one into your pocket and get it back to the dorms, they were a highly valued and tradable commodity. Getting them, however, was never easy. The peanut butter was closely guarded by the drill sergeants who sat at a long table called the Snake Pit. They would watch as you walked by, and they picked on airmen at random. Being caught with anything in your pockets was a punishable offense that carried a sentence of two weeks of dust bunny duty. Using one flip-flop, you would sweep the entire dorm, army crawling on your belly under each bunk in search of dust bunnies. We were given about five minutes to eat for the first few weeks before being yelled back into formation. To this day, I still eat too fast.

The subsequent letters I wrote to you were short. We didn't get much time to ourselves those first couple of weeks. When we did retire for the night, we usually tried to catch up on sleep, but we were always in a deficit. I locked myself in one of the bathroom stalls and cried in my second week, mostly out of frustration. I hated everything about the experience and didn't have the skills to cope with it as I had usually relied on music, skateboarding, or alcohol. My friends at the Creek View Apartments in Austin had tried to talk me out of joining. They said it would "change me," and I was "too much of a hippie to join." Now, crying in the stall, I feared the only way to survive was to change, and I was frustrated that they were right. The first two weeks of basic training are designed to break you down, and the people they have working there are very good at their jobs.

# Part 5: Beaten and Shot

I always had long hair growing up. I'd occasionally style a mohawk or shave off dreadlocks when I grew tired of them, but I preferred having long hair. I felt I had better intuition and was more connected to myself when it was longer. Your hair is a remnant of the person you were the day before and is composed of everything you've experienced. Shaving my head always felt like cutting away some history. Without my hair, I felt uncomfortably vulnerable. When the military shaved my head bald, I visualized the last bits of my previous self falling all around me as I became just another clone trooper, ready for the front lines.

As you learn the rules and expectations, you are shouted at less, and things become more manageable. Around the end of the second week, you start making friends with the other people there as you get used to the chaos of basic training together. It still sucks, but the fact that it sucks for everyone creates a bonding experience akin to Stockholm's syndrome. Again, once you start to put your guard down, that's always when they like to strike.

We were all brought into a room and had to sign more paperwork. Three overly angry sergeants spent thirty minutes investigating whether or not any of us had ever done drugs, even once. There were people who had said they never did it, like me, and there were people that admitted to "experimenting with weed once." Anyone outside of those two admissions was disqualified from joining the Air Force in the first place. Out of forty-eight people, someone was definitely lying. The people who said they never used drugs were treated mildly, relative to those who had admitted to some use. What was scary in MEPS was terrifying here. The stakes were higher for being caught. Now the Air Force had spent money on you; if you were to admit it now, you were in much bigger trouble. They also made it abundantly clear that if you continued to lie now, and it came out later once you were out of Basic and performing a job for the military, the potential consequences were military jail or dishonorable discharge.

People in both admission groups cracked and admitted to some use. A drill sergeant would immediately drag them out of the room, some never to be heard from again. Depending on the severity of their omissions, I assume they were either discharged or recycled into week zero of Basic Training. Still, their being beaten and shot didn't seem too farfetched either at the time. The fear of somehow being discovered scratched at the back of my eyeballs. I knew it was the truth, trying to get out of my head to end the suffering and anxiety. I told myself to hold firm and stay the course of refusing to admit anything, but the "what if" stayed with me every day. Every time a drill sergeant looked pissed and wanted to talk to me, which was every time a drill sergeant wanted to speak to me, I thought to myself, "Welp, here it comes."

By the beginning of the third week, I was doing better emotionally and started feeling as if I had a handle on things. I had written a few letters, but we couldn't send them out. Your first letter to me finally arrived, and you sent me scores of the NFL playoff games. Since you had named me after the Denver Broncos, the NFL felt significant to me. It felt like one of the few connections we had, and it reminded me of old home videos of everyone huddled around the TV on a Sunday. I loved talking about the NFL with you, but you started hating the league as I got older. You favored college ball, and I didn't have the same interest in it. There were a couple of times I got into a college team, like when I was living in Austin rooting for Colt McCoy, but the team changes completely when most of them graduate or draft out. The constant turnover of staff, coaches, and players made it hard for me to stay invested in any team. I found watching Brett Favre play in the NFL for 20 years more intriguing. Eventually, every time I'd try to talk football with you, you'd brush it off with, "I hate the NFL. Never even watch it anymore." Another one of our connections was lost, and I always took it personally. With my stupid name, I felt like someone's old tattoo of a band they didn't listen to anymore. Getting those letters from you with the NFL scores meant a lot to me.

Dad,

*Hey, I got your letter! We are still unable to send ours, but I'll keep writing until we can. I heard about the games. Saints/Colts would be cool to see, but I don't think you understand exactly where I am. There is no T.V. time. There is nothing but work. I'm actually writing to you now after lights out. That's the only personal time we get. It's either sleep or whisper with your wingman. Rumor spread around the base about the scores, and I finally heard, "Colts won, and it's 14 to 14 at halftime with the Vikings/Saints." That game was tied for three days before we heard any more news.*

*I'm finding a new sense of pride in the work I'm doing here and will eventually do. I had a class yesterday from 0800 to 1700, all about the history of the Air Force. The footsteps I'm following are some big shoes, and I cried during taps that night.*

*Well, anyway, I hate this hellhole and can't wait to get out!! Until then, I'm going to need my rest.*

*Love*
*Airman*
*Hamilton*

Week three of basic training is the most brutal; this is the week that separates the men from the boys, so to speak. So far, everything has been about how to act while they beat the pride and individuality out of you. If you make it through week three, the training changes to something that more closely resembles actual military training. You're no longer making simple mistakes, so you're getting in trouble less, but that just means the sergeants have to try harder to get you to screw up.

We had also started going to church. I rolled my eyes when they first allowed it; I hadn't considered myself religious since I was ten years old and going to Church Camp. My cousins went every summer, and they had invited me to go with them that year. It was supposed to be an exciting camping trip in the mountains for a few weeks. The first time I went, I had a religious experience that I thought would change my life forever.

# Part 6: 6,000 Years of Ear Infections

We were sitting around a large bonfire, and one of the camp counselors told us a story while having us all imagine ourselves on trial for a crime. The evidence was damning, and as the story went on, it became apparent that we would be held accountable and jailed. He went into detail about what it would feel like to have our freedom taken away and to lose our friends and family. He then introduced a new character to the story, a handsome man with long brown hair. He would walk into the courtroom and proceed down the center aisle until he got to the waist-high gate separating you, the judge, and the jury from him and the rest of the people watching. He would then take responsibility for your actions and take on your sentence. As you watch them shackle and drag this man away, you're reunited with all of your family and friends.

Being at the bonfire with my cousins and listening to the counselor tell this story with flames reaching high above his head, I was taken off guard by the emotions that swelled in me. I was under the spell of the moment, and a rush of chills spread from my spine to the tips of my toes when he revealed that man to be Jesus. I had never heard the concept of salvation explained this way, and I now felt so grateful for his sacrifice. I went home that first summer as a Christian and wanted to start going to church every week.

As I learned more about Christianity, I had many questions. Naturally, I went to my brother for his insight, as I did with most things. He told me religion was bullshit and made fun of me for believing in God. He wanted to know if I believed in the tooth fairy as well. He told me all the things he thought were loopholes in the religion and then did his best to explain string theory. Neither philosophy on our creation made any practical sense to me at the time, but I went back to Church Camp the following summer with a list of questions I couldn't wait to have answered. I was so excited to feel that presence from the bonfire again.

We had just eaten breakfast in the cafeteria, and the camp counselors released us to prepare for the day's activities. I grabbed the same counselor from the bonfire and told him I had some burning questions, and I asked him if we could talk. His story was so passionate, and his relationship with God seemed so well defined that I trusted him to have all the answers I sought. We found a gazebo on the edge of the woods and sat down, and I recited each loophole my brother had explained, starting with Noah.

"If Noah brought one of each type of species on the ark, there would be a huge issue with genetics, right?" I asked, unsure of the meaning of the words I was speaking.

"What do you mean?" he asked, obviously surprised that a young kid at a bible camp had questions about genetics.

"Well," I started, trying my best to convey what my brother had explained. "If you have any gene mutations, they're more likely to cause complications with inbreeding because there's no variability in the gene pool." I winced at the words; I had practiced them before I came, so I knew they were mostly correct, but I felt insecure. I didn't want him to clarify my understanding of genetics; I wanted him to explain God. I was ready to be comforted and provided the ammunition to debate my brother when I returned from camp.

"God wouldn't let that happen." He smiled and put his hand on my shoulder as if he had fully answered the question.

"God wouldn't let what happen? Mutations in genes? Don't they happen all the time, though?" I was frustrated that he wasn't spelling it out for me.

"You have to have faith! Faith is recognizing you may not have the answer, but you trust that God wouldn't have let those animals have those issues." Again, he was unwavering in his demeanor.

My eyes narrowed as I waited for him to finish. I didn't know enough about genetics to see whether he had successfully debated my brother's point or not, but I knew my brother would eat me alive if I came back with that as the only proof I could get. "So, the lions, for example, would have kids, and then those kids would have to have kids together, right? Isn't that wrong?"

"It would be wrong for us, but animals are different," he laughed at how simple a child's mind could be, but he didn't know I had walked him into a trap.

"Was it wrong for Adam and Eve's children?" My eyes were squinted so tight they were almost closed, and I looked for any signs he was cracking.

"No, no, no. That's different! That was their only option. Those rules had to be created later when there were more people." His smile had since faded as I bordered the line of a sweet kid with questions and hellion in need of flogging.

"So when Noah and his family repopulated the earth, it was okay then?" I crossed my arms and watched; the trap was set, and he had walked right into it.

He considered it for a second, realizing we were all direct descendants of Noah made him a more intriguing character all of a sudden. "Well…"

I cut him off before he could continue, "And what about the geological record? There is no indication there was ever a flood of that magnitude, and we can also tell that the planet is much older than 6,000 years." I felt in control of the conversation and could see why my brother enjoyed doing it to people.

"God works in mysterious ways, so you must have faith. It's like the rings of a tree. Science can predict the age of a tree based on the number of rings it has in its core. God can create a tree, on day one, with as many rings as he wants. Science can't explain everything." He plastered that same toothy smile on his face as he got up to leave; it just looked fake to me now. "Go get dressed. We have sack races today, and it will be fun!"

Sack races wouldn't have sounded fun to me before our conversation, but now they felt insulting too. I was here to learn and explore this religion. I didn't just want answers; I needed them. Blind faith had just shut the conversation down. There was no exploration and no discovery. Worse, there was no way I could use this against my brother. I was left to rely on faith and burlap, so I faked an ear infection and went home early. I left camp and Christianity in the mountains for good, so when the option of going to church at Basic Training came up, I stayed back in the dorms. I found my passion for Christianity again shortly after that when I realized staying in the dorms meant staying with the drill sergeant alone. I went to church every Sunday for the rest of Basic.

# PART 7: HAMILTON

Getting through week three was no easy feat, and I almost gave up during a fitness evaluation. The sides of my stomach were cramping, and my knees ached. I could feel my knees swelling as I ran, and with each stride, I could feel a slight popping sensation on the right side of my kneecap. I didn't think I could carry on any further and wanted to give up, but the thought of making you and Shannon proud served as the only fumes left in my empty tank. A need to impress my brother pushed me on the running track, and gaining your respect helped me fall asleep every night. You could tell by my letters in week three that I was learning to get through Basic and was starting to thrive, a sharp contrast from the previous weeks.

*Shannon,*

*Hey, what's up? Tell the babies I said, "Hi." I was doing a physical training evaluation two days ago and wanted to stop, but I started thinking about them. I just pictured their faces, remembered their laughs, and continued to push. I started thinking about graduation when you'll see me in my blues and dad will be there. I pictured you with a big smile because I have the WORST glasses ever, and I imagined Dad crying, just enough to notice. I pushed through and took 2nd. I made "Liberator," and next EVAL, I'm shooting for "War Hawk" 8:55, 1.5 miles. That seems out of reach right now, but I get stronger every day. I can do 55 pushups and 60 sit-ups in a minute each. If I get it, I get Sunday off when graduation rolls around. I'm living from chow hall to chow hall- Sunday to Sunday. I want out of here so bad, and I hear week 3 is known as hell week. Week 4 is when we shoot our weapons and go to the gas chamber, so it should start being fun soon.*

*LOVE*
*A1C Hamilton*

You can tell how much it meant to me to impress Shannon and how obsessed I was with making you both proud. My letter to you in the same week was more vulnerable and less braggadocios.

*Dad,*

*The first official day of week 3. Five more weeks, and I'm out of here! I'm really excited about graduation. I keep my*

*hopes up and my mind right by thinking about finishing strong.*
*I took my fitness EVAL and took second on the run. I got passed*
*on the last straight away. I can be a thunderbolt if I knock a*
*minute off my total time for the 1.5 miles run. I feel like I could*
*easily do it. I've already passed the standard, but I want to push*
*myself further. Like they say here, excellence in all we do.*

*Love A1C*
*Hamilton*

Getting through week 3 is like a mini-graduation because you get your nametag on your uniform. The first three weeks are about breaking you down and removing all individuality, but in the end, you get a piece of yourself back, your name. Tears filled my eyes when I saw my name for the first time. I had felt so alone this entire journey, but now, with my last name, I felt the support of our whole family. These sacrifices were no longer my own. It now felt like I was doing something honorable for my family, and I had earned the right to wear our family's name. I had also finally gotten to talk to you on the phone for the first time since I arrived.

*Dad,*

*Hey, it was good to talk to you today. Much better than last*
*time. We had more time, and I wasn't trying to keep from breaking*
*down. This place has pushed me in so many ways. I miss so many*
*things, but the longer I'm here, the older I feel. Each week we get*
*a new addition to our uniforms. 0-1 week, we had to wear our*
*civilian clothes, and then we got our ABUs, but we had to wear our*
*civilian shoes. 1-2 week, we got our haircuts. 2-3, we had combat*
*boots and received our issued glasses. 3-4 week, we get our names*
*and our blues. That's all to say that when you see someone march*
*by, you can tell what week they are. People in their first week,*
*we call them "Sneaker Weekers," and they look like kids. We've*
*all grown into respectful, well-trained men. It's strange. Being*
*here with some of these guys, though, makes me worried. Some*
*of them will be controlling the flights of million-dollar machines,*
*and they're idiots! We got dudes who will be responsible for entire*
*squadrons, and they can't even flush the toilet when they're done.*

*I've met some high-ranking people here. It's funny because none*
*of this mattered to me a month ago, but now they're like celebrities.*

*I was walking to work the other day and saw this guy in a flight suit*
*walking my way. I was marching a detail of three other guys, so I*
*called them to halt. Then I saw who it was. "Tench Hut! Present,*
*HARMS!" It was the commander of our training squadron. It*
*was scary at the moment, but we were all buzzing with excitement*
*afterward. I went to a speech given by a major general, and we*
*met a chief master sergeant today. Crazy stuff. It's incredible being*
*a part of the most extraordinary military power in the world.*

*We have a big week coming up. We have open ranks inspection.*
*They line us up and check us individually, from our uniform to*
*our knowledge of stance and memory work. They have "blue*
*ropes," which are SUPER drill sergeants. They suck! They get*
*in your face, yell at you and ask you questions, and you have to*
*get them right, or else... they rip out your heart or something.*

*It's Thursday night, week 3 of BMT. Only three more days,*
*and I'll be a Fourth Weeker! I got my name back, too. They'll*
*sew it on all my uniforms this week! It sucks that the first week*
*didn't count. Zero week was the worst, but I've made it through*
*four weeks of training. One month in this hellhole. It went by so*
*slowly in the moment, but looking back, it now feels like it has gone*
*by pretty quickly. The senior flights said this week is the worst,*
*but 4th week is when it starts getting good. We have to fold our*
*clothes perfectly. Seriously, it's sort of ridiculous. It takes forever,*
*and you fail if they find a piece of lint under your bed or a loose*
*string hanging from a sock. If it's not absolutely perfect, you die.*
*Sucks. Now in week 3, they do night raids. They come in around*
*midnight, throw our clothes on the floor, and flip the bunks. They*
*destroy the dorm that we worked so hard on, and then they make*
*us redo it. That's if we pass. Failing sucks so much worse. I hate it*
*here so bad. When we graduate, we get a t-shirt, and I was voted*
*to be the one to draw it. I'm trying to think of a good idea for it.*

*Gotta Go, AB Hamilton*

Week 4 and another Sunday service. Church had become something
we all looked forward to every week. It started as an opportunity to
take a break from all the madness but had now become a bonding
experience. Looking around the service, you could see trainees from
all the other weeks. The early weeks were all blubbering idiots crying
and wanting to go home, but the later weeks were all trainees that had

become used to the game and were linked arm in arm singing the same cheesy songs they played every Sunday. I loved the music they played. At any other time in my life, I would have hated everything about what they were playing, but church music had become the only music I was allowed to hear, and I rocked out to everything they played. When wholly deprived of all music, even shitty music sounds good.

*Dad,*

*I'm so glad we can send letters; it's such a boost to my morale. I semi-feel connected to the outside world again. The Super Bowl is tomorrow. I wish I could watch it. Send me a letter, tell me about it, and tell me some NFL news! Keep me updated on the Favre drama. I'll be in church during the Super Bowl, so hopefully, we'll hear about it. Church has been so nice. It's the one time nobody yells at you. It makes me miss music so badly because they have a house band that plays songs about going home! I'm like 20 feet from instruments, and I can't do anything!*

*I came up with an idea and tried it out a couple of days ago. I heard you could talk with a therapist if you requested it. I said I was depressed and needed to speak to someone, so they sent me the same day. I did my best to persuade the counselor to let me play the piano because it was how I coped with stress. He said, "Uh, no," and then sent me back to my flight. It was worth a shot.*

*I learned how to stay perfectly still for hours at a time. That's cool, I guess. I learned how to yawn without opening my mouth, and the other day I laughed to tears without making a sound. Sergeant Taylor is such a jerk, but I think he's funny as hell. The punishments he comes up with are excellent. To get our M16s, we had to sign a roster sheet. Two out of the fifty dudes in the flight managed to screw up the very simple task of signing their names. JUST SIGN YOUR NAME! They printed, so the roster was messed up, and we had to redo it.*

*Sergeant Taylor was going nuts. He would yell at them and then pace back and forth, trying to find their brains. This fuckin' guy was jumping up and down and throwing shit! He made the two trainees stand in front of each other and shake hands while repeating, "I can't follow directions." Then, "I don't know what's going on in normal situations." Then, "I cheated my way through cursive in 3rd grade." Then they started messing it up because they were still shaking hands and staring at each other, but their repeated sentences stopped making sense. So he had them start saying, "I don't know what I am saying," and then, "we're going to be best friends." Then he made them sing Kumbaya. They shook hands for like 20 minutes. I was doing my best to silently fight back the laughter so not to be lumped in with them. These things are always more funny when they're happening to someone else.*

*<3 A1C Hamilton*

The 4th week of basic is fun, relatively. In the 4th week, you get sprayed with CS gas, which seems fun compared to the previous few weeks. I had become daringly proficient at communicating with drill sergeants while maintaining my military bearing. When you're able to do that, they largely leave you alone. The drill sergeants start to feel more like ordinary people, and you can make small talk with them if you're brave enough to go for it. I always tried and was sometimes successful. I tried my hardest with Tech Sergeant Lewis, but I'd move my hands to make a gesture or accidentally give him a sir sandwich (where you start and end a sentence with sir). I'd be on my face doing pushups again, but I enjoyed the thrill of risking it all. I remember one time I screwed up my reporting statement, and he made me do pushups in the corner of the dorm behind the bunks. He got distracted and forgot I was doing them. I did pushups for 15 minutes until he happened to walk by me again. "Hamilton! Why are you doing pushups? Go clean something, you donkey!" he said lovingly.

# Part 8: Best Friends

*Dad,*

*Hey! This week has gone by super fast. I can now say I have been inside a gas chamber and survived CS Gas! It was crazy. We put our suits on, lined up, and I somehow ended up first in line. Ten of us poured into this small room with a center smoke pit. They fired up the gas, and the room slowly filled with smoke. We had to do some easy exercises like jumping jacks and running in place. Once we were breathing heavily, we had to remove our masks, place them on our chests, and say, "Sir, trainee Hamilton reports as ordered" then they let us leave once they saw the gas had taken effect. The worst part was getting out of the room. It was hard to breathe, it hurt my eyes and throat, and you know me, it hurt my ears. Boogers were pouring out of my nose once I stepped outside, and my entire head felt like it was on FIRE! That's some intense stuff. I experienced it for just a few seconds, but had it been real life, it's completely handicapping to every sense, and you lose self-control. It's scary to think I might one day be in a situation where I have to be around the real thing. The more we sweat during peace, the less we bleed during war.*

*Tomorrow is Friday. It seems like zero week was just a week ago. Sunday, we'll be Fifth Weekers! Amazing. So anyway, tomorrow we are going to the oak course. We'll be swinging over water, running through tires, and jumping down giant tree houses! Exciting!*

*So check this out; I thought this was cool today. It started two to three weeks ago. I was working, and I just so happened to be by myself. This 6 foot 5 Tech Sergeant comes walking in the door. I snapped to attention and said, "Good morning, sir."*

*He gets in my face and says, "What's so good about it?!"*

*"Sir, trainee Hamilton reports as ordered, sir, it's just a beautiful morning. I woke up early and got right to work."*

*He looked at me funny, "Where the hell are you from?"*

*"Montana originally, sir," I said, still not moving a muscle.*

*"Does everyone in Montana have a good outlook on life?" he asked.*

*"Not everyone, sir, but I want to be here."*

*He gets out of my face, relaxes, and asks, "Is it nice up there?"*

*We start having this water cooler-type conversation. Before he leaves, he goes, "What week are you, trainee?"*

*"Third week, sir."*

*He looks surprised and says, "Well, you have a lot of confidence for a Third Weeker."*

*"I wasn't so much first week, sir." He nodded and then left.*

*Fast forward to last week, I have self-aid and buddy care, a class I'm supposed to help teach with the instructor since I'm scheduled to be a medic (they don't know I'm a secretary). The instructor is Tech Sergeant Miller, the guy I met in the laundry room.*

*"Montana! How are you?"*

*"Good sir, it's good to see you."*

*He goes, "Hah, you didn't think I'd remember, did you?"*

*I said, "No sir, good job, sir."*

*He started laughing, and then the entire class laughed, "Well, thank you, trainee."*

*This morning, I was working in the laundry room with some new trainees from the third week. They are still acclimating to Basic, and we were showing them how they could sleep on the laundry bags if someone watched the door. Big ass Tech Sergeant Miller walks in, and everyone snaps to attention (this guy looks horrifying, mind you).*

*"Montana!"*

*"Sergeant Miller! It's good to see you. Good morning, sir."*

*"I'm glad to see you still got that good attitude. When do you graduate?"*

*"Three more weeks, sir."*

*"Keep it up, and let me know when you do."*

*"Yes, sir, take care, sir."*

*He leaves, and all the new trainees look at me with the most puzzled look, like, "What the fuck is going on?"*

*I have successfully made friends with one of the drill sergeants.*

*LOVE A1C Hamilton*

By the time I got to the fifth week, I was having fun. In the sixth week, you get to go to the shooting range. A guy in my flight was so excited about getting to shoot that he didn't use the restroom all day. He was so scared he'd miss the opportunity that he just held it in, hour after hour. On my first day at Basic, I realized that the Air Force loves to rush you around, only to have you sit for hours between activities. Holding your piss until the next task was always a bad idea. They had us shoot standing, crouched, and flat on our stomachs. We then had to repeat each task with gas masks on. By the time we got to the gas masks, this trainee had already pissed his pants. I guess it's easy to feel like you're doing well when the bar has been set so low that not pissing your pants is considered excelling. Despite never shooting a real gun before, I somehow made marksman. I feel relatively confident that someone else must have been accidentally hitting my targets for me.

Our drill sergeants started offering me the opportunity to get the new recruits off the bus each week. By this time in Basic, I had my name and rank on my uniform. Since I had an associate's degree, I qualified to be an Airman First Class with two stripes. When the new arrivals came, we looked almost legit, minus the blue M16s they made us carry, slung over one shoulder. Regardless, from the perception of a new recruit, the M16s could have been hot pink, and they probably wouldn't have even noticed. They are blind to everything happening around them because of the stress and uncertainty.

The first busload of recruits was rushed up to their dorms, just as we had been when we first arrived. The drill instructor told them to head to the bathrooms, shave their faces, shower, and then return to their bunks. We were barking at them, trying to get them to go faster. I was doing the thing I hated having done to me, but the difference was that now I understood the purpose of it all.

That level of uncertainty and stress is something you must learn to handle if you're going to be successful on the job, except for, most likely, my future appointment as a secretary. Despite the vanilla nature of my upcoming job, I needed a way to deal with stress and uncertainty in real life. I had been completely broken down within the first few hours at Basic Training, and it had taken about six weeks to rebuild me. The shit I had been through while in Basic felt like a rite of passage toward something better. I didn't want to take that journey away from these new guys. We rode them even harder than we had been, and it was for their benefit.

The showers were all turned off, and everyone was standing at attention back at their bunks. Some of them were crying, but every single one of them looked terrified, and they all seemed so young. As we walked around the dorm checking everyone, we found a large puddle of water in the hallway leading from the bathroom. We followed the trail to a naked trainee standing at the foot of his bed with his hands balled into fists, spine straight as a board, attempting his best impression of standing at attention.

Before we could say anything to him, our drill sergeant swooped in from out of nowhere and stood a few inches from his face. We were so excited to hear what he had to say. Clearly, this kid had not toweled off and hadn't gotten dressed like everyone else who had figured those things out independently. That universal urge to blend in and hide amongst your peers was immediately stripped from him, and he was now staring face to face with the meanest person I'd ever met.

# Part 9: Bars

The drill sergeant didn't say anything. He just stared at this kid for what felt like an eternity. We were standing behind the sergeant and couldn't see what he was doing, but we could see him slowly moving his head from side to side. He looked like a predator observing helpless prey, waiting for the best time to strike. I leaned to one side, fueled by my curiosity. I wanted to see this kid's face and attempt to decipher what was going through his head. My line of sight got around the side of the sergeant's hat, and I saw the kid's face for the first time. He looked like he was fighting back the tears. His eyes were darting around, looking straight ahead and then at the sergeant. When I came into his view, his eyes darted over to me, and that's when I realized this kid had shaved off his eyebrows.

Drill sergeants never point at anyone with just one finger because they'll be pointing their other three fingers back at themselves if they do. To avoid sharing any of the blame with the idiots under their supervision, they point all four fingers at you. He pointed his hand at the trainee's expressionless forehead and asked, "Where the hell are your eyebrows?"

The directions were simple, too simple, maybe. They had all been told to head to the bathrooms, shave their faces, shower, and then return to their bunks. I learned that night what stress does to the human brain. The more straightforward directions were omitted because only a crazy person would shave their entire face and return to the bunks naked.

Graduation finally came, and I had never wanted to see anyone as badly as I wanted to see you and Shannon. We marched in our blues to the graduation field. They had us walk by the stands, so all the families could see us in our formations. We were allowed to turn our heads in unison toward the stands, but we weren't allowed to look around. I walked with my head turned, chin against my shoulder. I did my best to find you in my field of vision, but there were just too many people. I knew you were out there, and I imagined you could see me. I did the only thing I knew I could do; I flashed my giant teeth toward the crowd, something I had worked so hard to prevent the past several weeks.

The ceremony ended, and we were allowed to search for our families. When I finally found you, it was everything I could have wished for it to be. You looked so proud of me, and so did Shannon. Not only did you look proud, but you also said you were. At that moment, something in my brain clicked, and my personality changed forever. I connected this awful experience to how I could make you both happy. The military didn't fit my personality, and I had been denied my favorite things for two months, but in that time, I had successfully made you and Shannon proud. The military had provided me a path to your acceptance and understanding, and I had reached a personal nirvana.

Shannon smiled at me and put his hand on my shoulder. He looked me right in the eyes and said, "I'll be proud of you when you put your bars on." He was referring to the rank of officer. That was the exact sort of backhanded compliment he always gave. Nothing could be taken away from what I had just achieved, so he instead reminded me of my position on the totem.

His comment could have been his way of saying, "Keep it up! Keep going! Get your bachelor's degree and become an officer!" I have a problem with what he said because it can also be taken as, "You haven't done anything. I'm not proud of you yet." At the time, I was crushed by it. I had built up these expectations of how this would go. After weeks of dragging my face through the mud, I felt like I had crossed a finish line, but to him, I had just started the race. I am no longer crushed by these things today because I've come to expect them. I've since learned that you cannot change people; you can only change your expectations of them. My expectations of him wouldn't change just yet, but I was learning to better anticipate his putting me down.

Seven years later, I gave up on those expectations when I got my bachelor's degree, but he was still unimpressed. I went through all the same emotions I had when I graduated from basic training. I built up those expectations for months in my head, and I couldn't wait for him to see me walk the stage. Not just walk the stage; walk that stage with honors. Undoubtedly, if I graduated with honors as a Biologist, he'd have no reason not to be proud.

# Part 10: Summa Cum Laude

When graduation came, Shannon was on his worst behavior from the moment he landed in California. He hates California, and I'm unsure if he genuinely hates it or if it's just another example of him going out of his way to show me he dislikes something I love. He stayed with us in our house, and as soon as he walked in, he looked around the room. The house was spotless, and Daphne and I decorated the walls with our art. I had my favorite skateboards displayed alongside my vast collection of random musical instruments. The house was an extension of ourselves and the things we loved. Taking it all in, he said, "Hmmm, less slovenly than I expected." Shannon wasn't enjoying himself and let it be known as often as possible. Luckily, you were more excited to be there. You were proud that I had finished school and were enjoying playing with my eight-month-old daughter, who was already starting to show her animated personality.

We drove to the arena where my graduation ceremony was held, and Shannon rode with me. He hadn't mentioned anything about me finishing school, and he hadn't asked me about any of the classes or experiences I had. I realize that some of my expectations for his reactions to my success may be unrealistic, but an hour's worth of driving in silence is a perfect opportunity to make some small talk about the thing we were about to attend. When that small talk never happened, I decided to bring it up myself.

"I'm so glad school is over; it's been so stressful," I said without taking my eyes off the road. We had just pulled into the city, and I was hitting light traffic for the first time on the trip. I made a stupid closed-lip smile as I sat in the silence of him ignoring me. I tried again, "I'm stoked I got these honors ropes. I worked hard to get them."

"What did you graduate with, cum laude?" he asked without looking at me. He was people-watching as we slowly passed the throngs of men and women busily weaving past each other on the sidewalks.

I cringed a little; this was precisely what I stressed about every semester. I would graduate, but my brother would be able to take something away from that achievement and use that as his excuse for not being proud. Of course, he would automatically assume that if I had earned honors, it would be the lowest one I could get. "No, actually, I got summa cum laude!" I said, and then with added emphasis, "The highest one."

"Mmmm," he said, slowly lifting his head in a single nod. "I would look so stupid if I wore every special achievement I got from school," he said.

I turned and looked at him to see if he was joking, but he was serious. He then listed off some of the things he'd have to wear and made it sound like the sheer weight of the material would make it impossible to walk the stage. The echoes of him reminding me I'd never be as good as him at anything.

"Well, I'm thrilled," I said, feeling that trigger activate, the one that makes me want to drink. I had significantly cut back on drinking and was going as strong as ever since meeting my wife several years earlier, but now I had that old familiar urge to drown out my disappointment with something deleterious and cold. "I'm glad Dad is here to see it too. I want to give him my ropes. I couldn't have done this without him."

"I didn't even ask him to come to my graduation." He caught himself and paused briefly. I assume he realized it made him sound like he didn't appreciate you. "I just mean, it's not that big of a deal; It's just school. Can you imagine if I made you guys come to see me every time I graduated? By the second master's degree, who cares, you know?"

I couldn't wait to get out of the fucking car. I regretted inviting him. He was moving the field goal again. Now a bachelor's degree wasn't remarkable enough. A master's degree wasn't even good enough for him; now, it would take multiple master's degrees. I saw a window and took the opportunity, "Man, multiple master's degrees? Sounds like a waste of time. I would rather have a doctorate."

The wound was unmistakable. I could tell he wanted to defend himself but was biting his tongue. I learned early on that he loves dishing it out, but he never does well with getting it in return. He doesn't enjoy the bitter taste of his own medicine. Unfortunately, that kind of behavior on my part isn't medicinal as it cures nothing and only increases the tension between us. He changed the subject by turning around and getting his daughter's attention, "Ollie, aren't you glad your mom's not here?" I had forgotten she was even back there with how quiet she had been. "You do so much better when she's not here. You have an opportunity to actually do things for yourself, for once."

He and Olivia had been in California for only two days. This marked the fifth time he had attempted to convince her she was better off without her mom. Olivia never responded; she always looked away or played on her phone. When he wouldn't get the reaction he wanted out of her, he'd look at the closest person and say something like, "Rene babies these kids. She'd wipe your butt still if you'd let her." He'd look at Olivia to see what reaction she would have. You could see the pain on her face mixed with embarrassment, and it would make me wonder if he could see it too. I hoped he was just blind to it because if he could see it and treated her like this anyway, that would be so much worse. I hadn't yet recognized that he did the same stuff to me about my mother; I just felt terrible for Ollie. Later that day, after I had walked the stage, I finally recognized his game.

Daphne rode with you to the ceremony, and her parents drove down on their own. My in-laws can be difficult during stressful events. My mother-in-law rarely leaves the house and seldom makes long day trips to the city. They were having a hard time finding parking, and they were taking their stress out on Daphne over the phone. My wife is a sweetheart, and she takes those interactions very seriously. Like me, she wants to make people happy and feels personally responsible if anyone is upset. After graduation, my in-laws were flustered by the city traffic and changing plans. They had decided to head back home, and Daphne had developed a shared anxiety. That stress was apparent on Daphne's face, and my brother saw his opportunity to share his mom-centric family advice.

"Your mom's giving you a hard time, huh?" he asked, pretending to care.

"Yeah, they don't get out often, and I think they're overstimulated with the traffic." The graduation ceremony had ended, and pedestrians were filling the streets around the stadium.

"You should just write her off. Seriously, you don't need her. You guys should move to Colorado," he said, motioning over to me with his head.

My wife didn't even respond to him because she is a bigger person than any of us. She didn't want to bad mouth her mom, but she didn't want to get into it with my brother either. For me, everything clicked in that instant. The way he treated Olivia didn't feel like it was my business because that's his daughter, and I have no say in what goes on there. My family is different; you don't get to talk to my wife or kids like that. I felt on the defensive, and as I prepared to respond, I recognized the words, "you should just write her off." Instantly, I was 15 years old again, and Shannon was calling me gay for missing my mom. "You should just write her off," he would say and then ramble off the same old tired list of reasons for why I should do so. It became clear to me that all of my mommy issues were *his* mommy issues. He was attempting to give those issues to his daughter. If he stayed any longer, he'd also try to give those issues to my wife.

My grand expectations of him collapsed under their own weight as the foundation they were built upon began filling with holes. The wall I built around the emotions I felt toward my mother also started to crumble. I wondered if I had any unique opinions about her. Was it possible that everything I thought I felt about her had grown from seeds planted by my brother? Every bad thing I had ever heard about her, I heard from Shannon. He told me all the nasty details of your divorce, the awful things she said about me, and what people around town were saying. I was wrong about my brother, which meant I might also be wrong about my mom. If I had the kind of patience my wife has for her mother, perhaps I'd still have a relationship with mine. I might feel better about myself if Shannon hadn't had such a colossal influence over how I saw the world. The urge to drink again started dragging me back into the pit. As always, I leaned heavily on my wife, and again she was there to pull me back out.

I hadn't spoken to my mom in years. She didn't know about my kids, the military, or college. Hell, I'm not sure she even knew I had graduated from high school, and she most definitely wasn't aware that I had almost killed myself with alcoholism. I had thought about her millions of times throughout that time, but I never considered ever reaching out to her. The walls I put up were there to protect me, and I was too afraid to tear them down, but the wall had begun to crack. That wall finally broke two years later, after a fight you and I had when Jade was born. After that fight, I started looking for ways to contact my mom.

# A Vision: Chapter 6

## PART 1: DIRTY LAUNDRY

My wife had placenta previa, which meant my son's placenta had fully covered her cervix, preventing any outlet to the uterus. There were serious risks to both mother and baby, so the safest option was to have a planned cesarean. Due to the high-risk nature of the pregnancy and the demands of our two-year-old daughter, we knew we would need help before and after the surgery. I had finished school and passed the licensing exam to become a clinical scientist. The local hospital hired me almost immediately, but I was paying my dues as a newbie on the graveyard shift. I was largely unavailable during the day as I tried to catch up on sleep. I called you and asked if my stepmom would be willing to stay with us for a little while until the baby came and we could establish a new routine for Pepper. She agreed, and soon she was living on an air mattress in our living room.

Everything was fine, and she was an enormous help around the house. Due to Daphne's condition, her doctor told her to lay in bed and relax until the baby came, which is impossible to do with a two-year-old and a sleeping husband. My stepmom cooked and cleaned, played with Pepper, and never expressed any concerns. Unfortunately, there were things both parties wanted to complain about, we just never brought them up to each other. They were left gently simmering on low heat.

When you arrived two weeks later, those issues started boiling over. Daphne was frustrated with the way my stepmom did laundry. It was a silly complaint, to be sure, but she was literally washing one outfit at a time. She would throw in a single shirt and a pair of pants. She ran the washer and dryer constantly and didn't want to wash her clothes with ours for some reason. I get it; not having her entire wardrobe and bringing clothes that require a particular clean cycle means we're going to run the machine more often. We can't always control what annoys us. We were grateful for her being there, but having roommates is hard, and sometimes even minor annoyances become significant issues. This was becoming a bigger issue for my pregnancy-hormone-infused wife.

A rule I have with my wife is that we deal with our own families if we have any problematic confrontations. I developed this survival technique after having several uncomfortable interactions with her family early in our relationship. Considering my wife's family all lived in the area, and my family lived much further away, it had been a rule put in place to govern interaction with her family only, but here we were, and I had to be the one to confront you.

Having kids had been a dramatically life-altering experience for me, and I wanted to share what I learned with you. I was looking forward to spending time with you and asking you countless questions about fatherhood. Unfortunately, I would have to interrupt that conversation with an ungrateful-sounding complaint about the quality of the maid you had sent us. If I pulled it off right, I decided I could still have both conversations, so I invited you out to my favorite place.

When I would get off work from the graveyard, Daphne and Pepper would still be asleep for another few hours, so I would drive out to the lake and sit among the Cedar trees. Sometimes I'd fish on my rowboat or run the trails around the mountain. More often than not, I'd just sit at the end of the dock and enjoy the sounds of nature. It was a peaceful place that I loved going to. Getting to take you there meant a lot to me, but I also hoped it might put you at ease.

I had so much to talk to you about that I wasn't sure where I should start in the conversation. I wanted to open with what happened at Basic Training and how much things had changed since getting to my new duty station. To tell you the whole story, I'd have to tell you about my addiction, and I wasn't ready to share that with you yet. I had grown so much in the past four years and was now seeing the world through the eyes of a father. When you have a small human being who is dependent on you and calls you Daddy, it changes your perception of life in so many ways. The Lion King used to be a story about a boy losing his father, but since I've had kids, that story is now about a father not being there for his son. That movie was once about you and me, and now it is about me and my son.

What I regret not getting to tell you that day is that I left for tech school after basic training with a new brand of unmanaged anxiety. I was completely clean of all drugs and alcohol, but I was now wound so incredibly tight by a determination to be the best. I had a taste of that sweet fatherly acceptance, and I was going to hunt that feeling down like a junkie. I didn't enjoy a second of tech school because I agonized over perfectionism every day. In the third week of tech school, you're allowed to leave the dorms and do whatever you want, so I attempted to cut loose, and a bunch of us went drinking for the first time since before Basic.

I wasn't actively trying to be sober. It still hadn't occurred to me that I had an addiction that was constantly trying to ruin my life. The only reason I hadn't had anything to drink was that I had been unwillingly deprived of the stuff since leaving home. Old habits die hard, and I drank that night as I did when I had a tolerance for it. It was barely thirty minutes into the night before I confessed my love for everyone. It was a Friday night, and I didn't have any responsibilities until 0200 on Saturday. I could get sufficiently plastered and be fully recovered by late next morning, long before the afternoon rolled around. I had CQ duty, which meant I would have to sit at the front desk, signing people in for a few hours. Worst-case scenario, I could do that with a hangover.

I got back to my dorms just before the midnight curfew. I stumbled up to my room and immediately passed out in my bed. At 0200 on Saturday, I was startled awake by the loud banging on my door. I was still very drunk, and I tried to focus my eyes on my watch in the dim light. It was two o'clock in the morning. Why would someone be knocking on my door? Then I heard the keys start to turn the lock in the door.

"Hamilton! You in here?" a voice came from the doorway.

"Uh-hm." I cleared my throat, "Yeah, just sleeping. What's going on?"

"You have CQ duty. You slept in." The voice sounded annoyed but young. I was relieved it wasn't one of the training instructors.

"No, there's been a misunderstanding. I have it in the afternoon. The CQ sheet said I didn't have it until two on Saturday." I rubbed my head; waking up after only getting a couple of hours of sleep when you're drunk is very disorienting.

"That would have been 1400 genius. Welcome to the military. Now get down there so I can go to bed." I could see the guy in the doorway now. He was propping my door open with his foot while motioning me down the hallway with a black flashlight that had a yellow cone covering one end.

"Hey, listen, dude, I… I am drunk. I fucked up, man. I don't know what to do." I started to panic. I had accomplished so much in my brief window of sobriety. Now, with just one night of drinking, I was about to throw everything away.

The airman shrugged his shoulders and said, "Uh… just don't say anything, I guess?" He had no skin in the game. He just wanted to go back to his room.

"Nah, dude, I'm still drunk. I'll get caught, and then it'll be so much worse," I said.

"Alright, uh, I'll go tell the T.I., I guess." I didn't protest; the only way out of this was honesty. I had to admit what happened and hope they understood my mistake. Needless to say, they did not.

I was right to fess up to my mistake and was allowed to sleep it off. The backlash came swiftly the next day, and I was made an example in front of thousands of people during the following base commander's call. My one night of CQ duty turned into a month of CQ duty, and I cleaned things that had never been cleaned before. They were throwing around the possibility of an article 112 and dishonorable discharge. I looked it up in the airman's manual, and it was a punishment for being drunk on duty.

Interestingly, my repeating 1s were guiding me again. I had been successfully wishing myself to success every time the clock hit 1:11 or 11:11, and now that I had royally screwed things up, I was given a sign in numerology that I had shifted off my path to 112. I took it to mean that I was almost on the right track and that it would be a simple adjustment to get back to 111. I also took it as a sign that the universe was trying to get me to stop drinking, so I didn't drink again for the remainder of tech school. Thanks to my good behavior and excellent grades, my article 112 was dropped, and I went practically unpunished.

School flew by, and as I approached graduation, I had to start looking for a place to live in California. I called a few places that fit my budget and were willing to accommodate my unique situation. I couldn't see the apartment or sign any paperwork until I arrived, but I also needed a place to stay when I got there. They would need to allow me to accomplish most of this over the phone and finish the rest later.

When I found the right place, I told the lady on the other end of the line that I'd like to move in. She gave me the address, 1111 Cable Car Avenue, apartment number 11. I was so happy to hear that the universe approved my decision, and I gladly accepted the apartment.

I got to my new base and met everyone at my new hospital. My supervisor, Sergeant Martino, gave me a tour and informed me that I'd immediately be headed back to school because they had a new assignment for me. As luck would have it, I wasn't going to be a secretary after all. "You're going to be the Drug Demand Reduction Manager," he said.

"Oh, okay, what's that, sir?" Being in a hospital setting, I assumed I'd have a role with pharmacy and disposing of their prescription drugs.

"You're going to be responsible for drug testing everyone on base and providing outreach to prevent our members from using illicit drugs," he said.

# PART 2: GRANDFATHER CLOCK

The lump in my throat felt like it may have been visible. There hadn't been a single day since I first talked to my recruiter that I hadn't stressed myself stupid worrying about my little drug secret. The Drug Demand Reduction Manager most likely maintained that mass surveillance database I feared. If I tested someone for drugs and they were positive, they'd have to go to court-martial. The defense attorney's only successful approach to getting their client off the hook would be to create doubt in the testing process. The defense would challenge the credibility of the person doing the testing, focusing not only on how I processed the samples but also on certain aspects of my personal life. If they could dig up some dirt on me to get their client off, they would. The anxiety I felt from my fraud complex quadrupled, and I overcompensated by working harder. Getting caught felt inevitable now, so I had to work hard enough in the meantime to build a good enough reputation that I could either erase all doubt or, at a minimum, avoid prosecution.

I became the hardest working alcoholic the Air Force had ever seen. Alcoholism is a weird thing. I hadn't attempted to get clean; it had been forced upon me when I was denied my freedoms in Basic. Leaving tech school, I was no longer dependent on alcohol. It would have been easy if I had chosen to quit for good at that time. Unfortunately, I hadn't made that choice yet, and I would have a harmless drink while watching football. Then I'd have a couple of drinks with dinner or socially with friends. Before long, I was belly up to the bar every night again. Luckily, I had so many responsibilities at work that I couldn't get blackout drunk every night as I used to. I worked nine to five and then went to night school from six to nine. That schedule isn't conducive to overdrinking, but I managed to make time for it by multitasking as I began studying at the bar.

With the return of my alcoholism came the return of my depression. I remembered my ultimate goal of dying on the job and returned to the work of trying to find a good way of doing so. Testing urine for marijuana didn't seem dangerous enough, so I started looking at deployments. I was hell-bent on going overseas when I met Dorothy.

Dorothy was a waitress at one of the bars where I liked to study. I would sit in the back of the bar with my books and read, but I'd order drinks and food regularly to justify taking up a table. "Nice hat," she said as she leaned against the back of an empty chair opposite my table. She had long brown hair with golden blonde highlights curling wildly against her shoulders. She wasn't my waitress, so I realized she had come over specifically to talk to me.

"Thanks," I said, taking it from my head and handing it to her. She snatched it out of my hand and put it on herself as she spun on her heels and headed back to the kitchen area. Ten minutes passed before I saw her again, and she tried to give it back to me.

"I don't want your hat," I said. "You can keep it."

"Seriously?" she asked, holding it against her chest, wrapped in both arms.

I didn't know Dorothy, but in the days following our hat conversation, I would learn that she was a free spirit who was always on the move. She had just returned from Australia, if "returned from" are the right words for it. More accurately, she had been deported for some mischief she would never tell me about and was permanently banned from the country. This was her modus operandi, and when she wasn't being deported from foreign countries, she was back in California, living with friends or family until she could save enough money for her next excursion. When I gave her my hat without a second thought, she assumed I was as free a spirit as she was.

She didn't know that I was a twisted ball of anxiety and depression. Constantly on edge about making any mistakes that would lead to me being dishonorably discharged from the Air Force, an alcoholic wallowing in self-pity and depression while also struggling through school to satisfy my still unimpressed brother. My spirit was trapped in a rusty cage of its own making; the door left wide open but too afraid to fly.

Dorothy called me one night and wanted to go on a date. I picked her up from her brother's house, and they decided to have some fun with me. Her brother was bald, but he had a shaggy Louie Barletta-style haircut the night I met him. Maybe it was nerves, perhaps the toupee was believable, but I didn't recognize just how bad the wig was. My ignorance came off as kindness, and her brother liked me immediately. I think they hoped I would be a good influence on Dorothy and she'd begin settling down.

We went to a Mexican restaurant and drank a bunch of margaritas before smuggling more tequila into the movie theatre. After the movie, we were nice and plastered, and Dorothy wanted to go to an antique shop. She removed her seat belt and shouted directions to me over the sound of her music while dancing in the passenger's seat. When we got to the antique store, the lights were off inside.

"Sorry Dorothy, it looks closed," I said, turning her music down.

"I know it's closed. Get out." She jumped out of the car and twirled in the street before running up to the store's large window.

When I met her on the sidewalk, she had her face pressed against the glass with her hands cupped around her eyes, blocking her reflection and allowing herself to see into the shop. "There it is!" she exclaimed.

I followed suit and looked into the window. There were shelves of random knickknacks everywhere, and you could see from the street that there was a layer of dust covering everything. I didn't respond; I couldn't imagine what she was so excited to see.

"Do you see the grandfather clock in the back?" she asked.

"The one with the acorns carved in it?" It looked to be at least 7 feet tall and had an elaborate woodcarving of acorns and leaves that surrounded three golden weights hanging from the center.

"Yes," she said with a sly smile, adding, "I want you to steal it."

"Steal what? The clock? What am I supposed to do, just put it in my pocket and walk out?" I laughed at her, thinking she was joking, but she looked hurt. She was realizing that I wasn't as carefree or reckless as she thought. That was the last time I ever saw Dorothy. She left me for not wanting to steal a grandfather clock. I wasn't too broken up about it. Honestly, she kind of scared me. Her energy reminded me of the path I had been on before the military. She was desperately searching for something while missing most of it in a drunken haze. Appearing to others as a free spirit, but never truly free, racing toward death.

A few years later, I heard from her brother that Dorothy had gotten into a drunk driving accident. She was in the passenger seat, likely dancing to her favorite song, when the driver swerved off the road and hit a light post. Her body was suddenly thrown from the vehicle, where she died at the scene. I went to the funeral, but it didn't feel right. They had attempted to make it a celebration of life party in her honor, complete with a photo booth. With the awkward mix of joy and sorrow, I couldn't help thinking that it would have been me driving under different circumstances. I had driven drunk with Dorothy too, but my resistance to breaking and entering meant she was with someone else the night they crashed.

Dorothy wasn't the only person I lost in a drunk driving accident. My cousin stole pills from our grandmother and mixed them with copious amounts of alcohol before swerving off the road and into a tree. In Texas, my friend Ricky said goodnight to his girlfriend as she was leaving the party early with her friend. She went the wrong way onto the interstate and woke up in the hospital. Her friend was driving when they left the party, but according to the police report, she was found in the driver's seat. She didn't remember leaving the party or switching seats with him, but she was now under investigation for the involuntary manslaughter of her best friend and the family of four, who all died in the crash. There's no reason, other than dumb luck, for my story to have not ended in a similar way.

I was sharing a beer with Dorothy's brother, Oscar, soon after she left me because of my reluctance to pillage antiques. He offered me a job at a mental health facility he managed. I was studying to be a medical assistant at the time, and the job description required the skills I was learning, but the thought of working around people experiencing a mental health crisis worried me. My own balancing act on the edge of psychosis had vastly improved since the last time I had taken shrooms. Still, I was concerned that one brush of the surreal could trigger my mental collapse.

After long and careful consideration, I accepted the offer and started working with some of the most fascinating people I've ever met. My fear of insanity by association was confronted on my first day of work. The aspects of my past drug abuse that I felt were my greatest weakness now served as a strength. While I had never met any of the clients before, I recognized myself in each of them. Some people were there because they were so depressed that they had been placed on suicide watch. I met people that had walked up to the line of drug-induced psychosis, but, unlike me, they weren't as lucky to have stopped just before falling over the edge. I met clients that felt they had failed their families and struggled with the weight of those expectations. I realized that I had something to offer those people, and I loved every minute of that job.

I also loved my coworkers. That job wasn't just emotionally

demanding but also mentally and physically challenging. All too often, triumphs and progress were replaced by setbacks and remission. Unfortunately, as with many social programs, the pay was garbage, and the turnover rate was high. Those that stayed did so because they loved the work and the people they helped. I was surrounded by the biggest hearts that were full of love and patience. I would occasionally also work with a cute redhead who wore band t-shirts.

# Part 3: Engelbert Humperdinck

She was thin, with an athletic build. Her hair was a dark brownish-red that shined vibrantly in the sun. She always wore it tied back in a tight ponytail, but she would leave a long strip of bangs that framed her beautiful face. Her name was Daphne, and despite her attractiveness, I didn't attempt to flirt with her. I was still looking for a deployment opportunity overseas and wasn't looking to be in a relationship. She also seemed well out of my league. She was stern, professional, and obviously had her life together. By contrast, I was always goofing around and didn't even have furniture in my apartment. You can imagine my surprise when she messaged me on Facebook to go on a date.

I took her to a Benihana-style restaurant, and suddenly, this girl that had seemed so confident at work and made the first move on me was now incredibly shy. She played with the hem of her dress throughout the entire dinner. After we ate, I invited her to my favorite bar on the other side of town. My ideal bar was one where it's large enough to get lost in a quiet corner, and the overall vibe is depressing with a hint of sketchy. The Creek and Meadow checked every box. It was karaoke night, and we enjoyed the drunken renditions of a surprisingly expansive collection of Engelbert Humperdinck's greatest hits.

I didn't kiss her that night, and I didn't kiss her on our next date either. Daphne was different, and I knew it. I was in no shape emotionally to be in a real relationship. Had I liked her less, maybe she would have been a fun fling until I left for deployment, but I could tell within our first date that I would fall hopelessly in love with her. I wanted to spend more time with her, but I decided I would never kiss her. Then I wouldn't have to fall in love with her and change any of my plans. She ruined my strategy one night after eating at In-N-Out when she asked me for a kiss, and as soon as we did, I knew my death was unquestionably on hold for a while. I thought about how I felt in Utah before leaving for basic training. Daphne was becoming what I had been longing for when I wrote "Old and Tired." Considering the change in heart, I decided to write a new song.

# Listen: Track 5
# "Lights up My Skies"

https://denverjhamilton.bandcamp.com/track/lights-up-my-skies-2

## Lyrics

I can't believe I left the city to move here,
The drive was long,
I should have known that this was wrong,
But as of late,
It's turning out,
Pretty great.
Without you, I'd be lost without a clue.

## Meaning

*I wanted Daphne to like the song I was writing for her, but she liked metal, and I didn't know the genre very well. My version of metal came off as more of a pop-punk than anything, but it's the thought that counts. The song starts with how I felt when I moved to California from Austin. I was living in the live music capital of the country but had now seemingly moved to the meth capital of California. I had left my things with you in Utah, and when I returned from tech school, I drove all those belongings to my new base. The drive was long and gave me time to think about everything I had accomplished. Now, at my first duty station, I regretted my choices and fell back into the old habit of drinking heavily again. Everything changed when Daphne and I started dating. My new duty station suddenly didn't seem so bad. Had I never met her, I'd still be lost without a clue of what to do with my life.*

(Chorus)
When I'm ready to go home,
I just look in your eyes
And I'm back in the city,
Under all those neon lights.
To turn them off,
You just close your eyes
And when you open them,
It lights up my skies.

*The chorus is a callback to "Old and Tired." While I was recording, looking out at the city lights, I longed for something I couldn't put my finger on. I had assumed it was the nightlife, meeting unusual people, and living spontaneously. The lights represented late nights on stage with an instrument or skating street downtown when all the businesses were closed and security was gone. "Old and Tired" was a song about letting that feeling go and growing up. Now, being with Daphne, I had that same feeling I got from all those neon lights. In "Old and Tired," the lights fade away as the dawning of a new day brightens to me being older and exhausted from another monotonous day of work, and I've since given up my favorite things. With her, I didn't need to give up anything. She was what I had been searching for my entire life, and looking into her eyes is what brightened the sky, both day and night.*

Whatcha doin',
Where ya goin',
And where ya at?
I miss your face,
Can I come over to your place?
The drive was long,
But it's nice being wrong.
Then just like this,
She looked at me and asked for a kiss.

*We couldn't get enough of each other and started spending every waking moment together. I wanted to go everywhere and do anything with her; I just wanted to be at her side every second. I was terrified by how hard I was falling for her, and I didn't want to screw it up. I wasn't prepared for a serious relationship, and I knew this would likely get very serious, so I refused to kiss her for the first several dates. Then, just like that, she asked me for a kiss, and I was hers forever.*

We drank every time we got together, and I think she was surprised by how often I wanted to. She wasn't a drinker but did her best to keep up. If things hadn't changed, my drinking would have probably become an issue. She never once complained, and luckily, my urge to drink began to die out on its own.

130

I woke up one morning after spending the night with her, and I couldn't remember everything we did or what we talked about, and I regretted it. I wished I could remember every second of my time with her. The next time we hung out, I got drunk again, but I felt guilty about it as soon as I started to buzz. I drank some water, hoping to sober up because I could tell I was losing touch with my clear head. I wanted to experience my night with her in the rawest and purest form possible. This was the first time I didn't want alcohol in many years.

I was so happy being around her that alcohol cheapened the moment rather than enhanced it. I had spent so many years relying on alcohol to make me more social and seem more outgoing. Daphne made me feel the same way by making me feel good about myself. She valued my uniqueness and admired my talents. Her concern was not what I had done in my past or what I'd do in the future; she was interested in who I was now. I also stopped worrying about what I had or had not accomplished as I started to feel better about myself. There was no stress about being better than I was and no shame for the mistakes I had made along the way. The things I had done in my past made me the person I am today. If that person could be loved by someone as amazing as Daphne, then I could learn to love myself too. The constant internal conflict pitting my need for creative expression against my longing for familial approval left me feeling ashamed of the things I was most proud of personally. That conflict was the trigger that would make me want to drink, and while I would still spend the next several years denying my real authentic self, Daphne became the higher power that gave me the strength to resist the urge to drink when I was triggered.

I had never been happier, and as I got further away from my alcohol dependence, my brain felt sharper, and my depression withered. I felt like I could accomplish anything. All because of the love and support she had given me. Our first date was on February 2, 2011, and by April, I was staying at her house almost every night. I moved in a month later, and we started throwing around the idea of getting married. Things were moving too fast, but we were both so madly in love that it felt right. When I realized that November would be 11/11/11, I decided to ask her officially.

Considering we had met at work, I devised a proposal that would catch her off guard at a company team meeting. I conveniently had the day off, so she wasn't expecting me to be there. Our boss, Dorothy's brother Oscar, was supposed to lead a team exercise on crisis intervention and de-escalation. He would call on Daphne to play the role of the responding staff member. This was one part prank, as I knew she hated doing things in front of a group of people, but it also served the purpose of getting her to stand center stage in front of all of our coworkers and mutual friends. Oscar picked another person from the group and had them walk outside to await their cue. They were told to reenter the room and pretend to be having a mental health crisis, to which Daphne would respond appropriately. Daphne didn't know that Oscar's decoy person was tasked with meeting me outside and holding the camera as I walked in.

The look on her face was priceless when she saw me come through the doors. The plan worked so well that she was utterly stunned despite having already discussed marriage and had picked out the ring I was now holding. I could tell she was confused about why I was walking toward the front of the room and why I had such a big smile on my face. She was likely under the spell of social anxiety as she was mentally preparing to play her de-escalation role that was about to commence at any moment. I was making the whole ordeal infinitely more awkward.

I had planned what I'd say to her for weeks, but my vision narrowed as I walked down the aisle toward her. Soon, all I could see was her, standing at the end of a long black tunnel. When I finally reached where she was standing, the words failed to escape my mouth. I fell to one knee and shoved the ring at her, hoping she'd get the idea. She said, "Yes," and by 11 a.m. on 11/11/11, I was married to my best friend after having dated for only nine months.

# PART 4: SENSORY DEPRIVATION

Daphne's middle name is Michelle, so I wrote a song with heavy inspiration from the Beatles' tune by the same name. I loved the bass line in that song and copied the style and tone. I also did my best to sing backup vocals for myself, like John and George. Almost every time someone hears this song, they ask me if a woman sang the backing vocals. I have decided to take this as a compliment.

# Listen: Track 6
# "I Want Her to Know"

https://denverjhamilton.bandcamp.com/track/i-want-her-to-know

### Lyrics

I'll admit,
When I'm wrong,
I didn't see you,
Coming along,
But I'm glad that you did,
When you did,
When you did.

### Meaning

*I wrote the second song for Daphne in a folky jazz-type style that I was more comfortable with, abandoning the idea of another metal attempt. The lyrics start with me remembering where I was emotionally when we first met and how I wasn't looking for a relationship. She had reached out to me and had made the first move, and I had honestly not seen it coming.*

You're the kind of girl,
That makes you wonder,
If there's any other man in the world,
Who loves anybody like I do,
I do,
I love you, girl,

You're the peaches on my,
Peaches tree,
I said, don't you leave me,
I love you too much.
I would do,
Anything that you ask,
All you got to do,
Is bat those little lashes, girl

(Chorus)
And I've got this girl,
She's out of this world
And I want her to know
There's nothing in this world
That means more,
To me.
There's nothing
That means more
To me
Than you girl

So I'd be happy if you
stuck around
Forever, forever, forever
Do you see now,
Why I run,
The air conditioner,
All summer long,
It makes you cuddle,
With me.

*There's an Easter egg of a line in this verse, "Do you see now, why I run." As I've said before, I rarely write lyrics first. I clear my mind and sing the first thing I think of until the song starts to come together on its own. A repeating theme in my poetry is running away from something or someone. In my song, "Three Different Things," a song I wrote about my mother, there's a lot of imagery about running away from each other. This is one of many songs where I've used the words "why I run." This line is a pun and a message to myself, asking if I saw why I had been running all these years. I always thought I was running away when in reality, I was running toward Daphne. Now that we had found each other, I was no longer running away. Instead, I ran the air conditioner to make it cold enough that she'd want to cuddle.*

Go to a movie,
Take you to lunch
Go play putt-putt
Show you that I love you a bunches
And bunches and bunches
Skee dop
Do op
Bededotdot
Boody day
I hope that I showed you
How much that you mean to me

Out at base, a position opened in the medical laboratory, but it required color vision. Our unit commander was an optometrist, and he worked his magic to make my color limitations miraculously disappear from my record. It was a mysterious loophole of sorts that allowed me to cross-train into the lab. We were only married a few months, and now I would have to leave my wife for over a year while I was training. Daphne made the sacrifice to leave the job she loved, the place we met, to follow me to tech school. Her family had not taken our marriage well at first. We had rushed into things, and I think they thought I would take her away on some military deployment. Although I was only cross-training and would be back in California at the same duty station in thirteen months, they felt their concerns had come to fruition, and we'd never return.

The two longest and most challenging tech schools in the Air Force are cryptic linguistics and medical laboratory. The course covers microbiology, blood banking, virology, hematology, chemistry, urinalysis, and other specialty lab techniques. The tricks I picked up in music school came in handy as I was tasked with memorizing entire textbooks. I had a tall garbage bag full of notecards and fell victim to perfectionism. Having been a cross-trained airman, I was the highest ranking in a class of all trainees fresh out of Basic, which meant I had to be the class leader. I took the role too seriously and shouldered the burden of ensuring everyone did as well as I did.

I had my first ever anxiety attack in phase two of training. In the first phase, we had about 80% didactic learning with only about 20% lab work. Phase 2 of training is split at about 50%, but the lab work is now with actual patients. We'd have to report to work at 0500 and draw blood on patients throughout the hospital. I already hated phlebotomy, but waking people up so early, only to jab them in the arm, made it so much worse. These people were also sick, so finding the vein in each patient was extraordinarily difficult. The stress of the ordeal amplifies when you miss the vein and have to try again. Now, the patient is pissed off, and you're running behind on collections.

As the class leader, I was the liaison between the students and the instructors. I struggled to maintain my grades and care for my patients, but I also had to put out little fires across the delicate landscape of near-teenage trainee emotions. I finally cracked one night after work when I couldn't focus anymore and could hear hundreds of voices in my head. So many people were talking that I couldn't make out what anyone was saying, but it wasn't like standing in a crowded place. All the voices were talking to me directly, expecting a response.

Daphne had been making use of her time volunteering on base and around town, so I had the house to myself. I tried to sleep it off, but the voices kept getting louder and more demanding. I would have drowned them out with alcohol in the past, but I was learning to cope in different ways. I was so overstimulated by the noise in my head that I decided to try sensory deprivation. I crawled into bed and then put on noise-canceling headphones and a blindfold. The voices became louder, and, at first, it was almost too much to handle. I tried to clear my mind and meditate, but they became more intrusive. After a few minutes of relaxing, I started to recognize one of the voices in the group. It was Airman Martinez, one of the trainees that had been in my phase 1 class. Once I picked it out as him, I could pretend he was in the room with me. Now I could focus on what he was saying. His roommate would cut his toenails in one corner of the dorm and then leave the pile of discarded nails there. Martinez refused to clean it for him, so now the pile had turned into a mound. His roommate didn't shower, never brushed his teeth, wore a wrinkled uniform, and would surely get them both in trouble at the next dorm inspection. I listened to everything he had to say and gave him some advice. I eventually promised I'd let the dorm manager know and see if I could get him transferred to a different room. Martinez was satisfied and went away. I immediately started trying to single out another voice.

One by one, I identified each voice and listened to their concerns. Some wanted advice, and others just wanted to vent before fading away. An hour passed, and I was sitting in bed in pure silence. I had successfully coped with stress without needing to drink. I now had another tool in my belt for dealing with anxiety, and I crushed the rest of my time in tech school. I loved my new job so much that I decided to take the necessary steps toward making it a civilian career after graduation. To be a scientist in California, I needed a bachelor's degree and had to pass a licensing exam. Armed with renewed confidence and additional coping skills, I enrolled at the University of California.

The classes were more demanding than anything I'd ever attempted before, and I was stressing myself out trying to maintain a 4.0 GPA that, to this day, has meant nothing to my career. Because I had taken so many classes outside of the Biology degree, I had zero electives to pad my schedule. I had to take all upper division math and science classes. Each semester, I spent more and more time in the study halls.

I was taking a genetics class when Daphne and I decided to start trying to have a baby. It was enlightening to put my homework to use and rather exhilarating to see my school project turn into an actual child. I had researched a few things that were supposed to improve your odds of having a boy, and I employed them all. I also cut out processed sugars and caffeine, two things that I read could damage your sperm or negatively impact cell division. When Daphne became pregnant, I knew in my gut that we were having a boy. There wasn't an ounce of doubt in my mind, and I focused on thinking of only boy names. I'd refer to Daphne's belly as "son," and I'd talk to the little slugger through her stomach. This is why my dream surprised me a few weeks before the gender-revealing ultrasound.

# PART 5: INSEPARABLE LITTLE BUDDY

I dreamt I was playing guitar and singing a song. The lyrics were about playing with my baby boy and all the fun things we'd do together, like playing baseball and digging up worms. When I got to the chorus, I sang, "You're going to be the most beautiful girl in the world." I woke up in the middle of the song and laughed at how clever it was. To lead the listener through each verse as if it's a boy, but then hit them with a twist because girls can do all the things little boys can. A little girl would love to play baseball and dig for worms. I considered changing the words to "You're going to be the most beautiful boy in the world," then I thought of recording two separate versions for a boy and a girl, but I ultimately decided to record the version in my dream. If anything, it'd be funny to explain to my son why the first song I wrote him was about a little girl.

## Listen: Track 7

## "Pepper"

https://denverjhamilton.bandcamp.com/track/pepper

### Lyrics

I can't wait to go outside,
And teach you to dig for worms.
Scrub the dirt out from under your nails,
We'll get 'em as good as we can.
I'll clean up your scratched-up knees,
Just look away while it burns.

### Meaning

*These are some of the things I remember you and mom doing that felt quintessentially parental. I remember riding my bike at the park across the street from our old house, the house with the crooked pine tree in the front yard that never grew taller than three feet until we moved out and someone else started taking care of it. There was a drainage ditch you could bomb down and ride up the walls, and I hit a patch of loose gravel and fell to my side. I jumped on my bike and went home as fast as possible to show Mom the road rash I had earned, and then I happily announced how big a boy I was for not crying. That all changed when she poured hydrogen peroxide over it, and my knees began to bubble and hiss.*

It's the bottom of the 9th
You got a ghost runner on 3rd
You hit one to left field
And I'll pretend I can't get there in time.
I can't wait to see you cry
When I tag you out at home.

*This verse is a callback to my brother. We used to play baseball all the time with just the two of us. If you got a hit and made it to the base, you would put a ghost runner on the first and return to hit again. The ghost runner would advance to the next base if you got another base hit. The reference to being at the bottom of the 9th is a callback to one of the last games Shannon and I played. The game was tied, and it was the bottom of the 9th. I had a ghost runner on third, which meant a base hit would win the game. I was standing in the hallway near the front door, and he pitched it from inside the living room. It was a curve ball, low and outside, but I swung for it. My bat went right through the sheetrock of your wall, just above the spot where you left your shoes every day after work. The last line is my favorite. While I believe it's important to let your children win, I also think it's equally beneficial for them to lose once in a while.*

(Chorus)
'Cause you're going to be the most beautiful girl
in the world
Gonna be the most beautiful girl
In the world.

And I can't wait to experiment,
On grasshoppers without legs.
Gonna love to see you squirm,
When you touch something slimy and gross.
Don't put that in your mouth,
There are other ways to learn.

*This verse was essential after the big reveal in the chorus that the song was about a girl. The following verses are about things considered more traditionally "girly," so I wanted to hit home the idea that my sweet little princess would likely also love playing with bugs and putting gross things in her mouth.*

I can't wait to dance,

While you're standing on my feet.

We'll break to have some tea,

With Mr. Squid and Mrs. Frog

I'll dress you like a princess,

And then we'll play with swords

*I also wanted to add some activities like playing dress-up and having tea parties to show I was happy to do "girly" stuff too. Daphne and I wanted to raise our kids in an environment that was as gender-neutral as possible. I was aware of gender roles and their impact, but I never realized the full extent to which those roles are forced on young children. There are so many products on the market that are unnecessarily gendered, like a hammer for women, but the only change is that it's pink and costs slightly more. I wanted to ensure I hadn't overcorrected and just forced male stereotypes on her. She would be allowed to be anything she wanted to be, even if that meant she wanted to be a princess.*

The song took on an entirely new meaning when the doctor told us we were having a girl. It now felt like my baby girl had visited me in a dream, and she had been the one who wrote those words. That little girl, Pepper Mae Hamilton, ended up being exactly like the kid in the song. That dream cemented our special bond, and she became my inseparable little buddy.

Daphne's due date was predicted to be at the end of the month, and by the time we were within a week from Pepper's arrival, we were trying everything we could to encourage labor. Daphne ate spicy food with every meal, danced to Beyoncé, and even drank entire spoonfuls of straight olive oil. During the week, I was commuting an hour to school, taking the most academically challenging classes I had in the program. I was enrolled in Pathogenic Bacteria, Immunology, and

140

Quantitative Chemistry. These were all courses with long lab hours. I was hoping she'd go into labor on a weekend because I couldn't miss more than a single lab. Starting Friday nights, we would spice up our food and do some light exercise to encourage labor. When Pepper hadn't come by the end of the weekend, we would slow things down, eat bland food, and try to wait it out until the following weekend. On September 10th, I got a message from Daphne just as I was pulling into the school parking lot. Knowing how Pepper turned out, of course she would come on a Monday, despite all our planning.

Daphne's water had broken while she was eating her breakfast cereal. She said it was undeniable what had happened but didn't want to freak either of us out by jumping to conclusions. She sent me an ambiguous text message that said, "Call me when you can." Regardless of her efforts to remain calm, I read this as, "ITS GO TIME! CALL ME IMMEDIATELY!!" As soon as she answered my call, I could tell she was in labor just by the tone of her voice when she said, "Hello." I told her to relax and that I'd be home as soon as possible. I turned around and jumped back on the highway. I thought it was hilarious that Pepper waited until Monday. Not only would I miss the most classes, but she also let me get all the way to school before deciding to make her grand entrance.

I was nervously laughing and fighting back the tears of joy the entire ride home. I called you, soon-to-be Papa Gene, and I told you she was about to arrive. At the time, you were living in west Texas and were waiting for that call before booking a flight to come see us. We had tested Daphne for Group B Strep, so we weren't worried about any infection risk to the baby. We had planned to do most of the labor at a hotel near the hospital, where we could have more privacy, and we knew it would be a very long time before Pepper would be close to being here. When you answered the phone, you sounded very concerned. This was true of every call to anyone the closer we got to the due date, especially once we passed the due date. I explained that I was driving an hour home, and then we'd drive an hour to our hotel near the hospital before checking into the birthing center. You were shocked we weren't racing straight to the hospital and expressed your uneasiness. Labor in the movies usually depicts a lady's water breaking, and then it's this crazy hectic emergency with a clueless father and a screaming mother. We were as prepared as we could be.

We had gone to every Lamaze class, researched hospitals, read books, and planned this day down to the go bag with everything we would need. Instead of a rushed panic, we went to Target and walked around before getting some lunch at Mr. Pickles.

When I got home, Daphne was cleaning the house with an anxious, yet stoic, look on her face. We gathered our things, stopped on our way out the door to take one last picture, and promptly forgot to grab our go bag and left it in the kitchen. By the time we got to the hospital two hours later, she had regular contractions about eight minutes apart. They hooked her up to a monitor, and we could hear Pepper's happy little heartbeat. Everything was progressing wonderfully, so they let us leave for our local hotel.

Daphne had been pretty cheerful up until we got to the hotel. The contractions were getting stronger, and the pain demanded her undivided attention. My in-laws got a room next door to ours, but they gave Daphne and me some space; they just wanted to be around when the baby came or if we needed anything. Daphne's sister Dani and her husband Jared also showed up to say hi, but they too stayed next door. By about 10 p.m., Daphne couldn't take it anymore. Her contractions were getting close to four minutes apart, and she had stopped talking to focus all of her attention on breathing. We said goodbye to everyone for the night and left for the hospital.

# PART 6: 13:13

We were checked in to the hospital, and again we monitored Pepper's little heart rate. I assume the nursing staff knew we weren't close to meeting her yet because they left us alone for several hours. Daphne closed her eyes at around midnight and didn't open them again until about 1:30 p.m. the next day, but she stayed awake, swaying from side to side. I could tell the pain was worsening, and she was starting to go into a primal survival mode. Her back was hurting, and constant massaging pressure was the only thing that helped alleviate it. I rubbed her back and did my best to be encouraging while Daphne gently rocked with her eyes closed.

By 3:00 in the morning, my arms were too exhausted to continue, and I was falling asleep. I would startle awake each time Daphne commanded me to keep pressing her lower back, and I think she was frustrated by the pain and my constant nodding off. Finally, she said, "Do you want me to just get the epidural so you can get some sleep?"

I sat up and told her, "The doula will be here in a few hours. Hang on. You've got this." Setting a goal of waiting for the doula gave us a little energy, and she pushed on through the night.

Finally, the doula arrived around 6:00 in the morning and didn't leave our side until Pepper came. I was too stressed and tired to remember the doula's name, but she knew exactly what we needed. She got Daphne up and moving around and gave us lots of great advice. We were also assigned a nurse, Vicky. Vicky was such a tremendous help that I was prepared to let her deliver the baby when the time came, but it was Doctor Bianca who had the honor of meeting her first.

Every time Daphne would push, I would get choked up. I had never seen anyone in that much pain, let alone the woman I loved, but she was so strong and dedicated to naturally bringing our daughter into this world. I was so blown away by her strength. We moved from the bed to the toilet, to the shower, and back to the bed for 28 hours straight. We eventually reached a point where Pepper was ready, but the only position working for Daphne was sitting on the toilet. To avoid pooping Pepper into the bowl, the doula gave us a birthing stool. I sat behind her and held her up while she pushed. This phase of labor was the most special to me because I felt like I was part of bringing Pepper into the world. I would squeeze Daphne close and push against her hands, giving her something to lean back on. With each push, I could feel our teamwork bringing our baby into the world. At 13:13, Pepper screamed hello as Bianca flopped her bloody uncoordinated body onto Daphne's chest. We couldn't do anything but cry-laugh.

We had prepared as much as possible for our new baby, but nothing prepares you for colic. Pepper wouldn't breastfeed, and she cried nonstop. We would try changing her diaper, breast feeding, burping her, and then napping. When none of those things worked, we'd start the process over and try changing her again. We would cycle through the classics until she cried herself to sleep. Not being able to comfort your child makes you feel like a failure. I can't imagine how Daphne felt when she also couldn't get Pepper to feed. Pepper's weight began to drop, and we had to pump the breastmilk and bottle-feed her. The more we bottle-fed, the less likely it became that Pepper would ever learn to latch on. We both knew how important it was that Pepper got natural breastmilk, but Daphne shouldered the burden and the lion's share of the guilt. Breastfeeding is talked about as natural and maternal, and mothers are often shamed if they decide to use the bottle instead. Since Pepper had such bad colic and refused to latch, Daphne felt unnatural, less maternal, and ashamed for using a bottle despite filling it with her breastmilk. She pumped every day and struggled with painful clogging milk ducts. She was working so hard for our baby, but none of it seemed to matter because of Pepper's colic.

I was trying to finish the semester, but I kept getting phone calls from Daphne. She'd be crying, worried about Pepper. Daphne was developing postpartum depression, and I felt awful having to leave them both every morning for school. I missed a few labs for my quantitative chemistry class, and I couldn't find time to make them up. I was so far behind that I couldn't move on to subsequent labs because I didn't have the reagents made from previous labs. I knew I'd have to drop my classes, but that meant I'd lose my scholarships, and it would extend my graduation date. Given the choice a million times over, I'd choose my family every single time.

It was six months of colic, just nonstop crying. Daphne and I had been together for five years when Pepper was born, and we had never fought over anything. There was no telling how we would do when things weren't going great. A major defining moment in every relationship is not how much you love each other at your happiest. It's how you manage to continue loving each other at your most miserable.

I was raised in a family that doesn't talk about emotions. As an artist, I learned to listen to my voice and find creative ways of expressing my feelings, but I always struggled with sharing those feelings with you. I can't imagine I would have stayed sober while trying to handle the immensely difficult combination of a colicky baby and a depressed wife if I hadn't worked on developing better coping mechanisms and maintained good communication with my wife. Bottling up our frustrations and not expressing our expectations of each other would eventually have blown up in our faces. I'm fortunate to have the wife that I do. We researched together, shared chores, and split responsibilities. Slowly, we got through it day by day. Notably, I never once felt the need to drink during this time. Daphne had literally saved my life, so I felt like I owed it to her to be the best partner I could be. That's the difference between having a problem and having a partner.

I was doing microbiology research and was learning more about the human microbiome. I was fascinated by how much our health depends on the diversity of our gut microbes. Several studies showed that the right combination of gut bacteria in infants could cure colic symptoms. We tried a variety of probiotics that we would add to the breastmilk in Pepper's bottle. Within two days, Pepper's colic completely vanished. She was now consolable and even started smiling at us and interacting more. We felt awful we hadn't tried it sooner, but we also felt like we had figured out a mysterious complication together as a family.

I felt more in tune with my wife and my child. We were a team and became acutely aware of what Pepper needed. We found she did better with a schedule. The more we could provide her with consistency, the happier she was. If Pepper were comfortable, then Daphne would be satisfied. I could ensure my family's happiness and emotional security by correctly managing the day's routine. When you would come to visit, my insistence on maintaining that level of routine appeared to be coming off as a personal attack on you and the things you wanted to do while you were visiting.

Around the same time, my eight-year contract with the military ended, and I was about to graduate with my bachelor's. I had to decide if I wanted to reenlist or pursue my new civilian career. Staying in the military until retirement had never been my goal, but I think you expected I would. I was almost halfway to retirement, and it represented that stability you always wanted for me. Unfortunately, two things happened the year prior that had soured my feelings toward staying in.

The first thing that changed my perspective of military life was in 2015, a Doctor's Without Borders-run trauma hospital in Kunduz, Afghanistan, was repeatedly struck by United States air strikes. General Campbell released multiple conflicting reports on why they chose to attack the hospital, only to conclude later that it was a "mistake." In the end, 42 innocent civilians were killed, but no charges were levied against anyone involved. A blatant breach of humanitarian law that amounted to nothing short of a war crime ended with an apology from Barrack Obama and an insulting $6,000.00 condolence payment to each family affected.

The second thing that happened was the following year when politics would polarize the country during the transition into the Trump administration. There was word that Trump wanted to send troops from my unit to guard the Mexican border and to help build the infamous wall. The military, and the country I served in, felt different than they had when I first joined. Had I not had any other options, maybe I would have made a different choice, but I was now licensed as a scientist, and I took it as an opportunity to start a new chapter. As I was walking away from the military, the presidential candidates were arguing about making college tuition-free. Reflecting on my own experience, it occurred to me why college had to be so expensive. The government's ability to amass an all-volunteer military force relies on tuition being so astronomically unachievable that people are willing to risk their lives for military benefits. I was fortunate to have the privilege to walk away from it all and focus on my family and career.

I'm not sure you could see past the fact that I was walking away from a stable career, a guaranteed retirement, and that I was doing so with a young family. You had been so proud of me for the last eight years, and now, it seemed things had changed between us yet again. I wondered if you ever treated my brother with the same concern or if you trusted his decisions. Admittedly, I hadn't exactly built a reputation for making great decisions, but I was leaving the military to begin a promising career as a scientist. I wasn't putting my family in financial hardship. We were starting the next chapter of our lives just as we had done everything up to this point, as a team. I felt like you always treated me like a little boy and couldn't see me for the man I was becoming. Worse, I couldn't just assume it was because you were my dad, and I would always be a boy in your eyes because you always seemed to treat my brother with respect and admired the man he had become.

These potential issues came to a head while floating on a tiny raft in the middle of the lake. I wanted to share my feelings with you, tell you everything I had been through, and express how I wished to be seen as a man in your eyes. I instead answered your question about how things were going with my stepmom and lost the opportunity. With a chuckle, I told you about how my stepmom had washed a single bra in the washing machine and how it was the final straw for Daphne. Maybe if I could make it light enough that you could bring it up to her in an equally playful way, she wouldn't get her feelings hurt, but she could also stop doing the thing disturbing my very pregnant wife. We could combine our delicates and live happily ever after.

You grew quiet and cold almost immediately. I don't know if you mentioned anything to her after our boat ride, but everything changed when we returned home. I assume you told her what I said, and she complained to you about some of the things that bothered her. You both eventually came to your own conclusions without us. I feel relatively confident that this happens every time we get together. Things always start out okay, but if I do something that upsets her, she talks to you about it, and then the rest of the vacation is disturbed. For example, she will expect us to help clean the house while visiting you, but she won't ever ask us to help. We will eat dinner and go to bed, leaving dishes in the sink. The next day, she is cleaning the dishes and ruminating on the fact that we're unappreciative and unamiable. Soon she talks with you, your attitude toward me changes, and then you grow cold. Since this family never talks about their emotions or expresses their expectations of each other, we walk on eggshells the entire time until the vacation ends. It happens so often that I stopped being as open with her, afraid that she was the reason I could never share my story with you. Eventually, my coldness is enough to trigger your conversations, and the vacation is awkward anyway. Daphne and I started trying to pick up on clues. We cleaned and over-expressed our gratitude, but hurting her feelings felt inevitable. You would become unexpectedly cold, the awkwardness would ensue, and I would feel too burnt out to try and decipher the cryptic messages.

Daphne and I had a good routine built for Pepper, who was now almost two years old. We knew there was a possibility of sibling jealousy, so we had everything planned out, down to the gift baby Jade would give her when they first met. We also had several rules for Pepper that we put in place because she was prone to irritability. We always joked about it but also believed on some level that this was a remnant of her colic. She had a semi-strict diet that limited processed foods and refined sugars. I had done so much research on the gut microbiome and had seen firsthand the effect certain types of food had on her behavior that I swore by it and rarely went against the routine we built. We also limited her screen time for phones and television, following the guidance of our doctor and every book we had read. Now that I worked the graveyard and slept during the day, these rules were left for Daphne to enforce. When you came to care for Pepper while Daphne rested, those responsibilities fell on you.

I fully understand why you would want to give her candy and treats, she loves getting those things, and you like being a fun grandpa. I know the joy it brings you when you take her to the store and let her have any toy she wants. What I don't think you understand is that when you leave, she expects the candy, she craves the treats, and she has a meltdown every time we go to the store, and we try to enforce our rules again. We are left to let you change our routine or fight with you over relatively benign, stupid little things. When it's a vacation, we usually let you do that sort of thing as much as you want, and then we fight with Pepper for the next three weeks until her body gets used to the old diet and routine again. This particular visit wasn't a vacation, though. You had specifically come here to help us enforce Pepper's rules so that when Jade came, it would have a negligible impact on the delicate structure we had built. We had a plan, and we needed your help sticking to it. I was sound asleep when Daphne woke me up in the middle of the day and chose the battle I'd soon have with you.

# PART 7: PRECIOUS ENVIRONMENT

It was noon, but for my work schedule, that was essentially the middle of the night. Daphne shook me awake, and I was startled, worried she was going into labor since Jade was scheduled to arrive in just a few days.

"What? Are you okay? What's going on?" I asked, seeing tears in her eyes. I feared the worst. If Daphne went into labor with placenta previa, we would have to rush to the hospital for an emergency cesarean.

"I'm sorry to wake you." She gave me a soft smile, but she still looked distraught. "Will you please talk to your dad?"

"About what?" I was now sitting up in bed, and the headache I'd have later was already brewing.

"It's Pepper. They have her watching a movie by herself."

"Why? Where did they go?" I assumed you two were busy with work or something.

"They didn't go anywhere, your stepmom is making a blanket, and your dad is just on his phone."

"A blanket?" I was so confused and decided it'd be easier to see for myself. I stood up from the bed and opened my door. The house was quiet, so I could hear a movie playing in the living room. I gingerly walked through the dining room on the cold hardwood floor. Years of skateboarding meant I'd always have at least 15 minutes of planter's fasciitis pain every day when I'd first get up.

I saw my stepmom sitting on the floor with the aforementioned blanket in her hands. It was a gift to us, a blanket I expect she anticipated we would wrap Jade in when he was born. As I got closer, I realized it was a Christian blanket with a sizeable hand-stitched bible verse from top to bottom. It was never any question about what our beliefs were; we were not a Christian family. A religious gift felt a little inappropriate, but again, I was able to pick my battles and didn't say anything. I'm sure she thought it might end up being Jade's first blankie, and she'd end up getting her feelings hurt when we didn't give it to him, but I was going to have to deal with that when the time came, first things first.

You were sitting on the couch looking at your phone, and I assumed you were checking emails for work. On the opposite couch was Pepper. At less than two years old, her little feet didn't even reach the end of the couch cushions. She looked so tiny sitting there by herself on a four-person couch. She was watching Trolls and didn't take her eyes off the screen when I walked in.

This was easily the tenth time we had asked you and my stepmom to limit the screen time with her, but every time we'd turn around, she'd be watching something on your phone or playing a game on the iPad. We were traumatized by Pepper's colic, and Daphne agonized about having to breastfeed again, not to mention the severity of the risks involved with her complications. We couldn't imagine going through that again, but now with an out-of-routine Pepper. After our fishing trip on the lake and my stupid laundry complaint, you seemed to be rallying hard against our plans. When we would ask you to limit screen time, it felt like you were intentionally rebelling against our wishes as if to say, "We came here to help you; beggars can't be choosers." This would have been entirely accurate; we can't ask you to drop everything you're doing, come to California, wait on us hand and foot, and then demand you follow our every request. Regardless, that was exactly what I needed from someone at that time, and you were the only person in the world that I felt comfortable enough to ask.

I didn't want to have this conversation. I just wanted to go back to bed. We had already talked about screen time, but it was always veiled as a request. You'd be playing games with her on the phone, and we'd let it go for a little while, and then we'd say something like, "Okay, no more games," or we'd change the subject, "Pepper, would you like to color?" I hadn't sat you down and clarified my expectations yet, and I honestly thought you would appreciate me talking to you man to man, so I decided to pull you to the side.

"Hey, Dad, can I talk to you outside?" My eyes were still squinted against the daylight. My room had blackout curtains that helped me sleep during the day, so waking up was always disorienting when I would realize it was closer to noon.

You had your head down, looking at your phone. When I asked, you didn't lift your head. You just looked up at me over your glasses. We locked eyes for a brief moment, and then you begrudgingly rose to your feet, put your phone in your pocket, and carefully placed your glasses in their case. "Everything okay?" you asked.

"Yeah, I just want to talk to you in private." I imagine my stepmom heard that and took offense; just another thing she'd bring up to you later, I'm sure. More eggshells I didn't feel like walking on.

You followed me through the kitchen and we stepped out onto the back porch. I sat down on the stairs, and a rush of anxiety filled my gut. I was going to try my best to make this confrontation unconfrontational. I failed immediately as the first thing that came from my mouth was, "So, what's going on with the screen time?"

"What are you talking about? We're just being quiet while you sleep." You had your arms crossed and already looked angry.

"I know that, and I appreciate that, but we've asked you guys to limit her screen time. Daphne woke me up because you have Pepper sitting on the couch, by herself, watching an entire movie." I waited for a reply, but one never came, so I continued, "At least sit next to her and ask her questions about the movie. Keep her little brain stimulated." I wanted Pepper to get the same level of care she would typically receive if Daphne and I were available. Had you been uncomfortable doing what we asked of you, I wish you had said no to us. It would have been fine. Daphne and I could have come up with a different plan. We could have asked her family to watch the kids or hired a babysitter that we could hold to a certain standard. It would have been sufficient, and we wouldn't have had to fight with you. Instead, we put you in a situation you didn't want to be in, and you could only see me as an ungrateful little boy. Then, as I tried to talk with you about it, you treated me like one.

"Well, I'm sorry we're poisoning your precious fucking environment. We'll be leaving soon, and then you won't have to worry about us anymore." You had this look of pure disgust on your face, and the hatred caught me by surprise. Again, I cannot stress this enough; I didn't want to have this conversation with you. I knew it wouldn't be fun, but I didn't know you'd get so angry. I thought you would be annoyed with my requests and probably roll your eyes, but you'd respect my decisions. I secretly hoped you'd be interested in how I came to those decisions. I had books, journal articles, apps on my phone, and guidance from our doctor, so if you were curious why Daphne and I had made these rules, I would have been more than happy to share our reasoning. You weren't interested in why I asked you to do these things. You were just pissed that I was unhappy with what you were doing.

Growing up, you would never explain any reasoning behind your rules. You would tell me what to do, and I'd ask you, "Why?" You would furiously shout back, "Because I'm the father, that's why!" Now here we were, but I was the father and had rules that needed to be followed for my kid, but you hadn't taken to the transition as gracefully as I'd hoped. Again, I wondered if my brother had asked the same of you, would you have been more careful to follow his requests? Would you have respected his wishes? Would you have been interested in the books and journals he was reading and asked to learn more? It's hard to imagine you yelling at him the way you had just done to me, and it's impossible to picture you looking at him the way you had looked at me.

The moment you stood up, arms crossed, towering over me as I sat on the stairs, I saw something in your eyes. They were so full of anger and disgust with me, and you wanted me to see it. There's a difference in the eyes of someone trying to hide their anger and disgust compared to someone who wants to convey those feelings. You attempted to intimidate and put me in my place, to show me I was just a little boy, and you were the father, a total alpha move. Looking back at you, I could see something else in your eyes that I had never seen before. It was subtle, but I could see the faint reflection of my mom staring back at me. The wind blew the leaves all around us in the backyard. I could hear them rustling wildly as they collected against the fence and blew against the door behind me. The sound suddenly stopped, and we were left in silence. I looked down to see that the leaves were gone, and I was no longer on my back porch.

# Part 8: Sherlock

It was a brief change in perception, a short glimpse into a memory that wasn't mine. Suddenly, I was my mother, at my wits' end with you, and realizing I was going to have to call you out for having an affair. I didn't have proof, but I had talked to several people you worked with, and they all told me you had been screwing around with that bitch Jo-Anne. Hell, one of the guys even told me he had walked in on you two fucking at work. Now you had flown to Texas for several meetings, but a few days before you were supposed to fly back, you called and told me some of those meetings had gotten delayed. As the meetings were all pushed back later in the week, your flight had to be rescheduled. It looked like you wouldn't be flying home until midnight. I guess you thought I was an idiot, though, because the local airport doesn't have redeye flights.

I called Trish, and I told her what was happening. We decided to hide at the airport when you were initially scheduled to arrive. Wouldn't you fucking know it? Here you come, bags in hand, walking off that fucking plane. I was furious, too furious to see where you were going to go. I wish I would have stayed hidden and followed you to that bitch's house, but instead, I confronted you in front of everyone. "You motherfucker," I shouted as I jumped out from behind the baggage claim carousel.

"Betty, what are you doing here?" you asked, shocked. "I got back early and was going to surprise you and the kids."

"Fuck you! This airport doesn't have midnight flights. You were probably headed to meet Jo-Anne. I have a copy of your fucking itinerary!" I hit you with the rolled-up paper I had nervously fidgeted with while hiding the past hour.

You crossed your arms, and a look of pure disgust filled your eyes, "Well fucking good for you, Sherlock."

My heart skipped a beat as it filled with the shock of the unexpected response and the accompanying anger associated with the deflection. I was here to confront you; how was I to blame in this situation?! As my blood began to boil, I could hear the leaves rustling again.

"Dad, are you serious? Poisoning our environment? That's a little much. I'm just trying to understand why you keep putting her in front of a television when we've asked you not to. I'm trying to understand if you have a reason. If you don't want to do what we've asked of you, that's okay, but let me know, and we won't expect that of you." I was doing my best to stay calm; I wasn't even mad at you. I just wanted to go back to bed. Taking you outside was intended to clarify what you were willing to do, but it hadn't accomplished anything. I had only upset you, and now I was on your bad side. I thought we could bond over our shared experience as fathers, but just like every other missed opportunity, you didn't understand or respect how I chose to do it.

Your arms never uncrossed, and the look of disgust never went away. That look stayed on your face for the next three years. This confrontation soured your opinion of me for a long time. Was it because I had left the military? Was it because of the laundry complaint? Was it for calling you out on screen time for a one-year-old? Whatever it was, you must have lost some respect for me, and all vacations after this were very awkward. Usually, you seem so excited to see me when we arrive at the airport, but you haven't been since that day. You're always happy to see the kids, but unfortunately, the kids have to bring me. That backyard confrontation changed your perception of me, but the out-of-body experience I had when you yelled at me changed my perception of you too.

I now empathized with what my mother had been going through. I don't think you ever had an affair, and I don't think you were fooling around at work, but what is certain is that my mom felt the need to confront you about something she was concerned about, and when she tried to talk to you about it, you hit her with the same look that I was now getting. Rather than taking the time to understand why we were upset, and regardless of your likely innocence, you showed us how disgusted you were with our accusations. How I felt in this moment is how she must have felt in her moment, and I felt bad for her. Shannon's behavior at graduation had cracked the façade around the emotional walls I built to enclose all memories of my mom. My recent vision had just knocked that wall down, and a flood of emotions for my mother that I'd not had since childhood came rushing over me all at once. A few days later, Jade was born, Daphne and I started establishing new routines for our kids, you and my stepmom went back home a week early, and I started researching how I could get ahold of my mother for the first time in almost 20 years.

# Mom: Chapter 7
## PART 1: CLOGGED SINKS

My mom and brother always had a complicated relationship, even when he was little. They would fight constantly, and she was hard on him. You've jokingly described my brother as the type of kid you'd have to follow around the house spanking as you'd repeatedly say, "No, no, drop that, no, stop, no, drop it." It's easier to joke about when you get to leave for work each morning. I've noticed this same paradigm in my own young family.

Daphne and Pepper are very similar, and now that Pepper is almost six years old, her teenage personality is already starting to show. Pepper has learned which buttons get a rise out of her mom and she enjoys pushing them. She can be downright evil at times. Pepper will say, "You're a terrible mom. I hate you." I know Pepper doesn't mean it when she says these things because she says it when she's frustrated with bedtime. We hear all the time, "That's normal kid stuff. They all say that kind of thing to their parents at some point," but it never makes Daphne feel any better because Pepper doesn't say that sort of thing to me. I imagine it's hard not to take it personally and not to feel terrible about it. I'd be crushed if Pepper said those things to me. Shannon also used to say that kind of stuff to our mom.

Unfortunately, it really is normal for kids to say mean things to their parents. They don't know what they're saying. All they know is that it got a big reaction the first time they said it. Negative attention is still attention. Kids lack the maturity and insight necessary to express big emotions. I know adults who lack the maturity and insight to express big emotions; that's the basis for this entire book. If I stayed home from work and was responsible for keeping the kids in line all day, I'm sure they'd hit me with death threats too. Instead, I come home after Daphne has fought the kids into taking a good nap. They greet me at the door, well rested, and I have dinner and desserts ready for them that I picked up on my way home. We eat, wrestle on the mega-bed, or play catch in the backyard. I poop them out, cuddle them into bed, and read books until they fall asleep. It's hard to imagine parenting is that hard when you come home and be a fun dad for only three hours.

When Daphne complains that Pepper wants her dead, I have a few options for how to respond. Based on my experience with the kids, it's hard to imagine Daphne isn't doing something wrong. It's compounded by the fact that Pepper is my little buddy. We are connected by some galactic force that introduced her to me before she was born via musical dreams. It also happens that her temperament and emotional state are cloned directly from my wife. Like familial magnets, Pepper and I are connected at the hip while she and her mom are naturally repelled. Again, the same can be said of my brother and you and his relationship with his mom. To assume the discord between my wife and Pepper is all Daphne's doing is unfair to Daphne and doesn't help alleviate any of the tension they will always naturally experience at some level.

A second, more helpful option I have in response to Pepper's terrorism is to listen to my wife and help her work through it. Our sink in the kitchen was once clogged, and the pipes began leaking under the sink. I removed everything, section by section, until I found the pipes were full of old decaying bits of food. Our sink didn't have a garbage disposal, so food that managed to get past the screen would clog if enough got through. I wanted to make sure Daphne knew she couldn't push food past the drain screen. Given the fact that I had just been forced to touch the most disgusting wad of filth, I felt it was time for a little bit of mansplaining.

When I shared my concern with her, she was immediately upset and went on the defensive, stating she had done no such thing. She suffers slightly from perfectionism and doesn't do well with criticism. Not to mention I'm complaining about how she does chores around the house; it's not as if she wants to do the dishes. All benefits of doubt aside, the accusation sent her into a pre-rage, and any smart man would know when to back off. Regrettably, for both of us, I took it as an opportunity to get her riled up and said something along the lines of, "Okay, but you really should stop doing it, though."

My wife didn't notice it at first, but Pepper has the same propensity for defensiveness. Daphne would send Pepper to timeout for hitting her younger brother and then wouldn't let her come out of timeout until she could first explain why she had been in timeout and what she would do differently next time. Daphne wanted Pepper to understand why she had been sent to timeout in the first place and wanted her to think about ways to handle it better in the future, something that works well for our son. For Pepper, it felt the same as being reminded about the food being pushed past the drain screen, and she would always get angry. My two perfect girls who hate making mistakes.

Framing this conversation with my wife was hard. She hadn't done anything wrong. She had gone by the book, literally. She watched YouTube videos, read child psychology books, and followed different parenting blogs on social media. It wasn't for lack of trying. As an outside observer, I could see something she hadn't yet seen. We approached the subject as a team, and I asked her questions. We talked it out and implemented a few things. I may or may not have reminded her about the time she would forcefully cram food past the drain screen. Eventually, we had a plan moving forward, which worked for a couple of weeks until we had to adapt again, as one must in parenting.

Most importantly, Daphne felt validated in her feelings, and even if the new things hadn't worked, she felt like she had been recharged. She had felt like she was at her wit's end and had tried everything, but now she at least had some more things to try. I also felt good about our conversation. I felt so bad I couldn't be there to help, but this is my way of helping around the house when I am stuck at work each day. I don't know if you and my mom ever had those opportunities to work through things the same way.

I imagine you did work as a team when Shannon was a baby, and you were rushing to weatherize the trailer as the temperature dropped well below zero and the water pipes were starting to burst around the trailer park. I wonder if you guys worked these things out together and the communication had just stopped at some point or if you managed to make it 20 years without ever communicating. If your relationship with me was anything like the one you had with my mom, I imagine you never really articulated how you felt. I also wonder if my mom's sour relationship with my brother was avoidable or if Daphne and Pepper are destined for a lifetime of fighting just like them. It may also be an apples to oranges sort of thing because Daphne is very different from my mom.

My mom had a difficult upbringing with abuse during her childhood and pregnancy at only seventeen. Based on my experiences with her throughout my life, she may have an undiagnosed borderline personality disorder with an attention deficit and dyslexia. Taking that into consideration, I recognize I have had it much easier as a husband to my wife and that our communication was likely less cumbersome than what you experienced with your wife. If every time I tried to talk to Daphne, she would blow up and go into a weeks-long depression while trying to push everyone away, I'd likely not have the fairy tale marriage I currently enjoy.

Something I find hard to understand is that I had a very different experience than my brother. I happened to have a great relationship with my mom. I was a momma's boy, and I think Shannon always took some offense to that. Not necessarily toward me, but his mom. To me, he probably felt some sibling rivalry and jealousy, but I think it was primarily directed at our mom. As we got older, his relationship with her got more physical, and his hatred for her grew.

# PART 2: CIGARETTES

I was walking home from school one day, climbing the hill toward our house, and I saw Shannon storming toward me red-faced. Furious, he said he was leaving before hitting our mom back. She had slapped him in the face, and he thought she was trying to kill him. I didn't know at the time that he had gotten caught sniffing glue, and she told him he wasn't allowed to go out anymore and that he needed to figure out what he was doing with his life. He replied by asking her what she had done with her life. Rude back talking doesn't necessarily justify what happened next, but she ripped the hat off his head and slapped him in the face with it before chasing him out of the house. He called you from our cousin's house to tell you that she had beaten him, and you said it should have been you. Unfortunately, it wasn't you, and he held it against her instead.

The first time I saw them getting physical was at the ice skating rink. I was playing with my cousins on the ice when I saw her enter the arena. I skated to the wall to say hi, but she just made a beeline to the top row of the bleachers, where Shannon was sitting with friends. She was yelling at him and backing him toward the edge of the bleachers. If I remember correctly, he had gotten caught throwing a party at the house over the weekend. She pushed him, and his back hit the railing. She stomped her way down the bleachers and went home, but Shannon was left feeling as if he had almost been pushed to his death, regardless that it was maybe ten feet high. Getting slapped and pushed around was very different from the childhood I was living in, but we had the same mom. With all the bullshit I pulled, it's safe to say that if my mom had been around when I hit my teen years, she definitely would have murdered me.

When you and Mom started having issues, she and Shannon were constantly at each other's throats. All this drama was unfolding around me, but you guys were doing a good job of hiding it. It reminds me of the first time I caught Mom smoking cigarettes. I remember playing outside of Pizza Hut with my cousins after eating dinner. I ran into the building to grab a drink of water and saw my mom and aunt smoking at the table. My world started to spin. All I could see was the cigarette in her hand with the red and white checkered tablecloth that served as the backdrop to this egregious deception. I remember struggling with the realization that my parents smoked cigarettes but also held secrets. That's exactly how it felt when I heard my mom crying in the bathroom for the first time.

The bathroom door didn't have a lock, so if one wanted privacy, you would have to open the cabinet drawers, and then they'd prevent the bathroom door from opening fully. I heard her sobbing and attempted to walk in, only to slam the door loudly into the drawers. Her crying became more frantic as she screamed for some peace. This only made me more concerned, and I repeatedly slammed the door into the drawers trying to get in. I realized more secrets were being kept when she finally let me in and she wasn't hurt or crying for any reason; she just assured me everything was okay.

I knew divorce was around the corner when I heard you both arguing upstairs when I came home from school. I burst into your room just as you pushed my mom onto the bed. She had just been hitting you, and you were trying to get her to stop. I would learn much later that this was the day after you had called her Sherlock for having investigated your itinerary from your trip back from Texas. I could see the look on each of your faces as you both realized you wouldn't be able to hide your metaphorical cigarettes from me anymore. The following Christmas, I woke up and learned my mom had left for good, and she had taken the Christmas tree out of spite. We had an old brass indoor plant holder that was maybe three feet tall, and we placed all of our presents around the base of it. We opened our gifts, and I played with my new toys, but I still didn't know what was happening or where she had gone.

When the dust settled, my mom would pick me up and take me to the arcade or the gym to play basketball. Even at such a young age, I knew she was trying a little too hard to make things fun. She would promise we would do this stuff all the time when I came to live with her. By contrast, you didn't seem to encourage me either way. You were okay with me choosing whom I wanted to live with, and if I decided to live with my mom, you went out of your way to ensure I knew you wouldn't be upset. The stakes didn't seem that high, considering we lived in a small town. I would see my mom all the time anyway. You stayed in our house, and Mom had moved out, so I stayed with you where all my stuff was. We lived closer to my cousins, the house was bigger, and I could attend the same school my brother had. There were so many reasons to stay with you. Considering my mom was just on the other side of town, I didn't think picking you would be such a big deal. That all changed when you said you were moving to Texas.

I had already decided to stay with you, but now I had to make that decision all over again. My mom was growing desperate, trying to convince me to stay with her since the stakes had increased significantly. On the other hand, you kept reminding me that everything would be okay. You promised to buy me tickets back home anytime I wanted to see either of you, no matter whom I picked. I guess you just supported me more, and it felt like the safer option. There was also the allure of the unknown, to go to Texas and travel to new places. My choice broke my mom's heart, and I don't think she ever forgave me.

After years of fighting fire with fire, my mom and brother had become pure enemies. He hated her so much and felt she was so critical of him. When it started to get physical, he wrote her off and couldn't wait to go to college. When you and my mom split, he didn't have to choose whom he'd live with because he was off to college anyway. My mom would stay in our hometown, my brother left for college, and you and I were headed to Texas. Our perfect little family had quickly fallen apart, and then we all separated from each other. I was packing my things, but I didn't know why. According to you and Mom, you both had simply fallen out of love, and I had taken that as a perfectly good excuse for it all. That is until we walked past Richard in the Smith's parking lot.

# Part 3: Sun Flowers

You and Shannon were walking shoulder to shoulder toward the store. We were there to pick up a few groceries for a barbecue back at the house. I was trying to catch up, lagging behind you both as usual. As I got closer, I saw the look on Shannon's face. He looked like he wanted to fight what appeared to be a random person in the parking lot. I saw you put your hand on his chest to calm him down, but the tension was palpable. The guy walking by had shaggy brown hair and a full beard. He was a real Al Borland-looking dude. Nothing happened, but I could tell something wasn't right. The guy was too old for Shannon to know from school. He seemed like someone you might work with, but why would Shannon want to fight him? Shannon was heated, and I started to pick up on some things, but you kept hushing him. I'd have to get him alone if I was going to get the scoop on this drama.

That night, Shannon explained that our phones had been tapped with some kit you had gotten from RadioShack. My mom had always been jealous, and you've often described your marriage as "constantly under the microscope." She accused you of things so often that you decided to protect yourself by recording all of her calls so you could hear what she was telling people. You listened in horror when you found the conversations she was having with her friend Trish, describing the affair. The man she slept with was our neighbor's son. The same neighbors whose yard collected all of Shannon's home runs. I remember the pitcher always had to get the homers, and considering I wasn't big enough to hit it over the fence, I was always the one that had to climb into their yard.

Our house was on a big hill, so the neighbor on the home run side had an elevated yard. We had a three-foot-tall brick ledge with a normal-sized fence on top of it. To a little kid, it was massive. It was equivalent to the Green Monster at Fenway. I'd have to climb our gate first. It was perpendicular to the fence and got me high enough to reach the top of the slats. I'd swing my leg over and start the descent into a yard full of sunflowers. Their yard seemed magical to me. The flowers were taller than I was, and their faces were bigger than my entire head. From the top of the fence, their yard was filled with vibrant yellow and orange. Once you climbed down, it was dark in between the thick green stalks and black soil. I would weave in and out of the giant flowers, quickly searching for the off-white whiffle ball. The faster I found it, the more we could play.

I've always been a competitive person, but I don't care when I'm losing. I'm not competitive because I want to win; I'm competitive because I want to compete. Winning is icing on the cake, but dropping down off the fence, down another run, into a field of giant sunflowers looking for the ball my brother just crushed over here, was my happy place. It meant I was playing with my brother; it didn't matter if he was winning. When I think of the Egyptian afterlife, A'Aru, instead of my soul residing in a field of reeds, I picture myself looking for a baseball in that backyard. That yard, our neighbor's yard, would be forever tainted by their son.

Our neighbors were an older couple who kept to themselves. I don't remember ever seeing them as I searched for baseballs in their flowers. They had a son who did home maintenance tasks. They volunteered him to do our tile floors in the house's entryway. Hiring him was a very you thing to do. It reminds me of when I dented the shit out of your truck, and you hired someone at the gas station to fix it.

I had taken Chuck's advice and started a lawn care company, but I was often getting called for jobs that required experience I didn't have. Unfortunately for the people who hired me, I am blessed with the willingness to try anyway. This particular job was evicting a family for not paying their rent. They were given time to pack their things, and then I was tasked with mowing the yard and cleaning out anything they left behind. I hired my friend Toad, and we borrowed your truck and rented a trailer. The trailer was extra wide, and I hadn't towed one like it before, but how hard could it be? When we got to the house, the driveway met the street like a "T" with ditches on each side. There wasn't enough space to get the truck and trailer down the driveway front first, so we decided that backing it in might be more manageable. We had smoked a few bowls on the way there, so by the time we made this decision, I knew it wouldn't be easy, but my competitive side was confident we could make it. I flipped that sucker into reverse, cut a perfect 90-degree left turn, and backed it all the way to the garage. Toad even complimented me on doing it first try.

We worked our asses off to mow the entire property, loaded the trailer with the abandoned belongings, and then collapsed back into the truck. As we were pulling forward, I realized we didn't have the option of backing onto the street. I couldn't pull out of the driveway first try; I had to back up and pull forward nearly twenty times before Toad decided to jump out and guide me. He was motioning me along with his hands as I slowly pulled around the corner. My wheels were teetering on the edge of the ditch, and now the trailer was full of heavy garbage. After what felt like an eternity, we found ourselves safely back on the road. I straightened out the truck and pulled over, waiting for him to jump back in. When Toad walked up to the passenger window, I noticed the color in his face had gone away.

He opened the passenger door and told me to get out and look at the truck, but I honestly couldn't imagine what it could be. Maybe someone had keyed it or accidentally opened their door into the side of it when we were parked at the hardware store. Whatever it was, I was expecting it to be relatively minor. I parked the truck and jumped out. I walked around the front and met him on the right side to see what it was. Above the wheel well was a humungous dent in the side of the truck.

"What the fuck is that!" I yelled. "What the hell happened?"

"I don't know, dude. I didn't even notice until you had finished the turn. Maybe it happened earlier today?" he asked.

"Fuck, maybe, but when?! That's a huge dent, and we would have known something hit us." I felt so bad this happened to your truck while I had it, but I was guilt-free because I knew it wasn't my fault. I was trying to think of what could have happened, but nothing was coming to mind. That's when Toad noticed the left side of the truck.

"Holy shit, dude! It's over here too." His eyes were just as wide as they were when we looked at the truck's right side.

I again walked around the front of the truck to see for myself. It was the exact same dent, in the exact same spot as the right side. The multiple possibilities of what had caused it became less numerous since it had happened to each side. I was the first to make the connection to the trailer. The end closest to the hitch had an extra wide bar in the front that appeared to be about the same height as each dent. I realized that the bar of the trailer must have dented the left side of the truck when we backed in and then had similarly dented the other side as we pulled out to the right at an opposite, but equally sharp, right angle.

It's easy to assume it happened because I was stoned, but I don't think it's fair to rule out being an idiot. The weed didn't make us reckless. In fact, it made me super cautious. I took each turn in and out of the driveway so slowly that we didn't feel the trailer gently denting the side of the truck. Arguably, had I been sober, I probably would have only dented the left side when we heard it crunch. In hindsight, it would have made telling you a little bit easier too. I remember you being so mad when I showed you the left side. It would have been so nice not to show you the other side.

It was about a month of driving around with double dents when we stopped to fill up at the Exxon by our house when the man approached you about fixing the dents. Maybe he didn't explain his process well enough, or perhaps you didn't ask enough questions, but something went horribly wrong. He first punctured the dent with something he considered a "tool," and then he pulled the dent out with brute force. Next was the stuff he sprayed onto the side of the truck to fill the hole he made, but the texture was akin to something more closely resembling a popcorn ceiling. Finally, he sprayed his work down with a tan color like the truck. Not *as* tan as the truck, but tan *like* the truck. It's not possible you approved of the work he had done. I have to assume your pride allowed that atrocity to be the final product. Hiring our sunflower neighbor's son was just one person in a long list of people you hired who didn't deserve to be.

# Part 4: Unlock the Door

I don't know how many phone calls you listened to, but my mom finally placed the call. She called Trish to tell her about the tile guy working at the house and the hotel they got together. A Monica Lewinsky level of convenience, she had taken the opportunity to have an affair with someone nearby. You hadn't just fallen out of love; my mom had cheated on you.

Shannon loved talking about it, and he enjoyed telling me just how awful our mother was, but you would never say anything bad about her. You couldn't explain why she was being so hateful, so you would always say, "Your mother is just sick." I started to understand everything that happened as less of a betrayal and more of an inevitable circumstance of being with someone with mental health issues. The constant reassurance that everything my mother had done was simply due to some vague mental sickness made me distrust women and built the foundation for the stigma toward mental illness I would have well into adulthood. At the earliest sign of drama, or anything I could maybe see as a sign of being even just a little crazy, I'd stop trusting them. It also had the effect of making her side of the story less credible to me. By trying to avoid having a difficult conversation and trying to spare my mother the blame, you unintentionally painted her as a crazy person who couldn't control her actions.

Soon, the rumors started to spread about you. They were all fabricated by my mom, but considering she was friends with all your coworkers, it made life in our hometown almost unbearable. Instead of defending yourself or spreading any rumors about her, you just took the first opportunity to transfer to Texas.

I was already struggling in school and was about to fail Mr. Ligerni's math class. Shannon had also taken his class, and he was a historical asshole. He once gave me a zero for not folding my homework correctly, regardless of the answers I had written on the paper. I had reasons for moving to Texas, but leaving Mr. Ligerni's class could be the simplest of those reasons.

We moved to Texas, and my mom hated me for it. When I'd return for summer break, she always had a chip on her shoulder about it, but I'd inevitably make it worse by asking her why she would have an affair. It was hard for her to explain, mostly because she was already defensive, but she also wanted me to understand that you were the one that had an affair first. Not unlike bible camp, I had come to this summer vacation prepared to ask her the questions my brother had already answered. There was more to the story, but since she didn't want to admit her side of it yet, everything she said sounded like lies. My brother had also prepared me for what she would likely say, so I was ready for battle when those lies came. I would need to have faith in her, but I wanted proof.

My mom was starting to drink more, and it got to the point that she wouldn't stop when I came to visit. There's a fine line between a cool mom who lets you drink a little bit and a mom who only lets you drink with her because she also wants to get drunk. With each visit, the time between landing at the airport and bringing up the divorce would shorten, and she'd have me back on the plane for Texas sooner each time. I remember one summer when she was spending a lot of her time at the new brewery in town every night. She would leave for work in the morning and then hit the brewery after, coming home late at night. I was constantly on the hunt for trouble as I freely roamed the city at all hours. I had an edge of bravery to my mischief because I knew I'd be on a getaway plane back to Texas at the end of the summer. My cousins were always left to suffer the consequences of anything we trashed.

It was a late night, and I was getting into bed at my mom's house. She had still not gotten home from work, so I knew she was likely out at the brewery. I always took offense to her spending our time at the bar because she didn't have many opportunities to see me, but I had other stuff I wanted to do anyway. I could hear gravel shifting under the tires of someone's car as they pulled into my mom's driveway. I heard some laughing and talking that was too loud for non-inebriated conversation but still too muffled to decipher from inside the house. I again listened to the tires as they pulled out of the gravel driveway and a jingle of keys began scratching at the side door.

My mom swung the door open and immediately started looking for a pack of cigarettes she would never find. "Denver, are you home?" she yelled through a bite of sliced white bread with American cheese.

"Yes," I yelled without moving from my bed.

"Drive me to the store." She hadn't asked, and she wasn't waiting for a response. I slowly dressed and moved my way out into the living room.

I reminded her I didn't have a driver's license yet, but she threw me the keys anyway. I unlocked the car door and got in with just enough time to lock the doors before she could lift the handle.

"Unlock the door!"

I looked at her confused and mouthed the word, "What?"

She relaxed her shoulders and pointed to the lock. I looked under the dash, in the glove compartment, and underneath the sun visor, but I couldn't find the door lock button. I looked over at her and shrugged my arms, trying to match her frustration.

Slowly, and as close to the window as she could get, she said, "Open the damn door."

"Ah!" I said as I finally discovered the locking mechanism. The door lock pin popped up, and she attempted to open the door, but not before I could lock the doors again. She started pounding the window with her palm and yelling profanities, but I just kept acting like the mechanism was faulty. She eventually bested my timing and got the door opened. If she felt like she needed a cigarette before this, I can't imagine how she was now feeling.

We didn't talk on the way to the gas station; I imagine she was still finding the strength she was asking the dear Lord for after the inexplicable car lock malfunction. She got her blue pack of Marlboro menthols and then instructed me to drive out of town.

She waited until we were on the interstate before saying, "Denver, I've been doing a lot of thinking, and I want you to know something." When I didn't respond, she continued, "I've been miserable ever since you left with your Dad, and I don't have anyone anymore."

I glanced over at her, and we made eye contact. She looked solemn, but I knew what was likely coming. My brother told me all the rumors she was spreading around town. She would tell people you used to beat her. She would tell people I was a little shit and hated it when I came to town. She told people you had convinced my brother and me to help you cover up your affair by dragging her through the mud. Every time I came to Montana to visit her, she'd tell me how bad of a husband you were and try to turn me against you. I'd ask her about the tile guy, Richard, and some things my brother told me, but she'd shut the conversation down and send me back to Texas. I assumed we were about to have that conversation again.

"Honey, I've decided to kill myself." She left the smallest window for me to reply, but all I could do was open my mouth in shock before she continued, "No, just listen, I've got it all planned out. I have life insurance at work, but they'll never give you guys the money if I commit suicide, so I have to make it look like an accident. I go camping all the time; no one would suspect a thing. I could get lost and jump off a cliff, and when they find my body, they'll just think I had fallen, and you and Shannon would get the life insurance money. What do you think?"

Looking back at this memory, having gone through everything I've been through, maybe it was a cry for attention just as mine was when I told my brother the same thing. Maybe she wanted me to cry and tell her how much I loved her, just as I was hoping my brother would have done for me. Then again, maybe she was just drunk and saying crazy things because she was "sick." Her reasoning behind establishing an after-death plan inspired my own plans as I got older. Her insurance scam is what motivated me to look for a job that would kill me but leave my memory intact as a hero in the eyes of my family. She seemed so crazy to me that night, but I've grown to recognize those same feelings she was having in my depression. I know things at 37 years old that I didn't see that night at 14, and instead of understanding her plea, I took it personally and got upset, just as I had learned from my brother when he yelled at me when I called on him for support.

"Why don't we just end it tonight then?" I yelled at her as I let go of the wheel and let us drift onto the shoulder while on cruise control, halfway to the next town. We passed the kissing rocks that once meant we were almost to the gorge where we all used to play as a family, but now they only symbolized how much longer I'd have to be stuck in the car with a mad woman. The car started to shake as we transitioned from asphalt to the dirt and uneven edge on the side of the road.

# Part 5: An Unusual Glow

"Stop the car, Denver!" She jerked the wheel back on the road, but I sat back with my arms crossed.

"Why? Why are you grabbing the wheel if you don't want to live?" Tears were streaming down my cheeks.

"Because I care about you, I don't want you to die too!" She was hysterically crying as we sped down the highway in the middle of the night, luckily the only car on the road.

I grabbed the wheel and pushed her back into her seat. I kept us on the road, but I told her, "You're so full of shit. If you cared about me, you wouldn't want to die. You'd want to watch me grow up. You're just drunk." Aside from the hum of the engine, the sound of the wheels speeding down the highway, and the occasional sniffling of noses, the car was silent for the rest of the trip. I took her back home and called my friend to see if I could stay the night. Thirty minutes later, we were in his room watching the Royal Rumble he had recorded onto VHS. I didn't tell him what had happened, but he could tell I was off.

"Hey, D, you ever smoked weed before?" he asked.

I was lying on the floor watching the television. I turned around and propped myself up on my side, "No," I laughed awkwardly.

"You want to?" He sat up on the edge of his bed and started digging through his bedside nightstand. I didn't answer right away; I just thought about my mom. I know she was going through a lot, but she had done it to herself. She had an affair and broke our family up. She had lied about everything and tried to make my dad look bad to cover up her own mistakes, and now she was going to kill herself. She wanted to know if I was okay with it. Would I prefer to have her life insurance money over her life? I felt like I had an excuse for smoking weed if I got caught. I could tell you what she had said to me and what happened on the highway. Who would punish me for coping with it inappropriately? Maybe if I did get caught, my mom would see how big of an impact she had on me by saying that to me, and she wouldn't want to kill herself. She would get her shit together and be a better mom. I would smoke so much weed that she'd have to pick me up from the hospital, and then she'd owe me an apology. "Yes, let's smoke it."

He found what he was looking for; a small dark purple spoon-shaped glass pipe with light blue swirls. "I don't actually have any weed, but I have this pipe, and we can scrape the resin out and smoke that," he said, as he showed me the bowl. I didn't know what I was supposed to look at, but I knew this wouldn't be my Cheech and Chong moment.

I watched in amazement as he took an unfolded paperclip and scraped dark black chunks of tar out of the pipe. He rolled it up into a sticky little ball and then stuffed it back into the bowl. He handed it to me with a small blue Bic lighter, but I stared at him with no idea what to do with it. He showed me how to cover the carb with my thumb while he lit the little ball. He told me to take my thumb off the hole when I had gotten some smoke in my lungs, and I did as instructed.

It tasted like butane and ashes, and the smoke burned my lungs. I coughed uncontrollably while he smoked the same piece of resin. One hit each, and the pipe was empty. It was a little anticlimactic, and I was disappointed because I didn't even feel as if I had done anything wrong. He turned off the Royal Rumble, and we went to bed, but my eyes were pulled to the unusual glow of his black light. Like a moth to the flame, I stared at that black light, unblinking, for nearly a half hour straight. I was maybe twenty minutes into that staring contest when my friend pointed out that I must have gotten stoned for the first time.

In hindsight, it was probably the best way to get introduced to weed if the goal was to get me hooked. It felt good, and after having the most dramatic night of my life, I could lay in bed and giggle. My mom sent me back home to Texas early, and I returned to my friends a self-proclaimed pothead, even though I had still never gotten my hands on any real herb.

It's a bit of a stretch to call marijuana a gateway drug, but it did change my perception of what I was willing to try. On a spectrum of illegal substances, cigarettes are well below marijuana, so I was now capable of smoking some cigs. My new badass attitude got the hook up on some cigars, and I was supposed to pick them up from a kid at school just before classes started the next day. I had it all planned out; I packed a toothbrush, toothpaste, mouthwash, and a bottle of Febreze. We showed up to school and, very obviously, made the deal as we looked around suspiciously throughout the transaction.

The cigar sat in a blue pencil box in the bottom of my bag all day long. I was so nervous that I'd get caught, and the anxiety ebbed and flowed as we moved from class to class. The longer it sat in my bag, the more the adrenaline replaced the fear and anxiety. The final bell rang, and we met at our top-secret undisclosed location, the drainage ditch directly behind our school. In Texas, it rains a lot, so deep drainage ditches separate the backyards in residential neighborhoods. Our smokin' ditch was flanked by the junior high and endless rows of houses.

We started smoking as soon as we got to the ditch, even though we could still see school buses picking up students and teachers were walking around. Those damned cigars had begun burning holes in our bags, and we wanted to smoke them as soon as possible. I had taken maybe five hits off it, not fully breathing in, just filling my mouth with smoke and then blowing it out, when someone's mom peeked her head over the fence.

"Hey! What are you kids doing back here?!" She yelled at us and made a move toward her back gate. We didn't wait for her; we just threw our cigars and ran in different directions.

I didn't look back once. I ran through yards, jumped fences, and cut through alleys. We would have vanished from sight by the time she had gotten to her gate. There is no way that lady gave chase, but that didn't matter to me. I ran two zigzagging miles through the suburbs before taking my backpack off, still in full stride. I slowed momentarily, just long enough to apply toothpaste to my brush before hitting top speed again. I knew how good your sense of smell was, so I attempted to bathe in Febreze, and I was surrounded by an aura of minty fresh breath. I didn't realize it then, but that would signal to you that either I had fallen in love with some girl at school, or I definitely smoked a cigar.

For the next week, I waited for the other shoe to drop. I was kicking myself for having thrown the cigar in the ditch right behind the lady's house that caught us. Undoubtedly, she had taken the evidence to the school, and they had identified us by our fingerprints on the cigars. We were as good as dead. The first day back at school came and went without any punishment. Similar to hiding the cigar in my backpack all day, the growing fear and anxiety of punishment were slowly replaced with more adrenaline and excitement. Once we realized we had gotten away with it, the gateway had been opened. Cigarettes made me feel sick, but weed made me happy, and alcohol made me fearless. I was getting away with using them, which pumped me full of adrenaline, something I'd also get addicted to over time.

About a month later, I got suspended from school for quoting Jamie Foxx from the movie Booty Call and was sent home. My shitty attitude and bad behavior had you at your wit's end, so you were ready to set me straight. A few weeks before my suspension, I was skating a parking lot gap and came up short. I was thrown forward and landed in what is known as the scorpion pose. My chest hit the ground, and my legs bent impossibly far over the back of my head. I sat up, immediately cringed at the pain, and whimpered at the sight of my collarbone, now deformed, bulging out of my chest. I was put in a sling that resembled backpack straps that were supposed to keep my shoulders back and my chest relatively immobile. Now that I was about to receive "the whoopin' of a lifetime" for getting suspended from school, you wanted to make sure that the sling was ready.

"You better tighten your sling," you said as you took your belt off.

"Why?" I asked, "Are you going to hit me in the chest?"

"No, I'm gonna spank you," you said to a 14-year-old boy who was too old to be spanking.

"You're going to spank me in the chest?" I was honestly confused.

"I'm gonna whip your ass, and I don't want you to hurt your collarbone if you fall down." You had folded the belt in your hand, and you again motioned for me to tighten the sling.

"How many times are you going to hit me?" I wasn't doing myself any favors. I could tell I was only making you angrier, but I was trying to buy myself some time.

"Until I get tired, now turn around." I was reluctant to turn around, wanting more time to negotiate, but you grabbed my arm and spun me around toward the T.V. in the living room. This was during the brief phase in my life when JNCO blue jeans were a thing. They were enormous pants that would cover your entire shoe. The bottoms were always torn ragged and were perpetually wet from dragging on the ground. We preferred them for skating because they were less restrictive of movement, but as I was about to learn, they also dispersed the energy from a belt, and the force wasn't enough to make contact with my body. The ineffectiveness of your blows was not only because of my thick denim shield but also due to my broken collarbone preventing you from holding me by that shoulder. You had to grab my opposite shoulder and spank me with your non-dominant left hand. Despite your intimidating threat, you only spanked my pants five

173

times before growing tired and sending me to my room. Tears filled my eyes as I walked away, tears of pure joy. I almost died laughing once I made it to my room. The only thing I learned from your lesson was that you were powerless to control me and were obviously in way over your head.

# PART 6: KARMA

Our bedrooms were on opposite sides of the house, separated by the living room and kitchen. You never came to my corner of the house uninvited, so I could sneak out of my window at night with minimal effort. One night, I slipped out my window with Hammy, and we skated out of the cul-de-sac. The Sigma Chi Fraternity was a few blocks down the street, and they had parties every weekend.

Hammy and I snuck along the tree line, perfectly concealing us from the view of the fraternity. Several people were playing drinking games and talking loud enough for us to hear from across the field between us. We had a laser pointer that we used to torment a single frat-bro that we had picked from the crowd. You could see them arguing with each other, trying to figure out who among them was doing it. They eventually triangulated our location, but there wasn't any chance they were catching us on our turf.

As we ran from them, we'd hop on a fence and pull ourselves up onto a house, lay just at the apex of the roof, and then shine the laser on our selected victim until they could pinpoint us again. We knew the neighborhood so well that they could never catch us. They eventually gave up, and we decided to entertain ourselves with more mischief.

The frat had chased us down the street toward that one church with the large ominous cross that was backlit with blue neon lights. We came out of our hiding spot in the ditch behind the church and realized our drunken pursuers had long since gotten back to desperately trying to get laid for the night. It was midnight, but a single car was still remaining in the church parking lot. It was a small blue Toyota Corolla with paint that had started to chip and fade on the hood and doors. Next to that car was a large gated enclosure that housed massive dumpsters. We checked to see if it was locked, and the squeaky gate slowly opened. Overjoyed, we used every ounce of our teenage muscle to push that dumpster twenty feet until it was behind the lowly Corolla, blocking it from leaving. We threw our boards down and headed for the next adventure.

We were skating past a house two blocks away and saw the garage door was open and all the lights were on. The garage was empty, and no cars were in the driveway or out on the street. As a test to see if anyone was home, we rang the doorbell several times. We waited a few minutes, and when nobody came to the door, we tried the handle. When the doorknob didn't budge, we decided to go around and check the garage. Quickly, we moved through the garage and burst through the unlocked door into the mudroom that led into their kitchen. "Hello? Anyone home?" I yelled.

"Dude, nobody is here!" Hammy shouted excitedly as he propped his skateboard against the wall.

"Let's look around!" I pushed him toward the back rooms as I turned around to cover the other side of the house.

I walked into the living room and saw they had a nice entertainment center with waist-high speakers. I hit play on the CD player and then turned the volume up to full blast. I cringed at the sound of Eiffel 65 shaking the cabinets and walls. In the entryway by the front door, I saw a yellow sunburst Les Paul sitting in an open guitar case and ran over to it. I carefully took it out and admired how beautiful it was before playing the opening riff of Stumped by Minor Threat.

In the back rooms, Hammy peed in their toilet and stole a Pepsi from the fridge. We decided we had better leave before they returned, so I carefully placed their beautiful guitar back in the case. We were more excited about them being confused by the music and mysterious pee than we were about actually taking anything from them. As we ran out of the house, the family who lived there was pulling into their garage. We cut across their lawn and skated down the street before jumping another fence and dropping into our getaway ditch. We lost them immediately and felt relatively safe as we came out of the same ditch from earlier, right behind the church.

We were laughing hard and telling each other what we had seen and done in the house. Just as we were hitting the pavement again to start skating home, we saw a frail old lady slowly walking toward her blue Corolla.

"Boys, excuse me, boys," she said with what sounded like a great effort. "Can you please help me? Someone moved this dumpster behind my car."

We froze. Of course, we were going to help her, but that dumpster took us ten minutes to move the first time, and we were hoping to get off the street before some pissed-off Texas homeowner with a gun found us. Hammy and I looked at each other, we were bad kids, but we weren't assholes. "Come on, let's just do it real quick," I said.

"Man, who would do such a thing?" Hammy joked as we grunted against the rusty wheels that didn't want to roll.

She was so tiny and looked so weak when she spoke. Why was she here so late? It was midnight; why was an old lady at the church at midnight? Why couldn't it have been some dude who could move this thing himself? I guess we were lucky, though, because that lady didn't know she probably could have kicked our asses.

We had just gotten the dumpster back into its enclosure when six police cars pulled into the parking lot from different directions. We didn't have time to run or formulate a plan. We were immediately blocked in and had gotten caught for any number of things we had done that night. The six police cars seemed a little excessive for a dumpster prank, so we thought there was a chance that it was just a coincidence. That is until the vehicle we saw pulling into the driveway of the house we had just broken into was following the last police car into the church parking lot.

# Part 7: Breaking and Entering

They immediately sat us down on opposite ends of the curb. Hammy got a mean cop that was screaming at him from the moment we sat down, but I had a lovely lady cop who asked me how I was doing. "You okay? You look nervous," she said, squatting on one knee to be at eye level with me.

"Yeah, I'm okay. Just surprised there are so many police here. What's going on?"

"Well, we just got a call about a home invasion by two kids with skateboards." She glanced over at my skateboard. "Look, if you tell me it wasn't y'all, I'll believe you. If it turns out it was y'all, and you wasted our time, then you'll be in so much more trouble. As you can tell, I'm much nicer than my partner."

I looked over at Hammy. He was wide-eyed, listening intently as the much larger officer was yelling in his face. "I know it was you! What the hell were you two thinking? What did you take? Empty your pockets, now!"

I looked at her and then back at Hammy, who was on the verge of tears. She leaned into my line of vision and said, "Hey, everything is going to be okay. Just let me know what happened."

I wasn't sure what Hammy would say to them, but we were caught red handed, and I trusted this lady. Besides, we hadn't done anything that bad, so I admitted, "We went in their house."

"Did you take anything?" she asked.

"No, but I did turn their music up. We were in there for a couple of minutes, and they saw us on our way out, so we ran," I said.

"Okay. I'm going to hear what your friend has to say and then we need to call your parents. What's their number?"

I gave her your number, and then she left to speak with her partner. Hammy and I scooted closer together. "Dude, we're so fucked," he said quietly.

"I don't know, man. I think we're going to be okay."

"Uh, no, we're not. That guy said we're definitely going to jail," he whispered through his teeth while slightly nodding his head toward the guy cop.

"Really? My cop was super nice."

He looked offended like it wasn't fair. "What did you tell them?"

"I told her we went in and then just left."

"I told him I took a coke, and he flipped. Who gives a shit about a coke, man? They would never have even noticed it was missing." He caught himself. Lowering his voice, he added, "I thought that cop was going to hit me."

"I thought he was going to hit you too," I laughed and then added, "She said we'd be in more trouble if we wasted their time, so I just told her."

"Man, why was that old ass lady here?" he asked.

I just shook my head at him and shrugged my shoulders. My lady cop came back over, and she asked me to get up and talk to her away from Hammy.

"My partner just told me your friend said he took something. Do you know anything about that?" She had her hands on her hips, and I could tell she was looking for any sign I might be lying.

"No, we were only there for about five minutes, tops."

"How about a coke?" She raised her eyebrows as if she had caught me in a lie.

"I don't know, ma'am. I don't remember seeing him with a soda. It all happened so fast, you know?" I knew he had already admitted to taking one, but I didn't want to unintentionally provide any additional information that might get him into more trouble, so I played dumb. I couldn't believe we would get arrested for stealing a soda. Hammy didn't even get a chance to drink the damned thing. When those people went into their house to see if we took anything, the fridge was the last place they would check. She was fishing for more information, or she was legitimately going to arrest us over a measly buck-fifty. When I saw your truck pulling into the parking lot, I considered asking them to take me to jail instead of having to talk to you.

Once the family had finished looking through their house and found nothing missing, they decided not to press charges over the soda, and we were allowed to go home. The police made us apologize to them before we could leave. Getting that close to being handcuffed and taken away informed all my future run-ins with the police. I would forever err on the side of honesty, focusing on what to admit rather than building a lie. Hammy's parents came and got him, and we were both grounded for a long time, but I kept sneaking out every night. A couple of nights later, the frat bros we were fucking with caught me alone in the middle of the night.

Shannon was back at home on a break from college. He brought his skateboard, a practically unridden complete with a red and white O.G. logo Shorty's deck. This was during the height of Chad Muska's fame, so I thought the board was super cool. He'd refuse to let me ride it, though; he didn't want to get any scratches on it. I couldn't understand the concept. Riding a skateboard without scratches is like owning a clean shovel. Either you're not using that shovel, or you're using it wrong. When you both had gone to bed for the night, I snuck out my window with his board.

The church we had recently almost gotten arrested at had a couple of small gaps and parking lot medians you could skate. I skated there for a while, waiting for my girlfriend and her friend to show up, but they never came. After thirty minutes, I finally left for their house and tapped on her window, but they shooed me away and said they had been caught sneaking out and were now grounded. Dejected and bored, I started skating back to the house.

I was skating on the sidewalk, pushing hard and carving each curb cut at every street intersection, when a big truck passed by me, close to the curb. They stopped about thirty feet in front of me, and two guys jumped out and approached me. They looked like your typical run-of-the-mill frat dudes, but I didn't recognize them. We had always picked our laser victims indiscriminately from the crowd and did it from far away. Considering how pissed they now appeared, it seemed pretty clear they recognized me.

# PART 8: YEAR BOOK PHOTOS

The first guy to speak had blonde hair tucked under a baseball cap. He stopped just in front of me, off to my right side, and asked, "What the fuck you say?"

"What? Me? I didn't say anything." I was standing with one foot on the tail of my brother's board, and I had my shoulders shrugged.

The other guy was off to my left side and said, "We heard you say something. What the fuck did you say?"

I looked over at him and scoffed, "Ha, I seriously have no idea what you're talking about. I'm just skating down the street." I turned and looked at the guy on my right. I was opening my mouth, about to ask him what he thought he had heard, when everything went black.

I didn't feel the punch; I just felt the ground. The world was shimmering at the end of a black tunnel. That tunnel was closing when one of them kicked me in the middle of my back, and I immediately regained my awareness. I grunted and instinctively recoiled into a small ball just in time to block the kicks that would have hit me in my face. They kicked my arms, trying to get past them at my head, and they alternated from kicking me with the toes of their boots to stomping me with their heels. It wasn't until they had started kicking me in the ribs that I realized I was getting my ass beat. It had all happened so quickly, and I was just reacting without knowing what was happening. By the time I realized I was in a fight, the fight was over.

They ran back to their truck and drove off. I jumped up, hoping to see a license plate, but they were too far away, and I wasn't wearing my glasses. My hat had fallen off at some point. I started looking around for it, but it wasn't anywhere nearby. I couldn't believe they had taken it, an unnecessary insult to injury. I gave up looking for it quickly and decided to head home when I realized my brother's board was also gone. "Oh shit," I thought. "No, no, no," I frantically started looking around. Afraid I was going to get my ass beat twice that night, I began hopping fences near where I had fallen, hoping they had tossed it over. I looked for as long as I could, but my head was throbbing, and I wanted to go home.

I hiked through the ditches, trying to stay off the main road. The street that took you back to the house was the same street that would take you past fraternity row. I got back to the house and quietly knocked on my brother's door before walking in.

"What do you want?" he asked in a groggy, sleep-filled voice.

"Hey, I lost your board," I was standing motionless in the dark.

"What? What do you mean? My skateboard?!" I could hear him sit up in the bed. I was starting to pick out silhouettes in the room as my eyes adjusted.

"Yeah, I'm sorry. I was skating it when I got jumped by two dudes, and they took it."

"Wait, what?! Are you ok?" He shot up out of bed and turned on the light. He inspected my beat-up face and had me walk him through what had happened. He seemed to forget about his board completely, and I was so thankful for that. To me, it had been the worst part of the entire ordeal. He threw some clothes on, grabbed a miniature Colorado Rockies baseball bat, and then woke you up.

You were equally pissed off that I had been jumped, and the three of us climbed into the truck to look for them. When I was walking back to the house, I thought about how much trouble I would be in for sneaking out. I thought about not telling you and attempting to cover it up somehow, but there was nothing that could have happened in my sleep that would explain the bumps and bruises on my face in the morning. I knew Shannon would be pissed about his board, and you would be angry I had snuck out again, but I also needed you both at the same time. A feeling I would later learn to live with as I struggled with addiction but was too afraid to seek help. I was not only surprised that I wasn't in trouble, but we were now going to find and beat these guys up.

I was sitting in the back seat, riding a fresh surge of adrenaline, scanning the road for the vague description of a red truck I had given. I had no interest in vehicles, so I didn't even have a good guess on the make or model. I was also colorblind, so the odds of us finding them were slim to none, but you and Shannon stopped every red truck we saw on the road at two in the morning. I felt so loved and protected that night. This was the older brother I expected and had largely missed out on when he left for college. This was the dad I wanted you to be. Skateboarding was my thing, and it was something neither of you understood. This could have been the perfect opportunity to point out that it wasn't safe or that I shouldn't be out at night. There was no "I told you so" or anything about how I had screwed up somehow. None of that mattered; it was about being there for me when I needed you, regardless of any mistakes I may have made. I was going to have my revenge, and I almost felt bad for these shit-kickin' frat boys. Almost.

We drove around for three hours with no luck and confronted several innocent people when you stopped the last truck of the night at the gas station. It was a good match, and Shannon excitedly grabbed his bat and jumped out. The older woman who stepped out of her maroon truck to pump her gas looked terrified as the two of you approached. You apologized over your shoulder as you hurriedly climbed back in the driver's seat, ready to keep looking.

"Dad," I asked as we started pulling away.

"Yeah, buddy?" You didn't take your eyes off the road. I could tell you felt bad that you hadn't protected me, and finding them would make up for that somehow.

"Can we go to the hospital now?" The adrenaline was all gone, and my top teeth were no longer lining up with my bottom teeth. My jaw had slowly shifted over the past few hours, and now I couldn't close my mouth.

"Yeah, you okay?" You looked back at me, and I saw the expression dawn across your face as you realized, maybe for the first time, that I had gotten hurt when they jumped me.

My brother dropped us off at the emergency room, and you and I waited for the doctor to arrive for about four hours. You filed a police report, and they continued our search, albeit in a likely more organized and legal way. When the doctor finally walked in, his hair was standing up on one side, and he appeared to have just woken up. He reviewed my X-rays and found that my jaw had been broken. You updated my case with the police officer assigned to us, and I slept all morning the following day.

I woke up to the sound of talking in the kitchen. The police had come by to update us on what they had found. They stopped at a party, and a girl had told them she overheard two men bragging about the kid they had beaten up. She mentioned them stealing my board, where it happened, and other details that removed all doubt of whether or not she had the right people. She gave them their names, and now the police were at our house to see if I could identify them.

He pulled out a high school yearbook and flipped it open to a page with a tab in it. He spun the book around and pushed it toward me on the table, "Can you identify one of the men from last night in any of these photos, son?"

I looked down at the book and tried to match my foggy memory with the grainy yearbook photos. It all happened so fast that I could barely recognize any solid features besides their hair color. Not to mention I had a head injury. This task felt unreasonable. These cops had a witness that described everything that happened and even gave them their names. How about you do some investigative work? Maybe you could talk to the guys involved. Any chance they own a red truck? Why am I trying to identify them by what they looked like in high school?

A kid with short brown hair was in the second to last row of pictures. He had a cheesy smile, but I could picture him scowling at me in the dark just before he sucker punched me. "That's him," I said, pointing to the picture.

# PART 9: TOXIC MASCULINITY

"Hmmm," our assigned police officer grunted. He took the book from me, closed it, and then turned toward you to say, "Sorry, sir, there's not much else we can do. Since he cannot positively identify the persons who did this, our hands are tied. Give us a call if any more information becomes available."

You followed him out the door, arguing that there must be something we could do, but there was no use. I wasn't getting justice, and their ineptitude would sour my opinion of cops for a long time after that. In hindsight, I would have gained nothing from those kids going to jail for jumping me, and I probably had it coming anyway. As for the police, I would go on to have many more run-ins with them, and I was fortunate enough to have been given my own second chances.

On my twenty-first birthday, we got caught smoking a blunt in a park, but the cop simply snuffed it out with his shoe and told us to go home. There was also the night Miho finally got his driver's license, and he was supposed to meet me at a party when he got off work. Just before he arrived, some overly aggressive UFC fanboy was trying to fight Kevin, our favorite little skatepark kid that had become one of the boys. Since I was already several whiskeys in, I told him I'd fight him if he wanted a real fight. He agreed and squared up with me. I immediately drove my right shoulder into his stomach and lifted his left leg with my arm. I picked him up and slammed him as hard as I could into the ground, smashing my own face into the gravel simultaneously. I scrambled to my feet and tried to shake off the stars, but fanboy was done. He was writhing on the ground, gasping for air. I spit on the ground, told him to leave my friends alone, and then I puffed out my chest as I basked in the warm glow of toxic masculinity. Miho was pulling up just as everyone was returning to what they were doing before the brief fight broke out. I was ready to leave and convinced Miho that he was too. I followed him back to his house and tailgated him the entire way, trying to make him nervous with his shiny new driver's license and lack of experience. We passed a cop on the way, and he sped up behind me with his lights flashing.

I started pulling over, and Miho turned down a side street, leaving the cop and me alone. He walked up to my window and shone his light in my face. "What happened to you?"

"Excuse me, sir?" I knew I was drunk, but his question confused me.

"You have much to drink tonight?" He waved the light in my eyes, moved it to the side, and then shone it in my eyes again.

"I had a little bit of whiskey earlier tonight, sir." I pointed to the bed of my truck where my guitar, amps, and keyboards were. "I played a show earlier tonight and had some whiskey onstage, but I never drink that much. It makes it too hard to play."

"What happened to your head?" he asked.

I glanced in the rearview mirror and saw my face was covered in blood leaking from a cut I had on my forehead. I was momentarily confused but remembered slamming the fanboy onto the ground earlier. "Oh wow," I said, "I was wrestling around with a friend earlier. I knew we had bumped heads, but I had no idea it was so bad."

"Step out of the car, please." He backed away and waited for me to get out. "Do you know why I pulled you over?"

"Probably because I was driving so close to that car, right?" I shrugged my shoulders, "That was the buddy I was wrestling with earlier. He just got his driver's license, and I was messing with him a little. He lives right around the corner, about one block from here."

"Well, you better call your friend to come get you because I'm not letting you drive tonight." He had me sit on the curb and call Miho. After I made the call, the cop just left me on the side of the road. He warned me that he would be driving back around, and if he caught me in my truck, he'd arrest me onsite. I followed his commands, not wanting to push my luck.

It's hypocritical of me to want justice for getting jumped when this cop had just let me off the hook. He pulled me over when I was obviously drunk, driving recklessly, and unaware that I was covered in blood. This guy had done me a favor that I didn't deserve. Had I not been caught by cool cop after cool cop, I would have a criminal record that would have prevented me from ever joining the military, something that changed my life for the better. There's a chance the cop we were assigned let these frat bros off the hook too. Considering all the times I was allowed to go home, I can't complain about the frat dudes getting their opportunity.

I made it back to Montana one last time the following summer, but it was starting to feel pointless. My old friends all had their own lives now. The first year I came back to Montana, I would hang out with everyone all summer. Now, it was just one night of debauchery, and then everyone would resume their usual routines. I'd waste the rest of the summer smoking weed in my mom's shed, alone in the backyard. The rumors about us were also starting to get worse.

I have a theory that when my mom started spreading rumors about you, she was showered with compassion and empathy for what she had endured. She then recognized that the love and support she was getting could fill the gap where her family used to be. Not unlike my hypochondriac ex-girlfriend, who faked a brain tumor for attention, my mom feigned physical and emotional abuse to gain the sympathy of those in town. Her story morphed from infidelity to physical abuse. Initially, the response to those stories was relatively extreme, and people were shocked to hear you could do such things. Their opinions of you had changed; now, hearing more about that story stopped eliciting the same response. My mother's craving for attention wasn't satiated, so she needed to intensify the egregiousness of your actions.

Once she had trashed your reputation, nobody was surprised by any story she could fabricate. To maintain the level of sympathy she was accustomed to, she started telling people how her kids were hurting her too. I couldn't be sure what was true when I heard things about the two of you that I had no personal experience with, but it was getting harder to believe anything she was saying about you after hearing some of the things she was saying about me.

I again left Montana early and had decided I'd not be coming back next year. I had my own life in Texas and wanted to spend summers with my new friends. The summer was the only contact I had with my mom, and when I stopped coming for the summer, I stopped hearing from her on special occasions too. Neither of us put in the effort to maintain contact, and life went on.

One night, back in Texas, I heard a knock at my window. I cracked the blinds and saw my friend Toad crouched in our bushes. I opened my window and crawled out to meet him outside. Toad had a hectic family life. I remember going to his house after school, and he fought with his brother. His brother hit him with a broom handle and knocked him unconscious. They always fought that intensely, but it was nothing compared to the beatings he'd get from his stepdad. This night, Toad feared for his life and didn't want to go home.

Toad and I both climbed back through the window, and he stayed with us that night. He stayed the next night too. A week turned into a month, and I decided to ask permission for him to stay so we wouldn't have to keep sneaking around. He told you about everything happening at his house, and you agreed to let him stay. He had my old room, and I took my brother's. We also became full-on MacGyver potheads known for building unique pipes and bongs.

# PART 10: WHICH NEIGHBOR?

Toad and I would wait until you were asleep, quietly sneak into the bathroom, and then start the shower. We'd let the room fill with steam and then block the gap under the door with a towel. This bathroom was in the middle of the house, so we couldn't blow our smoke out of any windows. We had to rely on the small ceiling fan to dispose of our evidence. We thought we had it all figured out, and you never once caught us. Looking back on it, especially with your insane sense of smell, I can't imagine you didn't know. You had to hear us giggling, two grown boys, in the shower together. Maybe you were scared we were lovers and were hoping we were just in there doing drugs.

Our smoking inventions started out of necessity because we didn't own any paraphernalia. When we couldn't get papers or blunt wrappers, we'd construct a makeshift pipe. Initially, they were crude, but we got better as we figured out the mechanics. We took a socket out of your toolset and taped it to a brass 90-degree elbow coupling. Smoking the galvanized metal gave it a weird taste, so advancements had to be made. We rummaged through old toys and used the water canister from an old super-soaker, the mesh screen from the sink faucet, and pen tubes. We used your tools to drill holes, glue pieces, and bend pipes.

One night we had taken a gallon milk jug and cleaned it out before cutting the bottom base off. We unscrewed the cap and inserted a handmade bowl that was deep enough to hold a good amount of weed but also wide enough to fit a mesh screen to keep the weed from falling through. We filled the bathtub with enough water to submerge the jug, leaving the top exposed. We would pack the bowl and light it as we slowly pulled the jug out of the water. The vacuum would pull air through the bowl and fill the jug with smoke. We'd continue pulling until just before the cut portion came out of the water, remove the bowl, and then one of us would clear the jug. You would have to first blow all the air out of your lungs and then inhale through the mouth of the jug as you pushed it back into the water, forcing a gallon of smoke into our tiny teenage lungs. We'd laugh our asses off while the other one coughed uncontrollably. It was always too much smoke for one person, but we'd try anyway. There is no amount of shower steam mixed with Axe Body Spray that could ever cover the amount of smoke that filled that bathroom on a nightly basis. Without any repercussions, we only got more daring as we became more complacent about hiding it.

Considering there's no way you didn't know something strange was happening, there are only a few options for what was going on with you. For one, you could have avoided having that conversation with me because you didn't know what to do about it. I remember coming home from school one day and blowing smoke out of my window in the spare bedroom where my drums were. The window led out to the backyard, concealing my activities behind the fence that blocked your view from the street. If you came home and I didn't want to talk while stoned, I didn't have to run back into the house. I could jump in the shower or lock myself in my room directly across the hall, which is exactly what I did when you got home early. I got in my bed and turned my T.V. on with the sound up loud, but I didn't hear you walk in the front door. I figured you were working on something before coming in, but I was too scared to peek out the window, a victim of my paranoia and not wanting to get caught. Uncharacteristically, you came straight to my room and wanted to talk when you finally came in.

"Hey, what are you doing?" you asked as you opened my door without knocking.

"Nothin', just watching the Simpsons." I smiled and nodded my head but immediately looked back at the T.V., afraid you could see the redness in my eyes.

"The neighbor said you were smoking weed. Is that true?" You had a look in your eyes, almost begging me to lie about it.

My brain was doing its best to figure out what was happening, moving slowly on the fresh high. My heart was pounding, and it felt like I had to hold myself down to avoid blurting out a lousy excuse. If I answer too soon, I will say something stupid, but if I sit here without responding, I might as well have admitted it. I decided to buy some time with a nonsense question and asked, "Which neighbor?"

"What does it matter which neighbor? Were you smoking weed or not?!" You had let go of the door handle and stepped a few feet into my room with your hands on your hips. I was thinking about how the neighbor would have known; he couldn't see me because I was inside the house. Then it occurred to me that I couldn't see him either. He must have been working in his backyard. Had I been standing outside, I would have heard him and left, but since I was in the comfort of the room, I had probably been blowing my smoke right at him. Again, it would have to be about what to admit rather than crafting a creative lie.

"Yes." I waited to see your reaction before offering any additional information. Better to see how this plays out, I suppose.

"Where did you get it?" You looked less mad than I expected.

"I got it from school. A couple of people were smoking it and offered me some. I said no, but I was curious. I got a small amount of it and decided to try it here where it was safer." I knew there wouldn't be any major consequences aside from losing some privileges. Considering I'd wait for you to fall asleep and then do what I wanted anyway, I wasn't too concerned about what punishment was coming. Still, I was anxious about this because I didn't know what would happen. This was unfamiliar territory, and I wasn't wearing my protective JNCOs.

"You've never done it before?" you asked.

"No, and I don't like it. I just wanted to try it once." I painted on a face of exhaustion as if it was terrible. I honestly don't remember what happened next. I assume you grounded me. Whatever it was, you didn't do much because I walked away feeling like I had again gotten away with a great lie. You didn't take the pipe or the rest of the weed. You didn't search my room for more, which was terrific because you would have found the pot plants I had growing in my closet. It just went away. Maybe you were avoiding looking for more weed in my room for the same reasons you were avoiding talking to me about giggling in the shower with Toad. A second option for why you would ignore our behavior is because I was such a weird kid that you didn't even question why we seemed so stupid in the kitchen after our shower, scrounging for food and mumbling through full-mouthed giggles. There's a lot of stuff I did sober that looked like I was on drugs.

My brother was in town and had been watching a lot of science fiction on TNT. On a whim, he decided I'd look better with a haircut like the Centauri from Babylon 5. I obliged and was even willing to let him dye it bright blue. I knew you'd be pissed and make me cut it off immediately, but I wanted to wear it to school for at least one day. Shannon shaved my head as close to the skin as possible but left a small square patch of hair on my forehead. The final coup de grâce was spiking what was left of the blue hair on the back of my head. I couldn't even look at myself in the mirror; it was so bad, but I laughed hard all night.

We would sometimes see each other in the morning while I was eating breakfast before school, and you were on your way out the door for work. I could have stayed in my room until you left, but I instead wore a full-faced motorcycle helmet around the house. When you came out of your room, I was sitting on the couch next to the hideaway table with a large bowl of cereal. You glanced over at me and said goodbye as you quickly walked out the front door. Did you walk by me pretending to eat a bowl of cereal, despite my mouth being covered by the full-faced motorcycle helmet, and brush it off because I was always doing weird stuff that you didn't understand? Is it the same reason you ignored Toad and me with the munchies, laughing at nothing while we ate raw ramen noodles in the middle of the night?

I made it to school with my awful haircut and had a good laugh out of it. I knew the sci-fi reference, so the style made sense to me. It didn't make sense to my computer science teacher, who had a very similar male-pattern baldness. He was sure I had done it to make fun of him, so I was thrown out of class and told to fix it before returning, but I didn't want to live another day as an ugly Centauri anyway. I still thought it might be fun to give you a hard time about it, so I pretended I wanted to keep it when you told me to shave it all. I put up a small fight and savored your frustration, but I shaved most of it an hour later. The dye had turned my scalp blue, and I kept the small patch on my forehead. You were so pissed that I had done it in the first place that my continued insubordination of not shaving everything sent you into a conniption. The small patch was much easier to live with than the blue crown, so I kept it for another day and hid it from you the next morning before school.

You came to my soccer practice after work and saw that I still had the small patch of hair you had ordered me the shave. You pulled me out early, and we headed home. I was giddy with excitement. Getting you pissed off about stupid stuff was a fun game for me, but I could tell I may have pushed you too far this time. We were still in the car when you told me you had enough of my disrespect, and then you threatened to send me to go live with my mom in Montana. I was in shock and felt like I had been mortally wounded. Up to this point, I felt there was nothing you could do to punish me, and I'm sure you probably felt the same way. Sending me to Montana never even crossed my mind as a potential punishment and the implications started racing through my mind.

First of all, this was all about a stupid patch of hair. Looking back, it was probably just the last straw of everything else I was doing, but at the time, I couldn't see past the fact that it was just a stupid haircut that I wasn't all that fond of anyway. You had let me wear a mohawk before, so why was this any different? I understand now that my defiance, not my hair, made you want to prove a point. I also didn't feel safe in Montana, and I felt like you knew that. Not to mention it meant you didn't want me anymore. I was crushed by it and ended up shaving that patch of hair into a small Ziploc bag that I kept as a reminder of how much I felt hated. A dramatic gesture for sure, but I kept that bag for three years.

# Part 11: Fuzz-Buster

We went to Georgia for Christmas one year to visit family, and Toad stayed at the house and took care of our dog. When we got back a week later, the place looked great. You could tell he had cleaned, nothing crazy, but it wasn't the pigsty that you feared it might be when we got back. I was still unpacking my things and settling back in when you called Toad and me to the kitchen. There was a corner of the kitchen counter that he hadn't wiped down and the beer that had spilled there was now a sticky brown circle that smelled like stale hops.

Toad denied everything, but he didn't have any good answers. He just played dumb. You were showing him the stain and pressing him for information when you moved the spice rack, hoping to uncover more of the spill. Under the rack were bits of weed. It looked like he had wiped the counter but pushed a small amount under the rack, just out of sight. You were furious with him, but he kept his denial about what it was or if he had thrown a party. We were both sent to our rooms, and I asked him about it. He lied to me too, but I told him I didn't care. If he didn't do it, I'd be willing to fight with you, and I promised to stick up for him. I asked him not to make me go through that if he really had thrown a party. I told him he was likely getting kicked out either way; the only difference was if I had to go down with him.

Toad came clean a few days later, and you kicked him out. Toad tried to go home, but his stepdad was even worse now that Toad had run away. Toad couch surfed for a while until getting an apartment with his older brother. Those two were pure chaos to be around and would often try to out-crazy each other. I hated going out with them because you never knew what would happen, but it would likely be bad. I craved having a mellow night for once, but one of them would inevitably get too drunk and then try to kill the other one.

Toad and I went to the bar to meet some chicks who had invited us. They knew a club they could get us in without IDs and promised to get us some drinks. I had a whiskey with coke and barely finished half of it by the time the girls wanted to head back to Toad's place. I was already feeling strange, so I left what remained of my drink on the table, and we headed out. On the drive back to the apartment, I felt drunk. Way too drunk for half a glass. I wanted to ask Toad, but he was making out with one of the girls. All four of us wound up in the bathroom, and the girls wanted to take a shower. Without hesitation, Toad ripped his clothes off, and he and his girl continued making out as they got in the shower. Sitting on the bathroom counter, I just smiled at my girl. Aside from the running water and weird noises in the shower, it was quiet. I started to compliment my girl on what she was wearing when the shower curtain flung back, and Toad came tumbling out, wrapped around his girl. They frantically grabbed and rubbed all over each other as they stumbled their way out of the bathroom and headed back to his room.

My girl and I met eyes again, and we laughed. I was starting to feel less dizzy, so I lowered myself off of the sink. I turned the water off in the shower and again was about to talk to my girl when we heard a loud crash. We both ran out of the bathroom and saw Toad's leg sticking through the door, and he was struggling to pull it back through the hole he had made. He punched through the top and then folded the door in half. The pieces left connected to the hinges were swinging pathetically as a very naked Toad stomped his way through the destruction.

Toad disappeared into the kitchen to get a drink of water, and the girl he was with came after him screaming that he had finished too quickly and was insulting his manhood. Toad's brother caught wind of what was going on and joined in. Toad tackled his brother, and they flipped over the back of the couch and crashed into the coffee table, splintering the legs and shattering the glass top. I looked at my girl, whom I had barely talked to all night, and waved goodbye. I grabbed a handful of clothes and broke up the fight just long enough to get Toad down to the car and away from the apartment.

We put it together the next day that Toad had finished his drink. The girls we met up with must have roofied us. His night was filled with holes and brief flashes of memory. He stressed for nine months straight that he had gotten her pregnant, and I was so glad I hadn't finished my drink that night. These things happened to Toad all the time, and you really had to be in the mood to hang out with those two.

I would generally buy pre-rolled blunts from Toad and his brother. You could get three for ten bucks; they were easy to conceal, smoke, and discard. Toad was getting his weed from Snoopy. We had all gone to junior high together, now we were in junior year of High School, and these guys were legitimately trying to be drug dealers. It was hard to imagine these kids you could remember from a few years earlier, now deep into the drug game. It's surprisingly easy to fall into, though.

When you smoke blunts, you eventually cut them open to pack a bowl or a bong and realize that three blunts don't contain ten bucks worth of weed. We could have bigger blunts if we bought the weed and rolled it ourselves. Then you realize you could buy extra weed, sell a few blunts on the side, and then you'd have enough left to smoke for free. Now you have a little side hustle with customers you know will buy every so often. At some point, you can sell it faster than you can smoke it, so you have to buy more at a time to have enough for yourself.

The guy buying the blunts from you eventually realizes three blunts don't have that much weed in them. Now he wants to start buying his own ten sacks too. The blunts that you're selling turn to grams, and then those grams turn to ounces. Snoopy was getting into some big deals and was becoming more secretive. He was all business and never rode his skateboard anymore. We stopped being able to call him for weed because he was afraid the police were watching him. Everything was in codes, and we'd have to meet up with him at different places. As he started dealing with more prominent clientele, he stopped doing small-time deals, and we couldn't get our ounces. Not unless we could make it worth his while.

Snoopy was running from his house to Austin, sometimes multiple times a week, to pick up weed. He was getting pounds of it and then distributing it to dealers in and around our town. I could get my ounces for free if I were willing to drive them to Austin. It seemed like a great idea to me at the time. He gave me a fuzz-buster that would pick up a signal of any cops that were nearby. They would leave at 1:00 in the morning and fly a hundred miles an hour, only slowing down if they saw a flicker on the fuzz-buster. They thought I had what it took to be one of their drivers.

On my first night driving, Snoopy rode with me so he could show me how to get there, introduce me to his contacts, and then show me how the deal was supposed to go down. The people that do this stuff, especially at the volumes they're doing it at, are not the chill potheads you see in the movies. These ones have guns, smoke potent weed laced with who knows what, and have little patience for people who look sketchy and don't know what they're doing. You know, with people like me. The stakes are too high for them. The cops don't care about the dudes buying blunts. They don't even care about the guy selling those blunts. They want to watch and see who's at the top, and that's the person we were driving to meet.

We hadn't even gotten out of town when they started passing around a bowl of hydroponic weed. We merged onto the highway, and I was doing a good clip, not the hundred miles per hour they were used to, but I was getting after it. We were listening to music, smokin' weed, and chillin'. I felt like I was sinking into a comfy couch, and the windshield might as well have been a giant television screen. Thirty minutes passed, and we were still inexplicably driving out of town. I must have let my foot off the gas, and we were slowly coasting down the highway off the momentum we had built. My coast turned into an idle as we barely hit five miles per hour in the fast lane. Luckily, I just didn't have what it took to be in the game. My career would have ended that night, but then you went to Africa for work.

# Part 12: Acidic Used Vodka

You would be in Africa for two months, but you let me stay in the house alone. You gave me enough money to get by and then gave me the phone number of one of your coworkers, Dan, whom I was supposed to call and check in with every night. You left, and I immediately started throwing my nightly parties. Everyone would have to be quiet so that I could call Dan, let him know everything was okay, and then we'd get back to partying.

I also transferred to Rosewood Academy at the Center for Alternative Learning while you were gone. Rosewood allowed students to work at their own pace to earn a high school diploma. It wasn't a GED program, and it wasn't for bad kids, but the school was full of High School dropouts and students who couldn't make it through the traditional High School. I tested out of everything and finished my senior year in two weeks. This gave me more time to focus on my crime spree.

It was simple economics; I had the contacts and the money, and now we just needed to sell it as quickly as possible. We could double the money and then have free drugs the entire time you were gone. Snoopy was long gone by this point. It turns out his house *really was* being watched, and they finally raided it after his last run to Austin. We now had to go to Sean for anything we needed.

Sean was our backup dealer, and I hated doing business with him. He was left in the care of his grandparents after his parents died. He was too much for them to handle, so they got him an apartment and gave him access to all the money he needed, as long as he stayed away from them. His apartment looked like a wealthy high school drug dealer lived there. There were surveillance cameras on the front and back porch, and you could watch the live feed from the living room. Once inside, you could choose from a smorgasbord of drugs. The worst thing he had there was his prescription Xanax that he would share.

Sean drank heavily and mixed it with his meds that he called "bars." He would become overly generous with his drugs while taking them, and that's why most people hung around him during his episodes, but it was too much for me. One night, Ricky and I were riding in Sean's truck, headed back to his Richie Rich-style drug compound. The red light stopped a small car in front of us. Sean honked his horn twice, but the little car refused to run the light. He started yelling at the car and then rear-ended them, pushing them into the intersection. The car pulled to the side of the road, but Sean floored it past them and then picked up where he had left off in the story he was telling. Ricky and I looked at each other with a shared horror. We were just two skate rats, and all we wanted was some weed so that we could get stoned and skate the mini ramp in the backyard. We agreed that if we bought enough drugs this time, we wouldn't have to hang out with Sean for as long as possible.

We bought a bunch of weed, enough hydroponic shrooms for one night of fun for a group of four, and a small amount of ecstasy and then decided we could make the most money selling Xanax because none of us wanted to take it. We set up shop in the kitchen and started our business. I maintained contact with Dan every night but would skip it if we partied too hard. He would then come by the house to make sure I was okay. I don't know if Dan talked to you and told you what was going on, and you just told him not to worry about it, but he eventually gave up on trying.

The longer it went on, the less we cleaned each morning. We were leaving beer cans everywhere, a large hookah-style bong stayed on the living room table, and other bits of party remnants were always all around the house. I was a better druggie than a dealer, so we quickly used all our drugs and spent the money. Dan came by one morning to check on us, and he either walked right past it all without noticing anything, or he was feeding that information back to you, and you were letting it go.

I almost died from alcohol poisoning several times while you were gone. On the worst night, I had finished a handle of vodka and was throwing up uncontrollably in your bathroom. This wasn't the first night I had drunk to this point, so my friends were getting sick of taking care of me. My girlfriend left with Ricky, and the party slowly ended, but I couldn't stop throwing up. Nothing was even coming out anymore as my body tried desperately to get the vodka out of my system. I painfully dry-heaved over and over. Nobody called Dan that night, but he had long since stopped checking on me.

Most of the people that came to the house that night were my friends, but someone always ends up bringing a stranger. When the owner of the house is puking his brains out in the bathroom, sometimes those strangers take advantage of the opportunity. I still don't know who did it, but they ransacked the house looking for something of value.

I woke up in your bed, unaware of how I had gotten there. Luckily, I had fallen asleep on my stomach because I had puked in my sleep. My face was lying in a wet puddle of acidic used vodka. My head felt like it had been split in half, and as I gingerly washed my face, I noticed I had burst a blood vessel in my eye from puking so hard. Everyone was gone, and I felt angry that they had left me there to die. Someone had removed your dresser drawers, and your clothes were scattered across the floor. You had a secret stash of porno mags under the bottom drawer, and those had all been taken. Someone had barbecued on your gas grill, but they had filled it with charcoal. The carpet had mysterious stains, the house was a mess, and what was left of the drugs and booze were all gone. When I got to cleaning my puke out of your bed, it had already soaked into your mattress. Covering up a months-long party was going to be hard, but I had learned from Toad's mistakes and was ready for the challenge.

When you finally returned, I had done about as well as Toad, but that was relatively impressive considering I had thrown a much longer party. You were pissed about your grill, confused by the large stain on your mattress, embarrassed about your porn, but you hadn't mentioned anything from Dan. You asked if I had anyone over, and I said, "Well, of course, I had people over. You were gone for a really long time. My friends came over almost every day. This is basically where we hung out." As you sat on the couch, your hand felt something in-between the cushions. You fished it out with genuine confusion and showed me my favorite glass spoon pipe that I thought had been stolen.

"What the fuck is this?" you asked but knew exactly what it was.

"I don't know. That's not mine." I shrugged. "Maybe it fell out of someone's pocket?"

You were obviously upset, but you didn't press. You let it go, and you threw my pipe in the trash. That night I snuck into the kitchen to get it back, and I saw that you had dragged the La-Z-Boy recliner into the kitchen and were sleeping next to the trashcan. Instead of keeping the pipe with you and disposing of it in the morning, you stood guard next to the trash like a clueless father just doing his best.

This avoidance of the issues I was having and the risky behavior I was taking part in allowed me to fall deeper into addiction. You wouldn't say anything about your whiskey bottles slowly emptying. I could get away with a single shot here or there, but I wouldn't be able to stop at just one. I would have to water the bottle down with tea to replace the volume I took. I was too dumb to realize that you would taste the difference, but I kept doing it because I kept getting away with it. You laughed it off when you had people over for fight night and found I finished the gallon jug of margaritas you had in the freezer. We fought about it, but I was out of control, and you weren't the one to get me back on track. I think you were relieved to get me out of the house when I turned eighteen.

After graduating high school, you made me sign up for classes at the junior college. I wasn't ready for college and didn't have a major in mind. I just wanted to play music and skate. The only career I could see myself in was owning a skate shop, so I signed up for business classes but never went. Not every profession needs a college education. In many cases, it's a terrible investment. My second try was a botched attempt at real estate. Now that I had failed two straight semesters, you were finally threatening to cut me off financially. I decided to ask my mom for money.

# Part 13: Corralejo Reposado

I hadn't spoken to her in years, so calling her now for money was doomed from the start. She refused to pay for my apartment, so I reminded her that she had never once paid child support. My attacks became more personal as I transitioned from reminding her she had failed her fiscal responsibility to me to how she had also neglected me emotionally. I pointed out that she had missed soccer games, my high school graduation, wasn't there to comfort me after bad breakups, and hadn't helped me with my schoolwork like a typical parent. Instead, I was alone, trying not to die from alcohol poisoning, and nobody cared. We went back to not speaking.

I saw her again at Shannon's wedding a couple of years later. Everyone was drinking on the night of the reception, and I was dancing the night away with my cousins. It was a good night, and I had a lot of fun, but I went to bed earlier than everyone else did. I learned from you and Shannon the following day that as the party continued through the night, my mom was up to her old tricks and told everyone who would listen about your infidelity and how you used to beat her. This was supposed to be a celebration. It was Shannon's night, but all of Rene's extended family was there, and they hadn't heard my mom's stories yet. Shannon was so pissed at her that night, but he conveniently forgets that he does the same shit.

He hates our mom for how she is, but he's more like her than he wants to admit. We recently had a family vacation in California and our stepsister Alexie brought her new boyfriend. Everyone flew in and crammed into a little bed and breakfast place for the week. We were there maybe two days before Shannon had the poor kid in a corner, spilling all his mom drama to someone that would never meet her, but it was someone who hadn't heard his story yet, so he had to share. He rushed through the classics: her affair, the rumors, faking cancer, how he'd never let her around his kids, all the things he had been reminding me of literally every time we got together. He tells these stories indiscriminately, just as my mom did that night with Rene's family.

You both told me what she did that night, but you asked me not to say anything to her. She was supposed to give me a ride to the airport, so we could spend a little bit more time together before I flew back.

You and Shannon were going to follow in a separate car, and we'd be flying back together. I got in the car, and as soon as she put it in to drive, I said, "Why did you tell everyone Dad used to beat you?"

She slammed the brakes, unlocked the doors, popped her trunk, and screamed, "Get out!" I sat there, waiting for an answer, but she reached across my chest and opened the door for me. You and Shannon looked surprised as I pulled my bags out of her trunk and started heading back to your car. We hadn't even gotten out of the hotel parking lot yet. Another two years would pass without any contact from her when I finally saw her for the last time at Olivia's birthday party.

We all came to Montana to celebrate and crowded into my mom's tiny house on 3rd street. My mom had a work friend over who was closer to my age. We drank heavily and were having fun getting to know each other. Out of nowhere, she asked me, "How can you live with your dad?"

I was mid-sip of a margarita that had too much Corralejo Reposado. "What?" I asked, licking the sour frost from my lips. "What do you mean?"

"You know, like, after everything your dad did to your mom. How could you live with him after all that?" She was sitting with her hands in her lap, staring at me intently, unaware of how deeply she had just waded into our family drama.

I could feel the heat in my cheeks as the tequila augmented my fight-or-flight response. Shannon had groomed me for this inevitability. Most of my interactions with my brother were of him retelling the same old stories about our mom and reminding me about the lies she was spreading. I once told him I was struggling with alcoholism and that there were things he said to me that acted as a trigger for my dependence. I told him it would help me immensely if we could talk about it and asked if he'd help me work through it. He ignored my messages and never spoke with me about it. On the other hand, if I were to suggest I wanted to talk about how much I hated our mom, he'd text me back nearly instantaneously.

He kept me informed about what she was saying around town, and I heard things for myself through the grapevine, but this was the first time I had been confronted with it so openly and under such a judgmental pretense. My hands were shaking. I was livid, but I wanted to hear what she thought she knew, so I asked her, "What exactly did my dad do?"

Her face scrunched, and she seemed confused. "Uh, you don't know?" she laughed, "Your dad was a total asshole to her."

"Oh? He was?" I looked dumbfounded.

"Yeah, he used to beat her and then told people she had an affair to cover up the abuse. Then you picked to go live with him anyway. I just can't believe you would turn your back on her like that." She shrugged and rolled her eyes while she sipped her drink.

I had never been so angry in my entire life. Her unprovoked attack solidified everything my brother had been telling me about our mom. It stung that my life, and everything I struggled with, had been boiled down to such simplicity. Tears filled my eyes, and I made the face Anakin Skywalker makes in Revenge of the Sith right before he kills the younglings.

All the resentment I had let build up in me about my mom, I unleashed on this poor woman. She was nothing more than an innocent spectator who was dumb enough to intervene. She didn't know either of us. All she knew was what my mom told her, and she had no reason not to believe her. It didn't matter, though; she had stuck her nose where it didn't belong. I caused such a big scene that everyone at the party ran into the house to separate me from this girl and to stop me from suffocating her with my verbal bombardment.

You and Shannon drug me outside, kicking and screaming, and we walked down the street. You and I had such a toxic relationship that we couldn't even be in the same room together for longer than a few minutes, but I still felt protective of you. I probably cared more about what my mom said about you than you did. I wanted the truth, and the longer this went on, the more it looked like my mom really was "sick." I told you guys what her friend had said, and then we laughed at some of the crazy shit I said in response. I eventually calmed down enough to come back to the house. My mom had kicked her friend out, but I felt so stupid walking back into the party. I felt everyone's eyes on me as they judged me for my inappropriate outburst. This would mark only the first time I would feel like the out-of-control alcoholic uncle.

After everyone left, my mom and I had a long talk. She couldn't avoid the conversation anymore because her friend had run her fat mouth, and she couldn't deny that her friend had to have heard it all from her. She tried to dodge the subject anyway, but I was persistent.

"No, tell me exactly when he used to beat you," I said with my hands on my hips, standing over her. She was sitting in her recliner, trying to maintain eye contact with me, but she kept looking away every time I pressed her for information.

"He used to get really mad at me, Denver," she said, and then tried to move past it by saying I was too upset to talk about it.

"No! When did he beat you? Tell me! I was there, and I don't remember that happening!" I was starting to pace, trying to expend some energy.

"The day after I caught him at the airport, you remember, you walked in on us."

"He was beating you? I thought he just pushed you onto the bed." I stopped pacing and walked over to her.

"No, but he was so mad, I thought he was going to." She shook her head as if she was reliving a bad memory. "I thought he was going to kill me."

"Wait, I thought you were hitting him?" I sat on the couch next to her and listened. I had heard this story before, but it seemed details about it had changed.

"I did hit him because I knew he was lying to me. I slapped him across the face, and then I was going to hit him again, but he grabbed my wrists and pushed me toward the bed. As I stumbled backward, my legs hit the footboard, and I fell onto the bed. I don't know what he would have done if you hadn't walked in. You walking in saved my life."

"So then that's it?" I asked, sitting on the edge of my seat. "That's the only time? You think he might have beat you if I hadn't walked in. He never actually beat you?"

"Well, I mean, he's gotten angry at me plenty of times." She looked frustrated that I wasn't getting it.

"Do you see how that isn't beating you?!" I shouted as I stood up, "You're going around telling people my dad used to beat you!"

"Well, it is verbal abuse," she said.

"That's not what you're telling people! You're not telling people he verbally beat you! Fuck, if anything, it sounds like you used to beat him! I can't do this anymore. You're just sick!" I left the room and decided Shannon was right. This happened every time I saw her. Her presence in my life was nothing but conflict, lies, and deception. I was better off without her. It had gotten too hard being around her, which meant it was easier to be away from her, so I wrote her off. I had Shannon's support. He said he was writing her off too. He vowed he would never let her around his kids, "All she does is hurt people," he'd say. He was proud of me for finally growing a pair and walking away from her. It didn't feel much different anyway, we went back to not talking again, but I planned to avoid her from there on out. I wasn't sure what to do about it when, two years later, I heard she had cancer.

# PART 14: POLYPS

I felt awful for her, but I didn't think she'd want to hear from me. I also felt like she was responsible for our lack of a relationship, so if she wanted to hear from me, she would have to call me first. My brother acted as if he didn't care, which made me feel less guilty for not reaching out to her. Every time I'd talk to him, he'd bash her for her lies and remind me how she wasn't ever there for me. He'd tell me I was right to write her off, saying it wouldn't be worth the pain if I reached out to her. That's why I was surprised to hear she was not only living with him, but he was taking her to all her chemotherapy treatments.

She had developed breast cancer and elected to have a double mastectomy. She started treatment and stayed with Shannon because he lived closer to her oncologist. At one of her appointments, the doctor explained her treatment options based on the staging of her cancer. According to Shannon, the described diagnosis did not match the staging she was telling people she had. On edge and untrusting of her, he concluded that she was lying about her cancer and started telling everyone. Considering everything that had happened until this point, I wasn't even surprised she would do such a thing, so I never took her diagnosis seriously. Assuming she was making it up for attention, I refused to feed into it and continued to keep my distance from her.

Looking back on it now, I don't think she faked her cancer. Insurance companies won't cover chemotherapy because you want attention. I believe Shannon expected too much from her at that moment. He loves to talk about her and say how stupid she is, how she hadn't graduated from high school and struggled to read. Despite her academic shortcomings, he expects her to have a good grasp of oncology and the staging of metastasis. I don't think there was anything sinister happening, but I do believe she likely exaggerated what she was going through for a very simple and very human reason. I was able to better empathize with that feeling after I had my own health scare recently.

I had used alcohol and drugs to silence the guilt and shame I felt for being different from you and Shannon. When I got off drugs and quit drinking, that guilt and shame manifested as an anxiety disorder for perfectionism. I started grinding my teeth at night and developed sleep apnea. I started having anxiety attacks, and my stomach was riddled with ulcers causing me to double over in pain after eating. The ulcers got so bad that the proteins I ate were coming into contact with my bloodstream from within my stomach. This caused my body to develop antibodies to the food I ate. The constant inflammation led to a diagnosis of eosinophilic esophagitis and gastroparesis. My doctor put me on an elimination diet that prevented me from eating peanuts, corn, soy, wheat, dairy, and caffeine. I had temporary relief with the diet, but within a few months, I started shitting blood and had to schedule a colonoscopy.

During the procedure, my doctor found five large pre-cancerous adenomas in my colon. Considering I was fifteen years away from having a routine check-up, I would have likely had advanced colon cancer if I had waited until I was fifty years old. Luckily, we caught it early, and they removed the polyps. I wasn't just cancer free; I never had cancer. That didn't change the fact that I was emotionally inconsolable. I had two beautiful babies, and I was so scared that my lifespan had been drastically shortened and I felt cheated that I might miss out on their lives. I remember sitting on the couch, unable to eat and feeling too weak to move, when tears filled my eyes as I tried to explain to Jade why I couldn't play with him outside. I was being overly dramatic. It's not as if I wasn't going to get better. I got a brief glimpse into the emotional toll my mother went through when she felt a lump in her breast for the first time.

Her stories about us had long since run dry of their juicy gossip and pity. For better or worse, her very real cancer provided a pipeline to more love and support than she could falsely generate by herself. Cancer is scary enough; there is no need to lie about your staging. Any discrepancies in her story are easily explained by an overly dramatic but warranted response to her mortality. It became more evident to me when I heard her botch the explanation of the colon cancer she said she had.

She told me she had an aggressive form of colon cancer that was removed. Upon closer inspection of her medical history, it turns out she had a few pre-cancerous polyps removed, just like I had. It's true; if you don't remove the polyps, they have the potential of becoming cancer. If they develop into cancer, colon cancer can be very aggressive, considering how easily it can metastasize. The fact remains, until those polyps mutate into cancer, they're just benign growths. When I heard her explain her colon cancer history, I didn't hear someone who was lying for attention. I heard someone over exaggerating about the severity of colon polyps.

I don't know if Shannon didn't want to let her be dramatic in her moment of fear or if he thought she was trying to get away with something, but the tension between them was balancing on years of repressed trauma, and he began to read between the lines of her actions. It came to a head when my mom tried to share her ice cream with a toddler-aged Olivia when she was still undergoing her chemo for breast cancer. She was with Shannon and Rene visiting Rene's family. They were all enjoying some ice cream in a cone. My mom offered Olivia a small bite from her cone, but Rene quickly reprimanded her. Due to the medicine's toxicity, she wasn't supposed to share food or drink while undergoing chemotherapy. Afraid it could give Olivia sores on her mouth, they asked her not to share.

My mom took it as an attack on her grandmotherlyness and thought they wanted to keep Olivia away from her. Not wanting to be treated like a pariah, she stood up and angrily slammed the ice cream cone onto the ground with a loud splat. They tried to calm her down, but she unfairly accused everyone of not being there for her, and she stormed out of the party and went straight to her email.

The letter she wrote was addressed to Rene, Shannon, and me. She wanted to let us know how awful we were and how we had never been there for her. She was removing us from her will and said she never wanted to hear from any of us ever again. I wrote the following song soon after that, but it still feels relevant today.

# Listen: Track 8

# "Three Different Things"
https://denverjhamilton.bandcamp.com/track/three-different-things

### Lyrics
I guess you're watchin' me,
And I don't know if you could ever see,

Just what I meant you to see.
And it's the cold, right?
It's been understood.
I guess I'm just trying to understand
And it's something I do.

## Meaning

*I tried to have a relationship with my mom. We'd have our time apart, and the absence would have restored our fondness for each other. It wouldn't take long for us to be reminded about why we fought so much, and we'd pick up right where we left off. When she wrote that email and years passed without contact from her, I started doing some soul searching, hoping to understand how my mother could give up on me. She kept tabs on my life through vague gossip that she could get through other people's social media. She knew I played in a band and some other bits of random information, but she didn't know anything about who I was as a person. I don't know that she could ever see the person I wanted her to see me as because she had convinced herself I was a terrible son, and anything outside of that jeopardized the story she was creating for herself to inhabit.*

*The cold that was understood was an admission that we were both giving up on each other. We didn't expect anything from one another, and it made it easier to deal with if we kept a certain level of coldness in our relationship. It would hurt my feelings if she didn't call on my birthday, but I would care less if I didn't expect her to call. The coldness became understood, but I could never comprehend how we had gotten to that point. If this book is any indication, I spend a lot of time and energy trying to understand why these things in our lives are the way they are.*

(Chorus)
And it's the culmination
Of three different things,
Two that I get
And one that I just can't see.

*When I started writing this book, I had lots to say about my relationship with you and Shannon. I had so much festering in my brain. Combined with my deep-seated dedication to improving our relationships, I agonized over my understanding of you both on a near-daily basis. Those chapters flowed out onto the page with little to no effort because I knew you both better than my mom. You and Shannon were the two that I felt like I understood on some level. As I started diving into the chapter about my mom, I hit something neighboring writer's block. I've accessed things in this book about you and Shannon that have long been hidden behind closed doors in my subconscious. As I tried the knob on these mental doors, the door would swing open with a violent whoosh, and all of the garbage crammed behind them spilled out freely. As I tried the knob on my mother's door, I found it was locked, and I had long since thrown away the key to accessing any of the memories I once had of her. She was the one that I just couldn't see.*

And she traveled a lot,
She walked right over me plenty of times.
And it's the walkin', right?
That she's always done?
She's done it so long,
It seems she's started to run.

*I felt like my mom had always walked all over me and had taken our relationship for granted. This verse is me asking myself if our relationship had gotten so bad because of her actions. Had our relationship soured because of what she always does, or was it me? It was all her fault, right? I was letting myself off the hook a little because I was certainly no angel as a teenager, but I had been so much worse to you than I had ever been to her. If she felt I had done anything so horrible that she could hold it against me, she would be shocked to learn what I had put you through every day. After the email she sent, it felt like she was no longer walking all over me; she was running.*

I guess it seems right away.
It seems I'm rushin' into something,
I don't wanna know,
I just wanna go,
And it's the walkin' I do.

*When I finally decided to walk away from her, I wasn't sure of myself and felt guilty. Especially after I heard that she was undergoing chemotherapy, I started doubting that she was faking her cancer, as Shannon had described. I wondered if I had let her go too quickly and if I should have tried harder to keep a relationship with her. Ultimately, I decided I didn't want to know, I just wanted her to go away, so I wrote her off too.*

I guess we're walkin' now,
I just wish I could keep up with you.
OH, can't you just settle down?
I don't know if I could even return,
I left so long ago.
And I don't wish it upon anyone,
HA,
I guess we've all sort of fallin' for something.

*After I decided to write her off, I often thought about how hard it was and if it was easier for her to let me go. She made abandoning me look so easy, and I wished I could move on so effortlessly. I would get angry, "Why can't you just be normal? Why aren't you interested in my life?" As more time passed, I realized the wounds being made would make it impossible to have a meaningful relationship ever again. When she was diagnosed with cancer, I think she thought she would get a free pass on everything that had happened. I think she thought her kids would shower her with love and compassion. Her husband would feel so guilty for having cheated on her that he'd finally admit everything he had done. She had found a glorious silver lining in a terrible diagnosis, and when that forgiveness never came, she had to pick which characters she would keep in the new chapters of her life that she would be writing herself.*

*On the outside, she played the victim of circumstance. A poor woman whose family had taken advantage of her was now being slapped with an unfair death sentence. She had convinced herself that she had been severely mistreated and that life was unfair. Her life had turned out so terrible that she wouldn't wish her circumstances upon anyone. Since you and I were in Texas, unable to defend ourselves, those around her fell for her stories. She was too caught up in playing the victim that she fell for her own lies and missed out on her children's lives. Nobody wins in these kinds of mind games when everyone falls for something.*

Don't you need,
One more time,
One more kiss,
Just one more piece of mind,
Before it's gone?
And I've been walkin' round,
Watchin' you,
And you've just been trying
to turn your back on me,
It's simply like that.

*Hearing the rumors and getting the email from her about how bad I had been to her made me angry at first. With time and age, I started rethinking who I was and how I was to her. She felt I mistreated her when she was going through her cancer treatment, but we had long since stopped talking by then. Not calling or visiting was the only awful thing that I did to her during that time. She forgets that we had gotten to that point long before the cancer. I didn't treat her poorly because she had cancer; she just happened to get cancer after I had decided my life was better without her. Regardless, I did try to reach out to her. I was leaving for the Air Force and waiting for my deployment in Utah. I tried opening that door again when I wrote her a letter and hand-delivered it to her mailbox.*

*I drove back to the city I grew up in but kept a low profile like an undercover spy. I didn't want anyone who knew me to see I was in town. I went to a bar under the big bridge six blocks from her house and attempted to work up the courage to drive down the street. I eventually got more drunk than brave and checked into my hotel instead. On the way out of town, I snuck up to her mailbox and threw my letter in before running away. I had written about how much I regretted that we didn't have a relationship and how I was nervous about the military. I hadn't told anyone the real reason why I was joining, and I had intentionally not planned an exit strategy. I was hoping for death, so this letter was me saying goodbye to my mother. I found out many years later that she hadn't even read the letter and just threw it away. She meant what she had said in that email. It was simply like that.*

# Part 15: Stigma

I never got over my mom, but I did learn to stop thinking about her. I locked every doorway that led to anything about her. I focused on my future and forgot about my past. Before long, I could barely remember my childhood, but this was preferred if it meant I could move on from the sorrow of my young adult life. I built walls around her memory, and she ceased to exist. When Pepper was three years old, she asked me why I didn't have a mom, and I was at a loss for words. I hadn't thought of my relationship with my mom in such simplistic terms.

Why didn't I have a mom? Damn, where do I begin? When I realized I didn't have a good answer for her, I told her I didn't know. I fought the urge to tell Pepper her grandma was "sick." I realized that might have been why you had said it to me. It would have been easier than trying to explain something I didn't understand myself. I told Pepper that I did have a mom, but I didn't talk to her much and it had been a long time since I had. Pepper wanted to talk to her grandma, but I was afraid. Shannon had scared me about letting our mom around our kids. I'm not sure exactly what I was afraid of, but I knew I didn't feel comfortable granting her that access. Pepper had begun to actively chip away at the walls I built to protect us. Daphne's mom was the next person to start weakening the barrier.

I had a rocky relationship with Daphne's family at first. They didn't trust me, and they thought I would take their daughter away on some military deployment. Our wedding was almost a disaster with how angry her parents were. We had another rough patch when the Air Force sent me to tech school to become a laboratory technician. When I finished tech school, we battled their emotions again when we moved an hour away. There were times I questioned whether or not I should have married Daphne. I had legitimate mommy issues, and now it felt like I was marrying into a similar situation that I had just navigated myself out of successfully.

Daphne's mom reminded me so much of my mom that I was scared to get close to her. She was lovely and creative, but she'd get emotionally aggressive and shut everyone out for weeks when things got stressful. I felt uniquely qualified to deal with it, having survived everything I went through with my mom. However, I quickly noticed

214

several things about how Daphne's family treated their matriarch. The first person I watched was Daphne.

Daphne was so patient with her mom. She never got angry with her mom when she was upset with us. Instead, Daphne would try her best to accommodate her mother. Sometimes she could calm her down, but other times, she'd have to walk away and give her mom some space. My mother-in-law would avoid us for a few weeks, but then the hard feelings would pass, and everyone would be okay. My wife's never-ending patience reminded me of the tolerance I once had for my mother. My father-in-law was the next person I learned from by watching his actions.

I used to get so frustrated with him because he would side with his wife regardless of whether or not he agreed with her. I'd have a relatively good relationship with him, my mother-in-law would get angry with us, and then he'd suddenly change his tune to match that of his wife. I would get so frustrated that he wouldn't stick up for us. I didn't think he had a voice of his own, but as I got to know him better, I learned to respect what he was doing and realized just how smart he was.

He was playing the role he was supposed to play, his wife's partner. I saw his unwavering devotion to her and realized how integral he is to keeping the family together. It would be easy to tell his daughters, "Your mom is just sick." It was never him and his girls against their mother. Instead, he would dutifully follow his wife and support her no matter what, and the girls were expected to do the same. I was inspired by watching them interact with each other's weaknesses by using their individual strengths to lift each other up. I couldn't help feeling guilty about not being there for my mom, regardless of whether she deserved it or not.

I had been trained to think of this behavior as coming from someone who was "sick" and undeserving of understanding. I had developed a stigma toward mental health that I had immediately applied to my mother-in-law. This way of thinking could have prevented me from being welcomed into a family I admire and love. Daphne's mom wasn't "sick." She was mad. She was being protective of her daughter and the family structure they had built. Her husband supported her, and they were rightfully unwilling to compromise that structure until they trusted me enough, as good parents should. To be comfortable supporting those you love, even when they force you out of your comfort zone, is the definition of unconditional love, and I saw Daphne and her dad live by that every day.

The longer I spent around her family, the better they got to know me, and they began trusting me more. I stopped being the source of their fears, and I felt that I had become part of the family. I grew close to Daphne's mom and started thinking of her as my own mother. She had become the mom I wished mine had been. She admires my creative side and consistently reminds me of how much she loves me. I feel so lucky to have her in my life, and I love her very much. Seeing Daphne's family work together, and having her mother welcome me as her son, was healing to my inner child. Her family unit had made a few more significant chips in the walls I had built to protect me from my mother. I stopped thinking of my mom as being "sick." When you and I had our argument in the backyard, I was filled with pretense, and the walls came crashing down.

# Perceptions: Chapter 8

## PART 1: COMMUTE

On November 4th, Daphne and I checked into the hospital for her planned cesarean. Her sister was a nurse in labor and delivery, and she had recommended a surgeon that was supposed to be the best we could find. Everything about the day felt different from when she went into labor with Pepper. We spent so much time planning and prepping for our first baby that we thought we knew what to expect. This time, we felt like we weren't in control of anything and were uncomfortably dependent on hospital staff. We were lucky to have her sister there to handle everything.

They took Daphne back for prep and got me outfitted in a protective gown with a hair net and gloves. When they were ready to start the procedure, they brought me into the operating room, and I was immediately overwhelmed by the number of people present. In the very center of the chaos was Daphne, laying on her back with just her head exposed. A large plastic tarp hid the rest of her body, and I could see her surgeon and his assistants getting ready on the other side. Several nurses rushed from station to station, and I felt like I was in the way. They motioned me toward a chair at the head of Daphne's bed, and I slowly walked over to her, happy that I had a designated safe spot next to someone I knew.

I sat down and said hello to her while trying to cover the look of worry on my face. I wanted to hold her hand or stroke her hair, but I was afraid, not knowing what I could or could not touch. Everything felt so intimate the last time we were in this situation, and time had slowed to a crawl. Now, it all felt strictly procedural, and within five minutes of sitting down, a nurse had already asked me if I would like to cut the umbilical cord.

I assumed she was asking if I wanted to cut it when the time came, but then I heard Jade cry for the first time, and I was stunned to find he had already been delivered. I most certainly did not want to cut the umbilical cord. It held no real significance for me. It's kind of gross, to be honest, and I didn't want to screw it up somehow. He was lying on a small table surrounded by medical equipment. The world around us was running at a speed that blurred into an indistinguishable mess of yellow and white. In the middle of it all was the most beautiful little boy I had ever seen. Everything in the room grew silent for a long moment. The nurse wrapped him in a blanket, and I brought him to the chair next to his mother so they could meet for the first time.

Jade was a super mellow baby, and Daphne was having an easier time feeding him, so it wasn't long before we were able to introduce him to Pepper. We were worried about how our princess would handle having a little brother, but she was so sweet and gentle with him. It's hard not to feel like we may have overreacted by trying to control so much of Pepper's experience. I regretted fighting with you about screen time, but we can't rule out that it may have gone so well because we had planned it out so carefully. I had finally worked long enough at the hospital that I could take paternity leave, so I stayed home and played with the babies. I also used the time to start applying to new jobs.

I had spent the last nine years working in human medicine, but I had always wanted to work with animals since I was a little kid. A few veterinary places were hiring, but the salary was significantly lower than anything I could find on the human side. Humans rarely get sick with anything interesting, so if you've worked in a large hospital for as short as one year, you've seen just about everything. Animals, on the other hand, are disgusting and are constantly getting sick with the gnarliest things. Not to mention all the variation between species. The more I learned, the more I was tempted to take a veterinary job. Luckily, a job with a top ranked veterinary lab came available that summer, and it was the only place paying veterinary scientists similar to the human-side pay scale.

I received a callback the same week and accepted their offer. The lab was in a cool hippy town about an hour-long commute away, but we had always hoped we could move there someday. I would make the commute for several years after taking the job because we could never afford to live there, but it was worth it.

The commute wasn't necessarily all that bad. With a newborn and a two-year-old, two hours of alone time was an opportunity Daphne would have killed to have. I would listen to audiobooks, podcasts, or good music. After you and I had a few more awkward vacations together, I started to prefer the silence. I would over-analyze every interaction we had as I drove to work. I'd think about my relationship with you, my brother, and my mom, just as I always had my entire life, but something significant had changed. I was now thinking of it from the perspective of a father rather than a son or little brother. I'd put my car on cruise control for two hours a day and reflect. I hated having to commute, but I probably wouldn't have taken that time for myself if I hadn't been in that situation. We often miss the silver linings in life when we're too caught up in actively hating the task.

While thinking of all my various relationships, I couldn't help comparing each scenario to what I would do with my kids. I couldn't imagine there was anything Jade could do that would make me want to abandon him the way my mother had done to me. Even if he felt I had failed him, and he didn't want me around, I'd still do everything I could to be there for him. I couldn't imagine silently watching Pepper fall into the grip of addiction. For drug use specifically, I felt more prepared to deal with it if Pepper ever went down that path. I also realized I am likely far more prepared for that possibility than you were, but we can sometimes compensate for our lack of experience by learning to be creative.

# PART 2: TOUGHEN THEM UP

I know I wasn't always the easiest to deal with, but I also don't feel like you tried to adapt when things weren't working. I suffered for so long, but I don't need to blame anyone for anything. I don't need anyone to be at fault for what I regret in life. All I need is to understand what happened so I can learn from it and use what I've learned to protect my children. If I can identify the mistakes you made, I don't necessarily need you to know you made them, nor do I need you to apologize for them. I need to figure out what mistakes you made and analyze what impact they had on my life so that I can make sure that the effect I end up having on my kids is as positive as possible. I have to be able to recognize my triggers and cope with my stress in healthy ways so that my children never lose me to addiction. I wrote this song about Pepper as I thought about her and our impact on each other.

## Listen: Track 9

## "Someday"

https://denverjhamilton.bandcamp.com/track/someday

### Lyrics
I can't wait to hear you say
that you love me.
That'll be the day that you hear me say
that I love you too.

And I love to hear you laugh
at the funny faces I make.
And I will do, anything for you,
just to hear you laugh, again.

Someday you'll need advice,
and I'll tell you everything that I know.
And let it be known, you're not alone,
cause I have been here before, too.

Someday you'll have a boyfriend
and he better be good to you,
'cause if he's not, well then he's got,
to answer to your mean ol' dad.

and you'll get older still,
if you ever need a thing,
all you got to do, is say you need me to
and I'll do anything you ask me to.

And then you'll go off to school,
you better do what your teacher says,
'cause if you don't, well then you'll have,
to answer to your mean ol' dad.

And one day, you'll be a mom,
with some children of your own,
and while they play, I'll love to say,
how much they remind me of you.

And one day I'll be old,
and you'll be right by my side,
and you'll say, what I hope you'll say,
that you'll do anything for me.

Understanding these things and going through this process is extremely difficult. So far, I've gone through the analysis and adaptation alone. In writing this book, I have made progress toward understanding my addiction, and I feel I've experienced significant personal growth in a short time. Faster alone, further together, as the saying goes. For better or worse, I want to share what I've learned during this journey. I want you to know about the good and the bad. I'm interested in going further than just awareness. I'd like to improve our relationships and, in doing so, bring our family closer together. There's also the chance that this book will only drive a wedge further between us. I cannot control how you will react to learning about who I am, but I'd rather you dislike me for who I am than merely tolerate me for who I am not.

With my brother, understanding him and the way he has made me feel about myself provides me a guide for which characteristics of his I do not wish to sustain in my behavior. His personality and demeanor have permanently imprinted on my subconscious reactions. How I mean-tease my wife and when I forget to show my admiration and pride in my children. On multiple occasions, my wife has told me she doesn't like to be teased. I have neglected her feelings a thousand times, saying I only tease her to get a rise out of her because I like getting her all riled up. I've even told her that it's a form of flirting. I must remind myself that it no longer counts as playing if she doesn't like it. If I don't stop after learning what she doesn't like, then I'm only choosing to bully my wife. Can an argument be made that she needs to relax and stop taking things so seriously? Sure it can, but who cares if you win that argument when you're all alone, wishing you had spent more time reminding her how much she meant to you instead? As a husband, it's not my job to toughen up her and the kids; it's my job to help them feel safe and happy. I failed to appreciate this about my behavior until I recognized my brother in that behavior.

I have learned that mean-teasing is how I deal with frustration and stress. When I come home after a long day, I want space and need time to decompress. I love my wife dearly, so I think I'm just playing around with her, but subconsciously I'm keeping her at arm's length by teasing her. It's a warning for her to keep some distance. Considering she doesn't like being treated that way, it would be better for both of us if I instead let her know what I needed from her with love and respect. I also want to model appropriate behavior for my children so that when they grow up, they will love and respect their partners and demand that treatment for themselves. I hope that if my children ever found themselves in an abusive relationship, they'd recognize it because I had set the standard of how a man should treat his partner. I can't live with the thought that I will have doomed my children to a life of abuse by making that sort of behavior feel like the norm.

Providing for a family is about more than just financial stability. We must set our children up for success by ensuring that the little voice inside their heads is confident and optimistic. What is the point in working so damned hard to surround our children in abundance if it leaves them empty on the inside? When I thought of leaving a child empty on the inside, a rush of emotions flooded my mind, and I spent most of my commute thinking about my relationship with my mom.

I watched my wife's life change drastically as she went from an independent, career-focused young woman to a stay-at-home mother. My life also radically changed when we had kids, but I got up early each morning and headed back to work. Work was a brief escape back into the life I had been living before we had kids, and I could focus on my career goals and interests. Daphne was left to focus on cleaning the house and providing non-stop education and entertainment to out-of-control toddlers. That selfless sacrifice to ensure our kids had the best head start in life wasn't always as easy as she made it look. It wasn't always easy for my mother either.

I remember her telling me about a party you had at the house. It was a bunch of people from work and their wives. She was having a good time socializing since you both enjoyed hosting and making your friends laugh. As she moved around the room, everyone was talking about places they had been and things they had accomplished. My mom became self-conscious about having nothing to add to the conversation. She hadn't traveled, she hadn't gone to college, or started some exciting career. She was stuck at home with the kids, for lack of a better spin on it.

My mother's feelings of inadequacy were just the first steps down a long road toward low self-esteem. Seeing you around the young and beautiful women in the office were the first sparks of her jealousy and poor self-image. As I sat in my car, driving the hour to work each morning, I couldn't help wondering if Daphne felt the same way. Working at the university has me surrounded by young college students in an exciting town far away from the dishes and crying babies. It's hard to imagine she doesn't resent me a little, even subconsciously. While driving, I quickly pulled my phone out of my pocket and texted her, "I love you, thank you for all you do for us."

I realized that I hadn't imagined my mother's timeline at any point from the perspective that she wasn't lying. My brother had painted so much of my perception that I never listened to anything my mother said. I wanted answers, but I only wanted her to tell me what I already thought I knew. Is it possible my brother had been gaslighting me, and the lies my mother told were all true? I know my brother exaggerated the truth and pressured me to adopt his point of view, but I'm less sure of his purpose. He hated his mom, so maybe turning me against her was part of his plan to stick it to her, or perhaps he just found it funny. He was no stranger to putting people down for laughs. For example, he once convinced his future wife that I had sex with our family dog.

# PART 3: THE ALAMO

My brother was working one day and noticed the house next to the property he was at had a small pen with pit-bull puppies that looked malnourished and abused. In the litter was a small white one with a black spot around one eye, not unlike the dog from the little rascals. This puppy was more intelligent than the rest and would wedge her little body between the doghouse and the fence and then wiggle her way up and over every time she saw my brother. The little dog would run into Shannon's arms, and he couldn't stand leaving her in such poor conditions. He called animal services and had the dogs rescued, but he kept the little white dog. Around the same time, Reggie Miller had busted his eye and missed the first few games of the 1996 NBA playoffs. My brother named the little black-eyed puppy Reggie, and she meant a lot to him, but you hated her.

You didn't want another dog, and she struggled with potty training at first. When Shannon left for college, he took her with him, but when he ended up living in an apartment that didn't accept pets, he asked you to take her. You initially refused, but I promised to take care of her for him. I would clean up the backyard, a task known as the tootsie-roll-patrol. Reluctantly, you allowed it, and I took on the responsibility of caring for his dog. Instead of being grateful that I'd help him out the only way I could as a little kid, he told his girlfriend I would have sex with that dog. He meant it as a joke, but his execution for pulling off the prank neighbored gaslighting.

Jokes and mean-teasing are meant to be in jest, but that doesn't mean they can't go too far. You can hurt someone's feelings with a poorly timed joke and push someone over the edge with too much teasing as it becomes bullying. Gaslighting is different. When you gaslight someone, you intend to get them to believe something that isn't true, and you challenge their sanity when they question your truth. Depending on the power structure, influence, consistency, and intention, gaslighting can rewrite someone's perception to serve any purpose the abuser wishes. His girlfriend knew me well, so she wouldn't have believed him if he had simply joked about it. For her to believe him, which she did, he would have had to convince her I could do such a thing by destroying her perception of my character. He had to rewrite my personality in her mind for her even to begin

225

humoring the idea that I would do that. He was likely just teasing and had taken the joke too far, but I sometimes wonder if there was an ulterior motive to his joking. I can't think of any positive reasons for saying it, so all that remains is a hateful purpose.

I have anxiety about the purpose of my brother's actions, and I know I shade his actions with my own projected insecurities. It feels like gaslighting because I think he wants to manipulate how Rene feels about me. If my brother would try to convince someone that I would fuck his dog, what would keep him from using that skill he had to turn me against my mom? He believes with conviction that she had intentionally hurt him, and maybe taking me away from her was a subconscious ploy for revenge. I was afraid that loving my mom would let him down. He would get so upset when I would defend her, and he eventually trained me to believe that writing her off was the only option. His actions were always calculated, so I think he had his intentions for trying to convince me I was crazy for loving her still. Then again, Shannon had also tricked Rene into believing that Bruce Lee died defending the Alamo. When viewed without my projected anxiety, he may have just enjoyed messing with his girlfriend and never considered the collateral damage. There may be nothing nefarious about his actions, and I've just been the butt of his jokes. I want things to be more complicated, but it might be as simple as him just being an asshole with a sense of humor.

My brother has created a narrative about our mother that he recites to anyone who will listen. When that narrative is questioned, he becomes defensive and gets upset about alternative points of view as if it is challenging his traumatic experience. Ironically, he hates his mother for doing the exact same thing. When I realized that much of what I knew about my mom came directly from his mouth, I asked myself, "What if I were to clean the slate, forget everything he has ever said, and approach these issues without his influence? How might I view my mom differently without all my preconceived notions about her actions?"

She may have hurt us both, but it didn't happen in a vacuum. My altered perception of her actions influenced my behavior toward her, and she may have been responding by attempting to indemnify herself. All these years, I might have been forming my opinions of her based solely on her retaliation for feeling attacked. It is illogical to judge people by the way they react to your mistreatment of them. We were stuck in a vicious cycle of pain that had spiraled out of control so fast that none of us could rightfully assign blame to anyone. The truth is, we all could have been better to each other, so I tried to imagine what life would be like if I had given her all benefit of the doubt and supported her more, regardless of right or wrong.

To do that, I had to go back to the beginning of the timeline and proceed as if you did actually have an affair. If I could believe my mother, everything she did after the affair would make perfect sense. I grew uncomfortable in the seat of my car and realized I had long since passed my exit for work. I had zoned out so deeply thinking about the implications of such a reality that I had auto-piloted my way into the next city. I turned around at the next exit and started thinking about it again, but I couldn't believe you could do it.

On the surface, this book may not illustrate how much I love you or show how much respect I have for you. It might appear that I hate you or feel like you failed me as a father. It's quite the contrary in actuality. You remain one of the most influential people in my life, and, as hard as it might be to understand, that is why I have written this book. I did not write this with the intent of describing in elaborate detail every mistake you ever made. The last thing I want to do is negatively alter anyone's perception of you when they read this book. That is not the message I wish to portray. The contents of this book represent a yearning for a level of intimacy I wouldn't be able to achieve with anyone other than you. I want to be as close to you as possible, and I don't feel I can truly do that if I am dishonest about who I am. No matter how close we get, you'll only be close to the person I am pretending to be, not who I really am. I know your heart and admire how good of a person you are. That's why I can't imagine you having an affair, even as a thought experiment.

The affair would be awful enough, but it would also mean you allowed my mother to take the fall. That you watched my brother and me lose our relationships with her so you wouldn't have to admit to infidelity. It would mean she was "sick" because you drove her crazy. While I may believe there are things you could have done differently along this timeline, I know you, and it's simply not possible that you hid an affair from all of us. Then I realized it didn't have to be true if it still felt true to her. For her, there's little difference between knowing you had an affair and believing you had an affair.

When we were leaving for Texas, your coworkers threw you a going-away party. One of the gifts they gave you was a photo album of people around the office. Included in these photos were several pictures of women from around the office posing together and wearing nothing but dark blue lingerie. Those photos were indicative of a very different place and time for the male workforce. Understanding the context of the gift, those pictures were likely an inappropriate gag, especially considering the circumstances for why you were leaving. It also highlights how comfortable everyone was with you around the office. Basing my judgment on those photos alone, I can picture an atmosphere of playfulness and near-harassment-type behavior that was the norm. If one of these women sat in your lap at work, would you push her off in disgust? Probably not, and it probably wouldn't have registered to you as inappropriate, either. You also can't deny that you are an attractive man, so any flirtatious behavior was likely directed toward you more than most men at the office. This can all be true without making your faithfulness to my mom false. Regardless, her perception of your loyalty faltered at some point, and you didn't do enough to mitigate her concern, letting those feelings grow over time.

I imagine you tried at first. You were probably shocked she thought something was going on and dismissed it. When she brought it up again, you probably became a little defensive. You probably started to get angry when she wouldn't let it go. It was likely too late by the time she was hitting you for calling her Sherlock.

# PART 4: ABSOLUTION

To be perfectly honest with you, it doesn't matter to me anymore. When I was younger, I wanted to know the truth about everything that happened. I needed to blame someone for it, but I know now that everyone was at fault at one point or another. A family does not fall apart because of one person, it's a failure of the bunch, and we all missed opportunities to be there for each other. My goal now is not to identify who was at fault; it is purely an endeavor to understand our actions and find ways to avoid making the same mistakes again. I suspect her actions before and after the divorce were predicated on her belief that you had an affair and got away with it.

She believes that you had an affair but that she only lacked the physical evidence to prove it. She was so confident that she decided to get you back by having an affair of her own. They say unwarranted marital jealousy is most often felt by those willing to do the thing they're worried their partner has already done. Maybe her poor self-image and feelings of inadequacy fueled a desire to search elsewhere, and when she started having those feelings, she projected them onto you as if you were feeling the same way about the women she feared. In the end, you were the one with that physical evidence she couldn't get on you.

Man, I bet her world was spinning. How could she be to blame? You had started it, and you were the one that had an extramarital affair. She was only having revenge sex. It wasn't fair that you were getting away with everything. She would have to clear her name by telling anyone who would listen what "really" happened.

I can't imagine what you were going through at the time. Your wife betrayed you in such a vile way and then attempted to slander your name. You handled the news so gracefully and you never once badmouthed her. Shannon would say terrible things about her, but you'd always stop him. Even to this day, you tell me how much you still love her, and I believe you. For every awful thing my mother did in response to thinking you had an affair, you would have had the right to do the same, but you didn't. When thinking about how things could have changed if certain people had acted differently, my mom had an opportunity to show us an example of how to have great strength during unbelievably tough times.

Had everything she accused you of been confirmed, but she had instead reacted with thoughtfulness and civility, she would be the strongest woman I've ever known. To be so fully confident that her husband was having an affair and to have just packed her bags, left his ass, and then found a job for the first time in her adult life. To eventually buy her own house and then travel the world after retiring from said job. To have done everything she ended up doing, but without the revenge and mud slinging. If she would have handled it as you did.

The divorce was ugly, and I watched as you let her have it all, down to the spice rack she felt so strongly about keeping. When she came for your kids, you again were selfless, thought only of me, and let me decide. When I chose to live with you, she couldn't believe it. Again, from the perspective of what she thought to be accurate, she couldn't understand how I could live with you, and she took it personally that I didn't believe her side of the story. The lies she spread about me were based on some truth if we assume the rest of her story also to be true.

Now imagine, her life has imploded, and everyone was gone. She was left alone in Montana and had nothing. She must have hated you for getting away with it, taking me away from her, and filling my head with stories. She was probably so mad that you wouldn't admit everything and started drinking to cope with the pain. I guess stress responses are hereditary. I can't imagine how much she missed me. It probably hurt so bad not to see me every day, as she had grown accustomed. She probably looked forward to the summers. Maybe if I had enough fun, she could convince me to move back home with her. She had likely built up such a high expectation of how it would go, only for me to come home angry, wanting answers to questions she believed to be false accusations. It was probably hard to explain that while she had done some of the things Shannon was saying, it was more complicated than that. She'd try and tell me what you had done, but Shannon had already warned me she would lie about those things when I asked her. I never once listened to her; I just wanted her to admit something she didn't believe.

As the years passed, I spoke to her less, and she assumed I didn't want her around anymore. She became suicidal, fueled by alcoholism, but not even that made me care about her. She confided in me, but I blew up and tried to drive off the road. She had told her stories for so long that she was starting to confuse reality and imputation. She was now telling people you used to beat her. She knew it wasn't true, but you had hurt her so badly that it felt like physical abuse to her. She wanted to convey that pain to people, even if her story was mostly untrue. Then she felt a lump in her breast.

As terrible as the diagnosis was, it created a pathway to forgiveness. We should have granted that absolution to her, but she had fostered so much bitterness that the reprieve never came. The doctor explained that with her condition, there existed a level of uncertainty around severity and outcome. While her prognosis looked good, there was potential for things to go poorly, as there always is in any diagnosis. She leaned in heavily on the worst aspects of the news and led with that.

Her sons were telling people she was lying about her cancer, the same disease that destroyed her body image when she had both breasts removed. An illness that brought her to the doorstep of the unpredictability surrounding life and death. She had finally had enough suffering and found it would be easier to let us all go. She didn't want the constant reminder of the deplorable family she once had; it was all too painful. Nobody believed her, and nobody cared about her. Without us, she started traveling the world and enjoyed an idyllic life for about twenty years until I found her number through a cousin in Montana.

My perception of her had changed, and now I had new questions for her. We talked about our mutual regrets and apologized for the things we had both held onto for too long. I immediately noticed that she was in a better place emotionally. She had moved on, didn't think about us anymore, and was genuinely happier for it. She was guarded initially but was thankful to see pictures of the kids she didn't know I had. She would comment, almost every time, how much Jade looked like me and how she regretted not being around to see my life. I was shocked by how much she had grown and how positive her outlook was.

Soon the rumor mill had spread back to Shannon, and he made an off-handed comment about me talking to her again. I had deliberately kept it from him. This wasn't about him. In fact, it was about doing this without his influence. I sent him a message and asked him if he had ever taken the time to consider how she felt. Not to imagine she was right about any of it, but to imagine if she sincerely believed she was right, how sane it made her perspective seem. He ignored every message I sent, but I wasn't surprised. At least he was staying out of my business, and I could try to have a relationship with my mother. Unfortunately, that didn't last long because my presence was too much of a sore spot for her.

I asked her to share her experience with me, but not as I did when I was younger. I was curious about her perspective, and I was a clean slate without prejudgment. She chose only to tell me how bad of a son I was to her and then decided not to share anything else. I apologized and clarified that I didn't want to fight with her. I wanted to hear her story and understand her point of view. She stopped replying and ignored my phone calls. I sent her nice messages on mother's day and her birthday, but I never heard from her again.

# Cups of Coffee: Chapter 9

## PART 1: WITHDRAWAL

I think there's a perception that I drank like I did because I liked living that life or just wanted to party, but that's not why. What I think would make this most relatable is for you to consider what you imagine your best self to be. If you have a deadline or an important presentation to give at work, who is the you that shows up? I bet that the version of yourself you're now visualizing is caffeinated. I guarantee that there are things you do every morning, if not the day before, to ensure that you are most likely to show up to work as the best version of yourself each and every day. You go to bed at a reasonable hour and set your alarm clock at the exact time where enough sleep and prep time converge. You slowly get dressed in the clothes you picked out the night before while you prepare your coffee with a precise amount of hazelnut creamer. Your hands instinctively pat at your pockets, checking for your wallet, phone, and keys as you finish ritualistically getting ready for the day. Being an alcoholic isn't much different, and if you disagree, I challenge you to skip your coffee tomorrow.

Let's be honest; you're not doing it. You'd have to plan your detox around vacation or a long four-day weekend because that first day will be miserable. Part of your addiction to caffeine is the fear of withdrawal. You've missed your routine before; you have trained yourself to expect the symptoms. Skipping your coffee means that I'm asking you to start your day with a headache that won't go away. To a lesser extent, you'd also be afraid of a drop in productivity. The reason you started drinking is now the least significant aspect of why you continue to do so.

Once you get past the headaches, maybe four days into the experiment, you're now functioning without coffee, but you're dragging ass all day, and it's noticeably worse after lunch. After a month of no caffeine, you're starting to perform reasonably well without it. You've broken your dependence, and you've established new routines. You're noticing the downsides, but there are a few positives too. You're a little less irritable and sleeping better at night. Then you're invited to breakfast with the team at a little Italian place downtown.

Everyone on the team has been singing the praises of the coffee at this place for months. You make the exception because it's just one cup of coffee, and you'll get back to your new routine in the morning. The barista places a small paper filter above the mug and slowly pours boiling water into the cup, just enough to wet the paper. She then spoons finely ground coffee onto the filter, and your mouth salivates unexpectedly. She slowly pours more hot water over the coffee, and a rich aroma fills the air as your pupils instinctively dilate in anticipation and the fondness of memory. The process of making one cup at a time feels equally special and frustrating. When that single cup of coffee hits your bloodstream, you're instantaneously reminded of the person you could be. How much better you'd be at work if you had a cup of this stuff every morning. You think to yourself, "I'll just have a cup before major deadlines or projects when I could use a small pick-me-up." Before you know it, you're a slave to the bean again.

Alcohol doesn't make you any more productive, and it's far more destructive than a cup of coffee, but the addiction is no different. I had gotten to the point that when I pictured my best self, he was buzzed. I was more loving and friendly. I was funny and outgoing with less anxiety. I didn't carry around the burdens of everything I've just described in this book, which was whom I wanted to be. Not to mention, just like that caffeine headache, I was afraid of withdrawal. Cutting out alcohol is a long and arduous process that some people say you never conquer; you just die before you can drink again.

When Daphne came along, she made me feel like my best self. She was like meeting someone who makes you feel caffeinated. Imagine working a job that inspires you so deeply that you don't need to have coffee to get you motivated. This is not the experience most people have with work. Most people drag themselves out of bed and take drugs to be more productive so they don't get fired from a job they wish they could quit.

Meeting Daphne helped me realize how important it is for you to be the cup of coffee in the life of those people you love. If you're not their cup of coffee, you just might be their reason for drinking.

Realizing this also helped me see that my journey through addiction was avoidable. All I needed was someone to help me feel like I was my best self and that everything would be okay, even when I made mistakes. Like Samuel Beckett said, "Fail, try again. Fail again, try again, fail better." I needed someone to help me stay on track, learn and grow with me, and to do so safely. I hope that illustrates why I am so protective of that feeling, just as you would be of your morning cup.

I don't want to drink as I used to or feel like I did several years ago. When I get triggered, it feels like I've skipped my morning coffee, and I'm not setting myself up to be the person I know I can be. I don't feel the way I know I can feel. I also get defensive and start projecting my trauma when I see my triggers activated in my stepbrother or my niece and nephew. I've learned that it is crucial to talk about these things because I've seen what damage they can do if left unaddressed. The remedy for the pain we are all experiencing is so simple that I have difficulty letting it continue this way. All we have to do is support and lift one another up.

John Gottman conducted a study on marriage success and found that couples who responded to even the most benign interests of their partners were more likely to have lasting relationships. While watching couples interact, he discovered that if one of them pointed out something like a pretty bird and the other didn't respond or simply brushed it off as nonsensical, those couples were most likely to fail. That doesn't mean you must be interested in everything your partner is, but you must show interest in your partner, regardless of whether you like the bird. When I think of couples failing because their partner gives them dismissive head nods every time the other finds something interesting, it reminds me of almost every interaction I've ever had with my brother. I feel so uninteresting to him, and I've literally spent my entire life trying to impress him. He has the power to be a stimulating cup of high-octane espresso in my life, but he has consistently and intentionally filled my cup with lukewarm decaf.

As for my mother, I don't intend to absolve her of any wrongdoing. She certainly has her issues, and getting along with her wasn't always easy. She was quick to anger and had a real vindictive side. There are things she has done that I have a hard time forgiving, but the thought experiment requires us to ask the question of ourselves, is it okay to be difficult? Is she still deserving of love and patience despite her flaws?

How different would things be if we were more patient with each other and showed interest in our unique differences? Is it okay for the people we love not to live up to our expectations?

As much shit as I've talked about my brother in this book, I've never wanted to write him off. I want to improve our relationship, and I want him to know that the consequences of his actions extend beyond just himself. According to what he has taught me, as someone that brings me pain, he should be written off and is no longer worth my time or admiration. This mode of thinking is a selfishly limited view of what it means to be a family. Likewise, I don't want him to write me off because I've proven to be more emotionally complex than he may prefer. To be written off because I wrote a book bad-mouthing everyone in our family. I want it to be okay for us to be our unique selves without worrying if we're going to love each other at the end of the day.

My stepmom is a great example. I like her just fine, and I'm glad to have her in my life. I can tell she makes you genuinely happy. I may have a difficult time with her, but it's not because of her. I know I'm the one with the problem. I'm jealous of her getting to spend so much time with you, and I want you to myself sometimes. As I explore my trauma, I don't want her around for that. I feel like she's making it harder for me to have these conversations with you. Without her doing anything wrong, I'm already annoyed with her the second I see her. Every time I call, she's on speakerphone. When we FaceTime, she's in the background. I am torn between being accommodating and wanting space. Inevitably, it comes off as irritable, and I hurt her feelings.

I also have some heavy mommy issues, and she has now been more of a mother to me than my biological mom, which brings up some difficult emotions. I've probably sent mixed messages over time as I have given her access to me as a mom, but then I've turned around and kept her at a distance, strictly as your wife. That's me being difficult, and I'm aware of it, but is it okay for me to be a little difficult? She knows me well enough and has seen everything I've been through growing up. She should recognize the awkward position she will always be in as my new mom. What I mean is, if I need space, can it please be okay? For her to know that it's not that I don't want her in my life, I just want my dad to myself for a week because I'm struggling with some things. There have been numerous awkward interactions that a simple clarification could have quickly resolved. That isn't possible without good communication, understanding, and acceptance of who we are, even when we're not our best selves. Likewise, I can work on adapting to how things have changed.

There was a time when it was just you and me. I was directly impacted by every decision you made, and you were always cognizant of that. When you remarried and adopted her kids, your priorities slowly changed. As I grew more independent, your actions stopped affecting me as much. It was natural for your relationship with my stepmom and her kids to become the focus of your life. I know that my brother and I will always be the most important people to you, but our family dynamics have changed. I used to be able to complain about her and share my frustrations. At some point, I was no longer complaining about my stepmom; I was complaining about your wife. I used to be able to tell you anything without judgment, but now I have to watch my mouth for fear of sounding ungrateful. Without the ability to vent my frustrations, the lack of communication fostered animosity. That subtle change happened so slowly that I didn't catch it until you took a laundry complaint far more seriously than you should have.

I recognize a contrast because I have that freedom of expression with Daphne's family. They try to understand me, and they've gotten to know my personality. Daphne's mom is a cup of coffee for me. I didn't think I could ever see someone as a mother figure again. If I did, it wouldn't have been in a good way. She has taken an interest in my passions, praises me for what I do well, comforts me when I fail, and provides me the luxury of being as difficult as I need. I don't have to change who I am because I'm unafraid that she'll write me off or give up on me. She will love me unconditionally, a feeling I've been too scared to try and experience with you and my brother. A feeling I'm hoping to gain by writing this book. The changes we now make can guide us toward growth and understanding. It's not about altering ourselves.

I don't want to feel the way I did when I was an alcoholic. I don't want to get triggered anymore. I have kids now; I never want to fall into addiction again. I have grown very protective of the relationships that provide me the strength to resist temptation. I may break from time to time and have a drink. In writing this book, especially the chapters about my mom, I had to sit down with a few beers just to access emotional memories I had kept safely tucked away in the dark recesses of my subconscious. The only reason I can be so vulnerable is that I have the love and support of my wife, whom I know will still be there afterward. I can be completely exposed but still feel absolutely safe. I'm happy to report that since finishing this book, I have maintained my sobriety. At the time of writing this, it has been three months since I had anything to drink and almost twelve years since I did any drugs. If you don't count the time I accidently ate those edibles last year.

# PART 2: THE METRIC SYSTEM

When I was working the graveyard at my first job after getting my license, I needed something to do on my days off when the rest of the world was sleeping. I started a skateboard magazine with photos, comics, and articles. The magazine opened the doors for me to meet interesting people in the northern California skateboard industry. Before long, I had a local press making us boards. We built a team and started filming for a skate video. I crashed more than I landed anything, and my body was feeling pretty haggard by the time we wrapped filming. There were several older skaters I knew who swore by taking CBD after skating, so I gave it a shot.

Cannabidiol (CBD) is an extractable compound in marijuana that is touted as being a potent anti-inflammatory without any of the psychoactive properties of THC. I started with a cream I would rub into my knees, and the placebo seemed to help with the pain the following day. I experimented with oils, tinctures, gummies, and smoking the flower. I noticed a significant difference quickly and made CBD part of my routine every time I skated. I kept trying different methods of ingesting CBD, and I had the idea of getting some from a marijuana dispensary. I figured they would have the purest CBD if they could legally sell marijuana.

When I talked to the young kid at the counter, I told him I didn't want any THC and didn't want to feel stoned. I was only looking for something that would help with my knee pain. He convinced me that one milligram of THC was so low that I'd probably not feel it but that it would improve the body's ability to absorb the CBD, and the pain relief would be more effective. They didn't drug test at work, so it didn't matter if I had a negligible amount of THC in my system. I only feared feeling mentally out of control like I had so many years earlier. I looked around the shop and saw a fridge with psychedelic-colored energy drinks. The bottom of each can read, "10 mg THC." My general knowledge of the metric system identified that this drink was a power of ten more potent than the gummies I had been offered, so I convinced myself I could likely handle a tenth of a dose. I nervously paid and then ran to my car.

I ate two gummies on my drive home without thinking much about it. Thirty minutes into my commute, I was singing loudly to my music and felt unusually relaxed. I was home another thirty minutes later and took the family to a Mexican restaurant. Daphne was driving, and we were halfway to Salsa Town when my face started melting.

I was suddenly stoned and hadn't told anyone what I had taken. I wasn't expecting to be dazed at all. I thought I would get a little giggly at worst, but now I was staring out the window, trying to gather myself. Like waves violently crashing on the beach, my level of stoned kept increasing, and I was scared Daphne would be upset with me. I turned around and looked at my kids and gave Pepper a warm smile. She smiled back at me, but I quickly turned around and thought to myself, "She knows."

I was crippled with anxiety, and I fought back the panic of heading to a restaurant with my wife and two young kids, too stoned to know if I was breathing too loud when it occurred to me that I didn't have to go to the restaurant if I didn't want to. I turned to Daphne and said, "I don't really wanna be in public right now. I'm super stoned."

Daphne slowly turned to look at me. With a confused expression on her face, she said, "What do you mean?"

"I took some CBD with a little THC in it, and I think I took too much." I cringed, not knowing what she would say, but her eyes widened, and she laughed it off. We went back home, and Daphne cooked dinner while I played with the kids on the floor. That feeling of my reservoir spilling over the edge into psychosis had returned, and I was abruptly thrust back onto the edge of sanity. Surprisingly, I noticed something about my personality that was very different now. The anxiety would swell like a painful reminder but then harmlessly subside as I played with my children.

Taking a page from what Carl Jung described as one of twelve archetypes of inborn personalities, I imagine we all have a shadow of ourselves composed of the things we want to hide. The shadow self is made of what we're ashamed and scared of, and it controls our triggers. Most people ignore this shadow and push it down, deep into their subconscious. As we continue ignoring our shadow self and feeding it the emotions we don't deal with, that shadow gets stronger. That rush of anxiety I got, worried that Daphne would judge me for being stoned, was my shadow self. I had now just awakened that shadow from a dormant sleep with edibles after an irresponsible application of the metric system.

I recognize now that I was never on the verge of losing my mind but that I had gotten to the point where the shadow self was transitioning into my true self. My shadow self was becoming the dominant perception of whom I thought I was. Depression, and sometimes addiction, is a symptom of the imbalance that occurs when the shadow self takes over. That feeling of overfilling my reservoir was a change in perception. My self-identity was altered, and I convinced myself that I was the sum of all my worst qualities.

Now that I had awakened the beast and those feelings started to rush back over me, it was Daphne who helped me process that shadow again. By merely accepting me without judgment, the shadow was instantly starved of its power and died off again. I did recognize that while the support of my wife granted me immunity from the pull of my shadow, it still existed deep in my subconscious and would continue to trigger my alcohol dependence. Now that I had the power to face that shadow without the fear of being taken over by it, I knew it was time to face it for real.

# Part 3: The Doldrums

I went back to the dispensary and explained that I was looking for something a bit stronger, but I was writing a book and wanted to maintain a certain level of awareness and concentration. The kid behind the counter suggested a vape pen with a high ratio of CBD to THC. He said the product wasn't all that popular because the high wears off too quickly, but that was precisely the experience I was hoping to cultivate. I took my new pen and checked into a hotel room after work. The plan was to smoke a bunch of weed, awaken the shadow, and confront it face to face.

I propped pillows up on the bed in the shape of a large recliner, and I got comfortable with my laptop. I struggled to figure out how to use the vape pen, and then I took a few hits and started writing. When the high came on, I could feel the shadow as it slowly cast over my mind, and then I immediately regretted not being home with my family. I thought about my wife taking care of the kids without my help. I thought about missing out on an opportunity to be playing with my kids as I sat in a hotel room, wasting my time smoking weed as an adult. I thought of what my brother would think. Would he think of me as a lousy father and write this process off, assuming I was a druggie? I immediately felt so overwhelmed with depressive thoughts that my first instinct was to push that shadow back into my subconscious. I tried to focus on the book and the chapter I was on, but then it dawned on me that this was why I was here. I was supposed to be conquering this feeling that was enveloping me, not continuing to avoid it.

Once the shadow had cast its darkness across the entire room, I found myself standing in a forest of trees blackened by ash. They were mostly decomposed and hollowed out by the beetle infestation that had stripped each of them down to bare trunks with sparse projections of crumbling branches. There was a light blue mist hanging in the air, and no matter how long I ran, the scene never seemed to change except for a small clearing where I could see the pit I had crawled out of many years ago. Partially covered in moss and decaying plant material was the rope Daphne had given me to climb out when we fell in love with each other. It seemed appropriate that she gave me the strength and courage to use that same rope to climb back in, not out of depression, but on a search-and-destroy mission. The edges of the pit were slippery, and I shuddered at the memory of how difficult it was to get out, and then I cringed at the thought of how much easier it would be to fall back in. Now at the bottom, I did my best to get comfortable as I sat among the things I had left there so many years ago. I could feel the weight of the lethargians pressing me against the walls of the pit as I again started to become one with the doldrums. The darkness was overwhelming, but I caught a glimpse of my daughter's face.

Earlier that day, Pepper had a dentist appointment that we had both been stressing about for weeks. They were filling one of her cavities, and we knew she would have to have a Novocain injection into her gums. I was expecting the worst because we had done this with her before, and the last time, she bit the doctor and kicked a dental tech. I left work early and drove an hour to meet her and her mom at the dentist's office. I talked her through the process so she would know what to expect. I told her she could squeeze my hands as hard as she wanted if she were scared or in pain. I convinced her that doing so would transfer her pain to me. It wouldn't hurt either of us very badly if we shared the discomfort. I sat in the chair next to her, and I held both of her hands. She completely trusted me, and I felt her squeeze my fingers when the dentist arrived. I distracted her through the entire procedure, and she didn't notice she had gotten the shot. It reminded me of when she had spent a week in the children's hospital.

Daphne and I woke up to Pepper crying in her bed. When we entered the room, we found that she was covered in puke and had a low fever. I stayed home from work to take care of her, and Daphne took baby Jade to her mother's house in an attempt to keep him from getting sick. I pulled our bed out into the living room and set up a sick day movie theater with chicken noodle soup and Gatorade. We were ready to cuddle all day and fight off her first little kid virus. She was in relatively good spirits until she started screaming in pain and holding her back right where her kidneys would be.

I rushed her to urgent care, but I disagreed with the tests they wanted to run. There was likely a list of things they automatically test for when any kid comes in with similar symptoms, but I knew my two-year-old well enough to know they were on the wrong track and wasting our time. It was clear they weren't going to move on without first testing her for strep throat and the flu. I eventually agreed to play the game and waited for the results. Everything came back negative, as I expected, so they finally started warming up to what I initially feared.

Pepper was potty-trained, but she was routinely weird about pooping. She would hold it as long as she could, and it would be painful when she finally went. This turned into a fear of hers, so she'd keep it in to avoid the pain of pooping. Soon a weird quirk had become constipation, and now that constipation was impaction. Her screams were coming in waves, and she only found relief after a short bout of explosive diarrhea. I figured she had a stomach virus in combination with impaction. The practitioner agreed and ordered an X-ray. They confirmed impaction but were unsure whether it was due to a twist in the colon or intussusception. We would have to wait a few hours for the ambulance to arrive, and then it would take us to the children's hospital, an additional hour's drive away. I declined to delay her treatment further and rushed her there in my car.

The waves continued, ranging from talkative, curious toddler to lethargic zoned-out zombie. This was followed by a blood-curdling scream, an explosion of diarrhea, and then back to a relatively normal toddler. We were checked into the ER and had just gotten to our room when she suddenly and unexpectedly crashed. She had been talking to the nursing staff and flexing her knowledge of animal sounds when her eyes glossed over, and she turned purple. Her doctors rushed in to take her vitals just as the color in her face was returning. She realized where she was, screamed, had more diarrhea, and then went back to making playful animal sounds. The purple was a new sign that whatever was going on with her was getting worse, and we were potentially running out of time. I kept thinking about what would have happened if we had waited for the ambulance.

The doctor came into the room and explained that they thought her intestines were twisted and cutting off blood flow. They wanted to take her immediately to the operating room to do exploratory abdominal surgery to find the twist and correct it. I asked them how much pain she would be experiencing and asked them to clarify aspects of it that didn't seem to fit what I was seeing in her behavior. I was telling them they were wrong and that they needed to figure something else out when she crashed again. I was relying so heavily on paternal instinct and a hope that I knew my daughter better than a handful of doctors who had never met her. They were simply following some medical flow chart based on her symptoms. My confidence slipped every time she crashed. I eventually gave in to their method and agreed to the surgery.

# Part 4: Silhouetted Reflections

I was kicking myself, thinking I had let it go too long, as I carried her tiny body to the operating room. They wanted to rush her into surgery, so taking her there in my arms was faster than waiting on a bed. We passed the nursing station on the way to the O.R. when the doctor I had been arguing with stopped me. She hustled around the corner of the desk and told me she thought I might be right. She said another provider was only ten minutes away, and he suggested we wait it out and gave her some medication to try. The emotional rollercoaster I was on had me feeling overly vulnerable, and I would have agreed to anything at that point. I just wanted her to be taken care of, and she was now well past the care I could provide.

She continued to cycle through scary moments, but the severity and duration decreased each time. Her care team took us to the room that Pepper and I would stay in for the next week while she recovered. She was finally confirmed to have rotavirus, and her symptoms had been exacerbated by intestinal impaction. Once the impaction cleared, she had excessive diarrhea, but she was finally able to rid the virus from her system, and her condition gradually improved. We cuddled in the children's hospital 24 hours a day for an entire week. Her little arm was in a protective sling that kept her I.V. from moving, and she wasn't allowed to eat anything until they could confirm that her intestines were unaffected. As a show of support, I didn't eat that week either. She seemed so sweet and delicate in my arms. I could now see her again in that state as I lay in the pit that I had intentionally reinhabited.

The father that always shows up for his daughter, and the father that this shadow was trying to convince me I was, cannot co-exist. I realized that the guilt and shame I felt for not being there with my kids at this moment was similar to how I feel every time I'm away from them. I love my children so much that I regret not spending every moment with them. I was making myself feel bad about missing my kids, but there's nothing wrong with doing things without them. I'm not a bad father for having hobbies. Soon, the only thing I felt while sinking into my mattress of shame was the overwhelming realization that I really love my kids.

Suddenly, I was no longer lying on the pit floor with my back against the cold walls. I was standing on my own two feet, held up by the thought of my wife and children. The vines that had grown around me relaxed their grip and fell to the ground with a sickening thump, immediately relieving my shoulders of their weight. I recognized that I didn't need to feel guilty for leaving the kids with Daphne while I spent a night in a hotel because she supported me and was allowing me the space to explore my emotions. A bad habit I had developed of feeling guilty instead of grateful when someone helps me.

My wife and I agreed that the healing I would gain by facing my demons this way was a gift I could one day give to my children. I refused to hand my pain down to them just because I had never addressed it in myself. The pit started to fill in, and I was lifted as the ground rose below me. It was no longer difficult to climb out of the depression as I could now easily walk away.

The forest around me was still dark, but the mist had cleared. The pit I had been in was now nothing more than a mound of freshly turned soil. I knelt to scoop a handful of the loamy black dirt and let it slowly fall from my hand. As I watched it recollect on the ground, I saw my shadow mimicking my movements, and I no longer felt afraid of that silhouetted reflection. I was happy to see it as an extension of self and as much a part of me as anything else in my perception. My shadow was no longer something to fear or regret. It was a gentle reminder of who I am and where I've been.

I closed my laptop and set it on the bed next to myself. I swung my legs off the edge of the bed and ran into the bathroom. I wanted to see the person I had just become. I knew I was still me, and I knew what I looked like, but I hadn't seen what I looked like when I felt like this. I wanted to see past my shadow at my true self. I burst into the bathroom, and there, looking back at me in the mirror, was a goofy-looking man in his late 30s with long blonde hair and oversized glasses. I laughed at what a character I still am after all these years, and I couldn't help thinking about what it would be like if you had been an equally over-the-top character. How different would my life be if my brother, the person I looked up to most in my life, were an eccentric artist with a stupid mustache that says, "I take art more seriously than life?" What if my mom had been some gnarly surfer chick who wanted to help me make shitty skate videos? What would my life be like if I had been more understood and accepted for the weirdo that I am? To have known that the things I was trying to suppress about myself were my greatest strengths.

I had spent my entire life trying to emulate personalities that didn't match my own, and it made me feel like I didn't belong or that I had failed to be what I was supposed to be. You and Shannon had always represented not only what I considered the norm but also a sense of perfection. I was now looking at myself with respect and admiration for the first time in my life. My idea of what a father "should be" had expanded to include someone like me. I realized I had not only become the best version of myself, but I was also the best father I could be to the two artistic little weirdos I was raising. I was granted an opportunity to heal my past self by supporting my kids in the ways I felt I needed at their age.

The weight of expectations and the anxiety of perfection were all completely gone. As advertised, the high had completely worn off, and I was now standing in a very normal Best Western-looking hotel room. I had accomplished what I came for, and after glancing at my watch, I realized I had checked into the room only forty-five minutes ago. I had just spent three hundred dollars to be alone for forty-five minutes, and all I wanted now was to be at home with my wife and kids. I spent thirty-seven years trying to live up to two people that would never understand me, and it took me forty-five minutes to realize that the only person I ever should have tried to impress was myself. I wanted to thank Daphne for giving me the strength and support to learn that on my own. I was ready to play with my kids and squeeze them as hard as possible because they see more in me than anyone ever will. I also decided I was now ready to share my story with you.

# Another Awkward Vacation: Chapter 10

## PART 1: COMPULSIVE PEOPLE-PLEASER

I spent four years on this story, repeatedly telling it to myself, whittling it down, and perfecting what I wanted to say. I planned for what you would say and constantly edited with the hope that I could get the best possible reaction with the most precise level of understanding and acceptance. I was now flying to Texas to have this conversation with you, but unlike the other times when I had planned to talk to you before writing the book, this time, I felt entirely at peace with whatever reaction you might have. The book had begun as a medium from which you could better understand me but had since become the tool I had used to better understand myself.

This book would now serve as a gift I could give you, a way of introducing you to the man I had become by allowing you to meet the parts of me that I had hidden from everyone for so long. An introduction to a son you had barely met. Of all the possible reactions you might have to discovering my dark side, I hadn't considered that you might deny its existence.

Your first reaction was anger, which I had expected, so I immediately initiated plan A. I was able to redirect you and ease your concerns with specific examples and clarification. I had barely gotten through the summary on the back cover of this book when I noticed you digging your heels in, preparing a retort. I could tell you already had a mental image of what you thought was the entirety of the book's contents.

"Well, I know you're critical of your brother, but before you bad mouth him too much, you should know that your mom really did do some of those things," you said, with a stern look on your face. You were always so quick to come to my brother's defense. When I would complain about what he'd say to me or about me, you'd always dismiss it because you assumed the best in him. I didn't enjoy the same luxury, evidenced by the awkwardness in our vacations always getting sparked by you presuming the worst in me. I was prepared for this inevitability and wasn't letting Shannon off the hook so easily this time.

You and I already had this conversation in my head a thousand times, and it was as if you had memorized your lines from the plan B script verbatim. I reminded you of how I was as a kid. I would break a rule and then ground myself. You and Mom would find me crying alone in my room and ask me what I was doing. I would confess my minor crimes and then beg for forgiveness. I was such a compulsive people-pleaser that I was always so much harder on myself than anyone else could ever be. When Shannon was mean to me, he was being mean to that little boy who was still very much alive deep within my subconscious.

I noticed that the comparison had gotten through to you, and I saw you drop your guard a little. You admitted that my brother was unnecessarily hard on everyone and conceded that he could be rude. Still, you dismissed them both as part of his personality and then suggested our kinship justified his behavior. "That's just how he is, Denver. He's still your brother."

Obviously, we all have our flaws. I reiterated that, regardless of familial ties, those flaws could have consequences. Given the very nature of our relationship and the age difference, there was a power differential between us. My brother enjoyed his influence over me and often exploited it to his advantage. While I never experienced a major, singular traumatic event at the hands of my brother, his constant humiliation and degradation of my spirit accumulated over time and slowly broke me down. The fact that this was done by my brother, someone I trusted, makes his behavior traumatic and unjustified. My near pathological codependence fed into his narcissistic personality. Our combined disorders mixed in a way that made us both worse for being around each other. For the first time in my life, I finally understood and attempted to explain to you how his actions didn't just hurt my feelings. They had become triggers for me and were complicating my recovery. I confessed that I had been coping with those triggers with drugs and alcohol, and I briefly described how bad it had gotten at times. I also went into detail about how thoughts of suicide plagued my mind when the drugs and alcohol didn't work.

I took the time to make it abundantly clear that I did not write this book to establish some sort of innocence in my mother. My mother's actions have done more to damage my self-image and personal relationships than anyone else has. Fears of abandonment, trust issues, feelings of inadequacy, and suicidal ideation and inspiration were all gained from my mother. Even after extending the olive branch as an adult and introducing her to my kids, she again decided to abandon me, proving she hadn't grown or ever tried to learn from our collective mistakes. This book should not be confused as an attempt to rectify her wrongs, make excuses for her mistakes, or share in her guilt as our own. My mother only serves as a tragic example of what happens when a family doesn't take the time to communicate with one another and how bad things can get. We must all learn our own lessons, but we can do so after observing each other's mistakes, thus sharing the burden and growing together. Avoiding these difficult conversations only delays progress and alienates the ones we should be supporting. My mother is an example of what I am afraid to become and our family's response to it, a pattern I wish to break.

I thought you and I had made some real progress in our conversation. I felt like you were finally starting to understand how serious it was, and you were seeing the bigger picture of why I wanted to share it with you. I thought you were beginning to appreciate that I wasn't mad at my brother but that I merely wanted to be released from his grip. I wanted to share my experience so that he wouldn't make the same mistakes with his wife and children. I had learned how his actions affected me, so I thought I could help him and his family grow closer by sharing my understanding. To show him that we all love him but that we don't want to have to work so hard for his approval.

It was uncomfortable watching my brother acting so outwardly awful to everyone in an attempt to hide his insecurities. I felt like I had found the cure to his misery in my own self-reflection. I possessed the revelations that could end the suffering, and I thought you were finally starting to understand. I had planned this all out perfectly, and I had thoroughly explained myself. Four years of practice and I had finally gotten through to you, but then you surprised me by putting up an emotional wall I had never encountered from you before. This wall was painted differently on the outside, but it was constructed of the same bricks of repudiation and held together by the quick-drying mortar of defensiveness.

# Part 2: Iridescent Hue

We were driving to the waterpark, and you were looking forward to floating in the lazy river with the kids. You didn't know I had planned to trap you in the vehicle alone so I could unload years of trauma and recovery on you. You lived an hour from the park, and it had almost been the perfect amount of time to say everything. Daphne had intentionally ridden in a separate car with my stepmom and the kids, and they were waiting for us to join them as we pulled into a parking spot.

I continued our conversation, "Dad, I'm not sure you realize how depressed I was. Have you ever watched Seven Pounds?"

"With the Fresh Prince?" you asked.

"Yes, that's the one. I was so inspired by it that I decided I would dedicate my life to working dangerous jobs that would help other people, but I'd be risking my life doing them. Did you know that was my motivation for joining the military?"

You had turned the truck off and were giving me your undivided attention. Your demeanor and attitude had cooled off, and we were now having a discussion that mirrored those I imagined on my long work commutes. You said, "Well, no. I thought you just wanted to serve your country."

"That's a pretty extreme level of patriotism to develop out of nowhere. Don't get me wrong; I'm so glad I served. I gained the respect and discipline I needed, which changed my life." I saw Daphne unloading the kids from her car, and I recognized that the conversation would need to conclude soon. Nodding my head toward her and the kids, I added, "It introduced me to my wife and led me to my career, but I didn't know anything about the military when I joined, and I only joined because the Austin fire department wasn't hiring."

"I'm so glad you met Daphne. She has been so good for you. I was worried about you, but I didn't know it had gotten so bad," you said with a far-off look in your eyes.

"Yep, I guess I'm lucky to have been colorblind, or I would have had a very different job." I laughed.

"No, it wasn't luck," you objected. "I know you're not religious, but I believe things happen for a reason."

"I may not be religious, but I am spiritual. I'm a Jedi, so I also believe things happen for a reason." We laughed together to break the uncomfortableness of the conversation. We were in uncharted territory together, and defaulting to a joke is a mechanism I had learned from you.

When I was in Basic, they asked us for our preferred religion. If you were killed in action and your body was unidentifiable, your dog tags would ensure your remains were treated with the correct cultural rituals. I wrote in Jedi as a joke, but as I've gotten older, the internal conflict between altruism and selfishness feels more relevant every day. I was so proud of myself when I got my dog tags, and the government had officially documented that I was a Jedi. Reminding you of that special status helped alleviate a tiny bit of the awkwardness we were steeped in, but we were far from done talking about everything I wanted to share.

I needed to relate my addiction and depression to what I wanted from you moving forward. I needed your help getting through to Shannon so I could stop being triggered by him. I had admitted my insecurities, but what was to come next would be the hard part.

"The alcoholism I continue to struggle with gets triggered when Shannon is critical of me. I get overwhelmed with depressive thoughts when you grow cold with me instead of telling me what's bothering you." I stopped talking as we both noticed my stepmom walking toward the truck.

"Hold on," you said as you rolled your window down.

"Hi. Are you guys okay?" she asked, with a friendly smile.

"Yep," you said with a head nod that did nothing to explain why we were still sitting in the truck. A better option may have been to tell her we were talking and to ask for some time, but we both just sat there with our lame smiles waiting for her to figure it out on her own.

"Okay. I'm going to head in. Let me know if you need anything." She looked at us both and then turned around to walk away. I felt terrible knowing this was probably coming off as rude again. Here we were, on another family vacation you were paying for, and I was causing trouble. She hadn't done anything wrong and didn't know she was interrupting my life's single most important conversation. She really is a great person, but right now, she was just in the way. I was annoyed with her presence again, and it wasn't fair to her.

You rolled up the window and began gathering your things to leave, but I wanted a cleaner conclusion to everything we had discussed. I hadn't shared my journey with you for fun. I had put you through this for a good reason. I told you about my triggers because I wanted to eliminate them. I wanted a little more time with you before gathering with everyone again. You had rented a condo near the park so we could all get dressed and have lunch before heading in. Once we got up to the room, I knew our conversation would be over.

I don't know if it was the seriousness of the conversation or if you felt like I painted you in a corner, but the calmness I had cultivated in the situation had been lost in the brief interruption. You now had to choose between continuing to give an already long conversation more attention or taking the hint from your wife that it was time to go. I couldn't let you leave, though. I had worked too hard delicately laying the groundwork toward getting you into the most receptive mood possible. The next phase of my plan was going to require effort on your part, and I started to panic as it felt like I was losing the opportunity to gain your buy-in.

My plan was to share my drug abuse, alcoholism, and depression with you. The next phase was to show that you knew about that struggle and didn't do enough to help me through it. I didn't want to blame you for my issues, but I needed to make the correlation that what happened then was happening now. I wanted to know why you hadn't done anything when you knew I was using or when it became obvious I had a drinking problem. If we could identify why you hadn't acted back then, maybe we could deduce that it was for the same reasons you weren't acting now.

Why had you let me off so easily after finding pipes in the house? Why didn't you say anything when my car always smelled like weed? I had once drunkenly caught the refrigerator on fire and then covered up the evidence with layers of skateboard magazine photos. I was so drunk when I did it that it ended up being a surprise to both of us when you found it a year later. You were angry when you saw it, but you didn't make me replace it or threaten me with rehab. You unintentionally supported my dependence by allowing it to happen. I needed to show you that you were now unintentionally complicating my recovery by refusing to communicate and not stepping in to support me when you recognize that I am being triggered by my brother.

You were either completely unaware of what was happening, or you actively chose to avoid the conversations because you didn't know what to do or say. By providing specific examples, I could prove a behavior pattern that influenced each major event within this book. I didn't want to beat ourselves up for the things we couldn't change but instead recognize that we continue to make the same mistakes.

Our avoidant behavior with my mom resulted in losing her to a long, drawn-out, ugly battle. A consistent lack of communication made me feel like I needed to fill a hole in my chest that only deepened with my substance abuse. What do we do now to avoid the consequences that will be paid for by the next generation of our family? What can we work on in ourselves that will pay dividends in how my kids feel about themselves? I had to shift your perception of this being critical of you to me just being an overprotective father wanting to provide a better emotional future for his kids.

Once the cause of the avoidance was established, I planned to work with you on finally moving past the blockage. Like Pepper in the children's hospital, removing that blockage would lead to excessive diarrhea, but we could finally get better afterward. If you didn't know how to initiate those difficult conversations, I would be willing to stumble through the process awkwardly with you. Kobe didn't hit every shot he took, but he still refused to pass anyway. Unfortunately, that brief disruption had broken your concentration, and now I feared I would lose the opportunity to bridge this gap. I'd have to go in for a showstopper and snatch your attention back.

You climbed out of the truck and grabbed your swim bag from the back, and I jumped out to meet you on the other side. I strategically placed myself in your path and asked, "Dad, do you remember when you came home from Africa? Did Dan tell you any of the crazy stuff we were doing?"

"No, he didn't say you were doing anything wrong." You walked around me and started walking toward the condo.

I spun on my heels and caught up to you, "Well, even if he didn't tell you anything, you had to know something was going on when you got back, but we never talk about anything, and we just hope it goes away on its own. I'm trying to tell you that these things don't just disappear if we don't talk about them. I was struggling then like I am now, and I want to break the pattern." In my desperation, the words were coming out less eloquently than I had hoped.

You stopped and looked at me, "Son, if anyone were ever critical of me, I would be very upset. Your brother, your stepsisters, anyone except you. I would understand if you were critical of me. I know I didn't do a perfect job. I had my head in my butt after the divorce, and I always say that you raised yourself."

"See, that's such a good example. You say that all the time, but it bothers me when you say I raised myself. I really did in some ways, but I needed *you* to raise me. I still need you! When you say that, I feel like you're acknowledging that I was alone without dealing with the consequences it caused." I saw the look of defensiveness on your face, but it was mixed with pain, regret, exhaustion, and helplessness.

"I talk with you! You can tell me anything." You were walking toward the condo again, a posture that didn't come off as actively listening.

"Okay, for example, do you remember finding my pipe in the couch when you got back from Africa? You slept beside the trashcan all night instead of talking to me about it." It was such an old example, but it represented the most blatant breach of catching me doing drugs and doing nothing to stop it or inquire about how it started.

"Wow, Denver, that never happened." We had gotten to the elevator that would take us to the room where everyone was waiting before heading to the waterpark.

I laughed, "That definitely happened."

"Nope. I would remember that."

"Yeah, no kidding! So why don't you?" I laughed out of frustration. Your memory wasn't great, but this had to have made an impact on you when it happened. "What about when Toad lived with us, and we smoked in the bathroom every night? You're going to tell me you never smelled the pot?"

"Denver. You know, if you were really doing heavy drugs..." You trailed off and picked up your bags as the elevator doors opened on the top floor.

"What? What were you going to say?" I asked, honestly confused.

"Maybe, it didn't happen," you said as you started walking down the hallway.

I blinked hard and then scoffed, "Wait, you think I hallucinated all of it?"

"Yes."

"Pshh. Dad. That's not really how that works, dude." I was stunned and hadn't planned how to react to this. Was this denial, or did you really have no idea any of this had gone on under your roof? I had brought this up to show you how you had a history of deflection, and you had now just hit the deflection grand slam. This was the same old emotional walls you always raised, but with the fancy new paint of fantasy. I wasn't sure if I should move on or spend time trying to convince you that I hadn't hallucinated my entire life away.

In my confusion, I had lost the conversation. What was I trying to explain? I had not been hoping to convince you that I had smoked weed in the bathroom in high school. I wanted you to know about the weed in the bathroom because it would help you understand what I was going through back then. If you understood what I had been through, you would realize that I'm still dealing with those unresolved issues. At least, I think it would. What was happening? How had I gotten so lost in where this conversation was supposed to go?

As we got to the room where everyone waited for us, it was easier for you to assume I had made this all up and to absolve ourselves from having to work through the discomfort. No one would need to apologize or change their behavior. We could just treat this all as one rather long delirium. This was the same avoidance that has plagued our family since day one, only now it was tinted with the iridescent hue of "hard stuff." The lack of communication that crippled your marriage and separated me from my mom was now mixed with the dismissiveness that makes me dread spending time around my brother. A shared nightmare that will continue to haunt our family every night, but one that we will routinely wake up from and pretend never happened as we quietly eat our breakfast together, falsely comforted by the quaint escapism of vacation.

Our conversation ended on a semi-positive note, despite the pain I felt for having been rejected in a way I hadn't scripted and not knowing how best to respond. Part of me knew this couldn't be the end of our talk, and you'd have to have so many questions after learning so much more about me. You were only dismissing this conversation because it was time to go. I knew you'd want to hear more. I had told you about my depression, alcoholism, substance abuse, thoughts of suicide, and the contents of the book I had written detailing all of it. The timing was off, and everyone was waiting for us, so I understood your reluctance to continue. It hadn't gone the way I wanted it to, but it had gone better than any other time we had previously attempted. I wanted to see what you would do with the information I had given you, so I didn't bring it up again. I hoped you would ask questions or ask to read the book, but we never approached the subject again.

I gave you the tools and all the information you would need to help me, but you let it go. This conversation was supposed to change everything, but it became another example of avoidance. I thought our interaction would write the ending of this book, and it would be a happy ending. As we hugged goodbye and your last chance to ask those questions slipped away, I had to ask myself again what I was trying to accomplish with all of this.

I almost stopped writing. I wanted to give up because it hadn't worked. I felt like I had explained myself so thoroughly, but you weren't interested in who I was. I assumed you didn't care. I didn't start writing again until I realized this book was never for you in the first place. This book was for my mind's image of you. The imaginary friend I talk to on my commute to work. This version of you doesn't exist in the real world, so just like talking to myself, this book was only ever meant for me. You would only ever see this book as being critical of you unless you were willing to appreciate the growth potential in our mistakes.

As I drove away from your house at the end of our vacation, I saw you put your arm around your wife, and I could see tears fill your eyes. You were worried about me and felt guilty that you had let me down as a kid, but you sat silently with those emotions as I left. This book would forever remain a mystery to you. I had written a science fiction novel about drug abuse and family relationships.

The process of writing this book has given me insight I didn't have before our last vacation. I promised myself I could be at peace with any reaction you had, but denial wasn't on my list of possibilities, and I struggled to accept the outcome. I finally acknowledged in myself that I have an astonishing level of impatience that fuels near-manic levels of concentration. I can write and record songs in a single day. I often ruin paintings because I can't wait for sections to dry. I needed to leave your understanding of me up to the universe, and I would have to be more patient about finding a good conclusion to this story.

## PART 3: TEXT MESSAGING

I had zero concerns about discussing this book with my mom. I literally had nothing to lose, and while reaching out to her felt like picking at an old scab, I was left with the same relationship I had with her for the past several years. I was anxious about talking with you, but I also felt like I had nothing to lose. There has never been any doubt of whether or not you loved me, and there was never any limit to your support of me. Talking with you about all of this represented an opportunity to gain understanding, and in the worst-case scenario, I knew you'd always love me and support me regardless. Again, I was disappointed with how it ended up going down, but I knew it couldn't damage our strong relationship. There was only one other person I needed to talk to, and I intentionally saved it for last, knowing I had nothing to gain and would likely walk away feeling triggered and on edge. Nevertheless, I knew I had to have that conversation with my brother.

I had been dreading it for weeks, but as the book was nearing its end, I knew I had to talk with him. If he wasn't interested, I had to warn him at least that I had written many critical things about him and our relationship. Unlike my conversation with you, I wasn't expecting any understanding or support. I didn't want to talk to him in person or on the phone. I knew I would need to choose my words wisely, and I didn't want to get triggered and say something I didn't mean. Besides, he could ignore my calls, but I knew my texts would go through. In hindsight, doing it by text message was likely the worst of the options, but my plan wasn't to tell him everything in the book. I would only explain what I had done and why.

To warm him to the idea that I had written the book, I decided to lead with my recent decision to seek professional therapy. While I had been researching on my own, talking with my wife, and doing shadow work for the past four years, I thought he would take the professional component of my journey more seriously. I also wondered if he had ever been to therapy. If he had started his own treatment, maybe he would understand what I was doing. He wouldn't think of this as strictly being critical of him but as an exploration of the factors that led to me being the person I am today. I texted him in the morning and got straight to the point.

*Have you ever been to therapy?*

*Nope. You?*

*Yeah, just started*

*How is it.*

Something I'm going to do my best to describe is how even the slightest little things can cause a trigger to activate. I am fully conscious of these triggers and capable of free thought, but a history of interactions with my brother has trained my brain to squeeze the shit out of the glands in my head that produce a sloppy soup of emotions I cannot control. I know, for example, that I am reading into him saying, "How is it" with a period instead of a question mark. The rational side of me knows that it's a grammatical error, but the glands that were squeezed made me read the lack of a question mark as if it were a statement that merely fits the context of the conversation and wasn't an actual question that he would like me to answer. This barely registered on a trigger scale from one to ten, but the needle did bounce slightly.

*It's been good. Surprisingly*

*How many sessions?*

The needle on the trigger scale jumped up to two. Again, the rational side of me knows he may have asked that question because I said I had "just started" therapy, but I immediately felt the need to justify the work I had been doing. If the number of sessions was low, which it was, he would dismiss everything I felt. He would only respect what I had learned from this experience if the number of sessions approached what he felt was enough.

*I've been doing shadow work for four years,*
*will be starting regression therapy soon.*

Now that the trigger scale was sitting at a two, the self-doubt and uneasiness began clouding judgment. I expected him to think it was stupid and a waste of time. The rational side of me tried to help by pointing out that maybe he just hadn't read the text yet, but the longer I waited, the worse it got. I decided to tell him I had also been looking into past life therapy. The craziness of exploring one's past lives helps lighten the mood and brings a bit of intrigue to the conversation.

*Also had one past life reading that
was kind of bonkers*

I waited twenty minutes for a reply, and now I was swimming in the anxiety of losing the conversation. This unreasonableness is me at a trigger scale of only two, so you can imagine how I am at a ten. My past life reading was interesting but provided no information that helped me with my present struggles, and it had nothing to do with what I wanted to talk about with my brother. Deciding to do this via text meant I had agreed to wait for responses. Still, my anxiety and the trigger scale reading were working against me, so I felt the need to pull the conversation back in the direction I intended it to go.

*Working on myself has made me
a better husband and father, but
it has also given me the tools to be
more prepared for when my kids go
through anything similar.*

Another excruciating ten minutes passed before he finally replied.

*Nice. Past life?*

*Yeah, you know, the one I had
before this one. Apparently*

*It was also not the only one I had,
but likely the most recent...*

I wasn't getting a response, and my anxiety was now through the roof. I didn't want to talk about my past lives; I wanted to talk about this one. I kept adding "Apparently" after each text, like a disclaimer. If he thought it was stupid, I could distance myself from it like it wasn't my own belief. I could pretend that I was just playing around. I decided to try explaining why I had brought it up and relate it to what I was doing with the book.

*Life is an opportunity to learn
things you can't learn in the next
dimension. We just keep coming
back, over and over again, until we
learn all that we need to before
ascending to the next plane.*

*Apparently.*

Nothing, there was no response. I was now digging myself deeper and further away from the intended conversation. I knew his complaints about Christianity and the fear-based teaching of most religions; maybe I could catch his attention with what I find is the most fascinating aspect of having multiple lives. A belief in the eternal pursuit of learning that has guided my journey through this book.

*No eternal damnation, just lessons to be learned. You either do or you don't. You progress, or you don't. Just spirits having a human experience together.*

Two hours passed without a response to my grand revelations. Interestingly, the trigger scale jumped to a five, all on its own. So far, he hadn't said much of anything in the conversation. I was operating on a lifetime of experience that was painting every punctuation and each perceived slight. I know that a possibility exists where he hadn't left me on read; he just hadn't had the opportunity to reply. As I waited, I thought of the times he had rolled his eyes as I explained something I found interesting. I pictured the times he would get up and walk away while I was talking on our family zoom nights. I felt relatively confident that the silence I was now getting was based on his disinterest in what I was saying. What made it worse was that I had deviated so far away from what I wanted to say in an effort to lighten the mood and catch his interest. He was now ignoring me, and I wasn't even saying what I wanted to say. It was time to get it over with and rip the band-aid off.

# PART 4: ADVANCE THROUGH THE PROGRAM

Our conversation continued via text messaging. I was ready to tell him everything I needed to say, and it didn't matter if he ignored me again. If he wasn't curious about what I had written, then he forfeits the right to critique what I have to say. You can lead a horse to your book, but you can't make him read it.

*Shadow work consists of thinking back on times in your life when you needed support but didn't get it (or in the way you wanted it). Imagine going back, knowing what you know now, what would you have done or said to your younger self*

*Those critical moments shape our fears, self-doubt, shame, regrets, etc. By reliving them and acknowledging them, you can heal past wounds and move on.*

*There are a lot of things that came up about our relationship that I've asked to talk with you about in the past, but it never worked out. I kept going anyway*

*I compiled it all into a book. It's my journey through addiction to drugs and alcohol and how I overcame them both, and what I learned from it*

I waited another fifteen minutes for a reply, now swimming in the chaos of admitting the book, partially airing my confessions, and being left to sit in the swarm of anxiety and depressive thoughts. Since I had done much of the work alone, I assumed he'd never respect it, so I would have to justify my work's validity by bringing in a professional source.

*I have a friend that is a licensed
family therapist who is reading the
book and discussing it with me.*

Another hour passed with no reply, and I was ready to give up when he finally replied.

*I look forward to talking about
it once you've advanced further
through your therapy.*

The needle on my trigger scale almost broke as it slammed into the tenth mark. Not only had he completely glossed over everything I had said, but he was now dismissing it all. He was deferring the conversation to another time when I had "advanced further" through my therapy. I was well aware of how his sliding scales worked, and I knew that once I had "advanced," I would always need a little more work before he would be willing to talk.

*Haha, but not until then?*

*Shouldn't you advance through
the program to a more complete
understanding and then seek out
conversations?*

*Growth is a lifelong process
and there should be many
conversations. That also assumes
that I'm in therapy because of
things I don't understand.*

*Or that I'm in therapy because I
have a problem*

I waited for ten more minutes. My anxiety was too high to wait for a reply.

*I overcame my addiction over ten
years ago and have since been
working toward learning better
coping mechanisms and skills.*

*Reading, talking to professionals,
and doing my own writing to explore
triggers. I understand very well how
things mom did have manifested
themselves into my insecurities.
I'm now great at my job, a good
husband, and a kick-ass dad.
Therapy isn't a sign of weakness,
but of strength and a willingness
to improve. I've come a long way in
the program.*

I thought relating any of this to his impact on me would only put him on the defensive. Linking it to our shared experience with our mom might open the door to him being more willing to accept the conversation I wanted to have. My triggers showed as I tried to defend my journey through therapy. My only regret was letting my pettiness also show by throwing the vagueness of some unknown "program" back at him. I waited for thirty minutes for another response before I decided I would say my piece and move on. It was time to do what I had come here to do.

*I've looked up to you my entire life,
but you're always so critical of me
or my past. Lots of mean-teasing that
I internalize and feel bad about.
It's a trigger for me.*

*I don't need your praise, but I do
want you to know that your opinion
of me matters a great deal, and
when you put me down, even in the
slightest way, it really affects me.
Please be conscious of that when
we're together.*

He replied immediately.

*When do I put you down? You
mean when ninety-five percent of
our time together you're calling me*

*ugly, make fun of my walk, tell me*
*no one likes me because of my*
*personality. You and I have two*
*very different views of things.*

This came as a welcomed surprise to me. I wished it was a breakthrough and not a simple deflection. Regardless, I learned a great deal from his response. I hope I've not represented myself as some innocent victim being mistreated by his family as I blindly stumble, unguided, through life. In actuality, I've attempted to show how flawed I am and how I've spent a lifetime coping poorly with things.

When my brother is critical of others, I've seen some people shy away and curl like a pill bug while others dismiss him outright. On the other hand, I've been known to fight back with him. The longer it has gone on, and the angrier I get with him, the more I fight on behalf of those who allow him to go unchecked at their own peril. When he makes fun of our stepbrother, I'll reply with how that seems to be particularly harsh criticism from someone who looks exactly like Steve Buscemi.

We have all been hard on each other for so long that the wounds are now deep and intertwined. It has become too hard to establish who started it or does it more. In the end, none of that even matters anyway. From my perspective, he doesn't like how I treat him after he mistreats me. If he truly feels the same about me, I'm open to ending that cycle and moving on without spending any time establishing who needs to say sorry. The problem isn't that we are talking about it now; it's that we haven't talked about it yet. None of this would be nearly as difficult to discuss if we had talked about it on day one, in the moment. A new process that I hope we can adopt moving forward. In my defense, I know he only said this out of evasiveness. I may be willing to change my behavior, and I'm happy to discuss any wrongs I have committed, but I know he was deflecting because he didn't want to acknowledge what I said.

*I'm sure we do have a different*
*view of things if we don't talk*
*about it. That's why you don't wait to*
*have those conversations.*

*I do retaliate and try to hang in there. I realized I do it to my wife, too. Just like I see you do it to Rene. Last time I talked to you, you said she looked like the drummer from Twisted Sister when she tries to look nice. When I mean-teased my wife, she said, "Hey, stop that. I don't like it." And I thought, wow, I never considered just asking you to stop.*

*When we were vacationing in the bay, you called Rene a stupid bitch in front of the kids because she had to run back into the house to grab something when we were leaving. I think sometimes you're teasing, but then sometimes it goes way too far. I've fought fire with fire. I don't want to anymore. I don't like doing it and don't like hearing it. If you feel I'm bad to you, I'm sorry.*

# Part 5: The Triad

I waited a month for a response from Shannon, but one never came. I didn't need to give him examples of what he had said to me because I had written an entire book about it. I don't remember telling him that nobody liked him because of his personality, but I can see myself telling him at some point that he was too critical of people or that he was mean to someone. I regret giving him the example of the time he yelled at his wife in front of all of us, something that sat uncomfortably with me for a long time. It has always been more upsetting to me when I see him do it to others than when he's just doing it to me. A part of me feels like I need to stick up for her, even if it's not my responsibility. If I was attempting to gain his support, I should have kept the conversation just about us.

I didn't tell him that I called Rene to apologize for him after that vacation. When I told her some of the things he had done to me to relate my experience to her, she also apologized for him. When I tell you about him, you also apologize. Everyone he surrounds himself with supports him unconditionally and apologizes on his behalf. I've never once heard him apologize for himself or show any appreciation for the love he is embraced with consistently. I don't know if it is an inability to see or an unwillingness to feel.

I recognize that I probably expect far too much from my brother. He didn't volunteer to be my brother or the person I would idolize. He didn't ask for the power to influence my life so absolutely. I may view him as a father-like figure, but I am not his responsibility. You can't change people; you can only change your expectations of them. I again found myself returning to the concept of setting expectations.

I have always felt that my family's expectations of me were unfair. Those expectations made me feel like I wasn't good enough, which contributed to my developing a personality dysmorphia that I struggle with to this day. Half the battle of working through my addiction has been managing my family's expectations of me, and the other half has been me realizing that I do the same thing to them.

Is it possible my brother is hard on me because he feels inadequate compared to the pedestal I put him on? My near-worship of him has put him on a path of excellence he could never truly obtain, and it has manifested in him a sense of anxiety and insecurity. Pushing me away with his mean-teasing keeps me at arm's length in a subconscious attempt to break my unfair expectations of him. Maybe my feeling of inadequacy that I see in his eyes comes from my failure to live up to the excellence he feels I'm capable of achieving. A sibling rivalry that our self-doubts and mutual admiration have made increasingly complicated to the point we are today.

I have gotten used to the feeling that I perceive the world differently than most people. I can't differentiate pitch, but it hasn't prevented me from playing or writing music. When I'm recording, I feel satisfied with the final product, thinking everything sounds perfect. My ear isn't good enough to hear when I'm slightly off key or, depending on whom you ask, way off key. Watching someone cringe as they listen to the mistakes I recorded is always embarrassing, especially when I can't hear what I did wrong.

I pushed through the awkwardness and kept making art, but the more my music was rejected, the less it became something that helped me cope. My art would eventually trigger me, stressed by my own coping mechanisms. My perception of life is a lens painted with mixed emotions and painful experiences. I am proud of the music I make, but I'm also too self-conscious to share it because the world doesn't hear it the same as I do. That warped lens influenced my relationship with my family, friends, and coworkers.

No matter how successful I am, I will always have imposter syndrome fed by a fear that even when I'm doing well, I assume everyone else only sees my mistakes. I try to improve and push myself harder every day, but I eventually collapse under self-inflicted stress. I'll never fully recover until I learn to be okay with imperfection and realize I don't have to be the best at anything. Our failures are sometimes our greatest gifts if we're dedicated to learning.

I feel like I've worked so hard and come such a long way in understanding the circumstances that have made me the way I am, but as I conclude my story, I can't help but feel as though nothing has changed. You don't understand my addiction any better than before, my mom is gone again, and things have only gotten more awkward with my brother. Luckily, the experience hasn't been a complete waste of time. I now have a rough road map to guide me through the next chapters of my life, the ones I'm currently writing with my wife and kids. I've also learned more about myself. I have a better grasp on how my brain works, and I've developed new ways to cope with my triggers. I'm better for having written this book.

I've learned that one must be cautious with the expectations we set for our family and the unspoken expectations we subconsciously have of them. Regardless of whether we use caution, those expectations can be damaging if we don't communicate effectively and consistently. Still, with fair expectations and excellent communication, the weight of life and unexpected misfortune can derail even the closest bonds between families. Ultimately, the family must support and forgive each other unconditionally along the way.

Mistakes happen, but we also make the wrong choices intentionally from time to time. It's okay when we don't always understand, communicate effectively, or support each other. As long as we don't fail on all fronts and take the time to correct, relationship strength can fluctuate while remaining intact. I've begun to focus on three pillars of action that I imagine work in unison to hold a family together and form a relationship triad. The three points of the triad are understanding, communication, and support.

Like a three-legged stool, the triad can only support the weight of any relationship when all three pillars are actively working together. The stool becomes wobbly when the pillars are uneven, but the relationship can still survive. If any one or more of the legs are missing entirely, the triad cannot sustain the connection, and the structure falls apart.

The triad philosophy can be applied to any relationship singularly between two people or viewed as a guiding mantra within groups of people, like teams and families. A fully activated triad creates the highest level of intimacy attainable in a relationship. This activation level is often reserved for romantic partners, families, best friends, and in situations where teams are required to be highly cohesive.

Lower activation levels are achieved by activating at least one pillar of the triad. These relationships are easier to maintain but prevent the participants from achieving higher levels of intimate connection. Most of our relationships exist within this activation realm, and the entropy of relationships naturally deactivates any linkages operating at a higher plane than this. Maintaining a fully activated triad requires constant upkeep and diligent participation from all parties.

A growing and developing child requires a fully activated triad to feel safe and to reach their full potential. The advantage of using the triad philosophy within family relationships is that a family can act as a single unit. Considering that individual pillars of the triad are easier to sustain than all three, each family member can serve as the key contributor to a particular point within the triad. A family unit can provide that child with everything they need to reach self-actualization by working together. This was true of our family early in my childhood, and my needs were satisfied. Our family's triad was maintained by an intricate network of relationships. I was supported by you, felt understood by my cousins, and I could communicate with my mother. When you and I moved after the divorce, I lost that network, and the triad became your sole responsibility to maintain. Like all things in the universe, our family moved from order to disorder. I eventually compensated for the imbalance with drugs and alcohol, like a sugar packet stuffed under the leg of a wobbly stool.

The first pillar of the triad is understanding, which includes learning about each other and showing interest in one another. Setting realistic expectations of each other without first understanding our personalities, capabilities, and motivations is impossible. To understand each other, we must use the second pillar of the triad, communication.

Communication involves checking in with each other, learning by listening, and having difficult conversations when they're necessary. These two pillars are connected to one another and create synergy as they are both improved by one another. For example, we fail to communicate effectively when we misunderstand each other. Issues arise when we set unfair expectations or say things we don't mean when we're angry.

As we learn and grow together, one should expect that we will miscommunicate or misunderstand each other from time to time. We can work through the discomfort by using the triad's final pillar, support. Nobody comes out ahead when we get caught up tallying who started what, pointing fingers, and name-calling. A functioning family must allow themselves to be vulnerable with each other and forgive. Setting boundaries and holding each other accountable are the uncomfortable but necessary linkages that triangulate support, understanding, and communication. A family functions best when all three are firing together.

Since the divorce, our family has attempted to function exclusively on support, devoid of understanding and communication. I feel closest to you because you have always supported me unconditionally and did your best to maintain the rest of the triad. I wrote this book to help bridge the gap I perceive between our understanding and communication.

The relationship I have with my brother is consistently getting worse the longer we misunderstand each other, talk without listening, and as we allow a trivial sibling rivalry to keep us from supporting each other. My mother cut all communication with us years ago, we both refused to understand each other's perspective, and the support withered away with time. Without any active triad feature, she ceased to be a part of this family. I believe that it is never too late for a family to be revived by implementing the triad, but these connections cannot be sustained by any one person alone. The sides of the triangle that connect each point are two-way roads that require both parties to participate. The triad cannot be forced, for it is merely a tool that can only be used by someone who wants to build a stronger relationship.

When I first put pen to paper as this story materialized, I thought I had to convince you to use that tool. I was under the impression that I needed our triad to be fully activated if I was ever going to be free of my alcohol dependence. I didn't know I possessed the strength to form my own triads to support myself. It wasn't until I had developed that bond with my wife that I realized I could feel whole again. My relationship with you and Shannon could improve because I didn't rely on you both to complete my support system. I could be satisfied with what you each do well as key contributors to the network I had rebuilt. I didn't have to change you; I could just change my expectations. I was relying so heavily on you to help me meet Maslow's hierarchy of needs that I didn't think I could reach self-actualization without you. I could only relax my expectations of you and Shannon once my wife had instilled in me a sense of love and belonging. I couldn't reach esteem and overcome my shadow until I learned to respect myself as a strong father. My goal now is to raise my children in a vast network of powerful connections they can rely on and teach them how to build on that network with the relationships they forge on their own so that they may also reach self-actualization.

# PART 6: JOY JAR

I can see this book coming off as overly dramatic and unfairly critical. You and Shannon have the type of personalities to think of my complaints written within these pages as too sensitive. I'm not sure I would even disagree with you. I have excelled in the arts because of my sensitivity, and you can never be too sensitive in the art world. That highlights our most notable difference; we don't value the same aspects of personality.

My greatest gift felt like a hindrance, and I never entirely belonged with you and Shannon because of it. Unfortunately, in my pursuit of making you proud, I worked my way into a career that went against my personality grain. I excelled in that career field, but my health began to decline as I became overburdened by the stress of living a life better suited to someone else's strengths.

Allow me to better illustrate my experience by asking you this; have you ever cried listening to instrumental music? By just listening to a drummer and a bassist backing a muted trumpet, I can be moved to tears. The notes of a melody, harmonizing in just the right way, will send chills up my spine, and my skin will ripple with goosebumps. The sound produces an emotional tsunami of feelings within me, and tears will fall from my cheeks. In my world, the ease with which I can be moved by subtle vibrations in the air is what makes me unique. That same gift became debilitating when I joined the management team in my new career.

Making you proud had always been my ultimate goal, and that anxiety guided me through college. It influenced my work relationships and encouraged me to take on more responsibilities in my career. Now, making you proud was all I could think about as I walked to the manager's interview. There were four people on the panel, and they would decide whether or not I would manage the diagnostic laboratories. In my gut, I knew I was too green in the career to take on such a responsibility, but my pride wanted to be able to brag about getting that position anyway. I sat at the end of a long table, and my ears buzzed from the nerves. I answered their questions well and felt like I was making a good impression until they asked me why I wanted the position. I took the long road to answering them.

I told them about growing up with you as a single father when we moved to Texas. I described how you always worked late and were stressed when you came home. I was frustrated with it as a kid and had difficulty understanding why you worked that way. Then I told them how we moved around a lot and that I had been to several of your going away parties.

At every one of those parties, I had a line of people who wanted to shake my hand and tell me how much you meant to them. They thanked me for sharing my time with you so that you could help them. I was always impressed to hear how many lives you had touched, and it gave me enormous respect for what you did and why you were home late so often. I was in the process of telling the panel that I hoped someone would say the same things to my children someday when I got too choked up to continue talking in what was the most important interview of my life. I was lucky that my tears came off as endearing, and they hired me, but my boss made sure to keep a box of tissues in my office and reminded me about it often.

One of my first responsibilities as department supervisor was to fire an old lady who was extraordinarily bad at her job. I was convinced I could help her, but I wasted six months banging my head against a brick wall and had to let her go. That emotional tsunami I get from music was nothing compared to what I felt when I saw her face as I sat her down with human resources. She packed her things while I puked in the bathroom.

I ran back and forth from that bathroom, stress-puking, for three years as I attempted to fit my too-sensitive personality into the rigid structure of management that I thought I was required to inhabit to make you proud. One of the many advantages of writing this book has been realizing that there was never a connection between my stress level and your acceptance. Making you proud wasn't a problem I could solve by working myself to death. I had pressured myself into a situation where I was becoming old and tired, despite my reluctance to do so.

I found there was more attention paid to what I did poorly than what I did well. With greatness as the expectation, there was no celebration after reaching the summit. When working that hard didn't get the payoff of making either of you any more or less proud, I reevaluated my intentions. I wanted my children to be proud of me, and my shadow was quick to insist that I had to be the boss. If I were simply a bench scientist, my kids would be embarrassed to introduce me at career day. The familiar feeling of creeping darkness tickled the hairs on the back of my neck.

I sat quietly in my office with the door closed. The walls were adorned with family photos and drawings the kids had scribbled for me. "This office will be the hardest part to let go of if I quit my job," I thought to myself. It had become the only safe space I could escape to when work was too stressful. I grabbed a decorated Mason jar from its spot on the bookshelf. For father's day, Daphne had created what she called a "joy jar" and filled it with lovely notes from the kids. I started pulling them out, one by one.

The first one I grabbed was a long strip of paper from Jade. On one side, it had scribbles that looked vaguely like an alligator eating the letter "H." I flipped it over and saw he had drawn six skateboards. Jade was my three-year-old mini-me. We looked nearly identical at the same age and shared the same interests. He was already obsessed with skateboards and loved playing the drums. I get choked up whenever he tells people I am his favorite skater. I placed the note to the side and randomly grabbed another from the jar.

*"My favorite place to go with you is* **THE PARK!***"*

*Love, Pepper*

The note was cut into a similar rectangular shape. Pepper had covered one side with patterned tape. On the other side, Daphne had written down what Pepper said. I instantly wanted to leave work to go play with them. I grabbed another note.

*W*ESHOULD PLAY *PLA*Y*D*O*H TOGETHER PEPPER*

The letters were messy and smooshed together, but I admired how well it was written for a five-year-old. Daphne had clearly helped her spell, but Pepper had definitely written this one. I was already smiling ear to ear. I pulled more notes out.

*A joke to make you laugh: "Why did you fart? ...*
*Because I'm a tart!"*

*Love, Pepper*

*"You're a sweet dad, and I'll love you forever.
That's why we're making all these great gifts for you."*

*Love, Pepper*


*"This is a picture of someone that is skating, but he's invisible,
so he can't see you."*

*Jade*


*"When you get HOME, I want to give you a hug and
tell you I LOVE you."*

*Love, Pepper*


*"I remember playing on the piano and DRUMS with you,
and that is super fun!"*

*Love, Jade*


*"I love you DADDY"*

*Pepper*

I placed the notes back into the joy jar and unplugged my laptop from my desk computer. I walked into my boss's office and thanked her for the opportunities she had given me. I told her my joy jar didn't have anything about management in it and that I would rather be someone's favorite skater. I quit my job and returned to being a regular old bench scientist who was just the right amount of sensitive with plenty of energy for his kids when he got home.

This book already feels as if it has served its purpose for me. I feel like an enormous weight has been lifted from my shoulders without having to give it to you. In fact, I've decided I don't want to share it with you at all. If you or Shannon misunderstood my intentions, this book would destroy our relationships rather than enhance them. Still, as I hold the manuscript in my hand, I feel I have written something that could serve a similar purpose for someone else like me. I wish I had read this book in my deepest depression or before I wasted another paycheck on alcohol.

After speaking with each of you before publishing, I was amazed to find that all three of you responded similarly. The initial reaction was one of genuine interest that quickly dissolved into suspicion as you realized I had not only held you partially responsible for my addiction but that I had also written it all down in detail. After the initial defensiveness, each of you attempted to dismiss it. My mom resorted to lying about the experience or stretching the truth. My brother played the "you started it" card from our childhood, and you just assumed I had dreamt it all in the basement of a metaphorical opium den. The final stage of each discussion, however, was the most eye-opening.

As I attempted to activate the communication portion of the triad, it would quickly lose steam and die off again. Each conversation I had, ended after the dismissal, and we never approached the subject again. I was disappointed each time, but it helped me understand myself more fully, and it helped me feel more prepared to serve my new growing family better. I hope that if any of you ever find this book, you'll get to the end and understand what I tried to do with it without taking offense. I hope it inspires you to explore the relationships in your life and seek to improve them. I hope it changes your perception of addiction and helps you find patience for growth. I hope you decide, as I have, to treat your family, both new and old, with the guiding mantra that summarizes all that I have learned from writing this book:

———

Create a safe place for communication
and never, ever stop trying to understand
and support each other.

———

# Aphantasia: Chapter 11

"That's it," I said as I closed the manuscript.

Ruby took the book from my hands. I had been working with her for three months. I had first walked into her office hoping to start regression therapy, but I was struggling with hypnosis. The first few times we tried, I just fell asleep. We had instead started reading through the book together and were now at the end. "How do you feel?" she asked.

I looked away from her and stared at the ceiling. She had asked me this question a thousand times during our past sessions, but I wanted to give it more thought this time. The process of writing the book hadn't fixed everything with my family as I thought it might. While it had vastly improved some of my relationships, it had put additional stress on others. I wasn't sure what I felt yet. "It's complicated," I said.

"How so?" she asked, urging me to continue with a wave of her hand.

Taking more time, I looked around the room. Ruby's office was always dimly lit with stained glass lamps and various candles. The smell of old fabric and menthol cigarettes hung in the air. I briefly met eyes with her again and then sat forward while resting my elbows on my knees. "I'm glad I wrote it. This process has been good for me, but I'm scared to share it with my family."

She slowly nodded and asked, "What are you afraid of?"

"I'm afraid they're going to be mad about it. They won't understand what I was trying to do, and I'm scared they'll write me off." I sat back in my chair and tried to relax, but my foot bounced to a nonexistent beat.

"Let's talk about that." Ruby placed the manuscript on the table and then folded one leg under herself to sit on her foot. Decorative pillows covered her couch in floral prints that didn't match. "What would your brother think about the book?"

A surge of anxiety coated my stomach in acid. "I think he would be pissed about it."

"Do you think he would disagree with how you described him?"

"Well, yeah," I chuckled. "I tried to be mindful of what I shared in this book. Every personal detail I decided to share, I made sure it served the purpose of explaining how I got to where I am. I wasn't trying to be persuasive about my brother being a bad guy. I don't even think he is. It's just that this book is mostly about negative events in my life. It's not a representation of who he is; it's about me. His greatest attributes were irrelevant to the particular story I wanted to tell."

"You don't think he'd recognize that?" Ruby asked.

"Absolutely not. I think he'd get upset within the first critical sentence and then slam the book shut. I don't even think morbid curiosity could get him to read the thing. He would see it as a hit piece and write me off." I crossed my arms and recognized the trigger that Ruby and I had been working on.

It must have been evident that I was getting upset. She put both feet back on the floor and then softened her voice, "What do you think *his* book would look like? Whom would your character be if he wrote a story about you?"

I smiled. I liked Ruby's questions. So much of our journey together had been about understanding perception. While I had attempted to write my story from the different perceptions of each member of my family, it was still my perspective of their experience. When I first started writing my book, I wasn't even the main character in my own story. It took four years of introspection to begin humoring the idea that I wasn't an extra in someone else's life.

I spun the ring on my finger while I thought about how best to respond to Ruby's questions. It suddenly occurred to me, "I wouldn't like the character he would make about me because he would likely be describing my shadow self, and that's why I get triggered by him so easily."

Ruby leaned forward, "Explain."

"I don't know how he actually sees me. I could be wrong about how he feels about me. What I've learned during this process is that my anxiety comes from how I think he perceives me. I get triggered when I read into his actions, no matter how benign they are. He has a way of highlighting my insecurities." I stood up and started pacing. I had improved my ability to tap into this zone where I could untangle my thoughts and self-reflect. "I feel like he only sees my worst qualities. I feel like the character he would write about me would be my shadow."

Ruby looked contemplative. "I thought you were at peace with your shadow."

"I am, but I guess the question now is whether or not I'm at peace with others seeing my shadow." I stopped pacing and stroked my chin.

"What do you think? Are you comfortable with him seeing you that way?"

I looked at Ruby without answering and studied her facial expression. She looked curious but also had a mischievous glint in her eyes. As I continued pacing, I said, "Yes. I think I've always been at peace with my shadow. The relief I gained from writing this book was my coming to peace with how my family sees that shadow. My guilt and shame were more about letting them down than it was about me being disappointed in myself. I thought writing this would help them understand that side of me. I realize now that I don't need them to accept me. I am worthy of their love and admiration. It's their loss if they don't want to know this side of me."

"Then I ask you again, why are you afraid to share the book with them?" The mischievous glint was now an aura of delight.

"I have written a book likely describing what my brother sees as his shadow. Reading this would be triggering for him, and I don't think he's ready to be that introspective." I sat down again across from Ruby. "This process served its purpose for me. It wouldn't have any positive impact on him. I won't improve our relationship by sharing this book with him. I can only improve it by acting on what I've learned from writing it."

She made a few notes on her pad and then looked up at me. "What about your dad?"

"He's different. I don't think he would be mad, but he wouldn't be interested, either. I think he would be disappointed in me. It would only hurt his feelings, and he wouldn't see the purpose in my writing it. It would do the opposite of what I set out to do. What's the point in putting either of us through that?"

"What if you're wrong?" Ruby asked.

"Getting this story off my chest has been liberating. I'm no longer ashamed of my past or stressed about future interactions with my family. I feel like I have the tools to handle my triggers when they come, and I can focus on enjoying my dad for what he does well. I was always so frustrated with his unwavering consistency, but I'd not be where I am today without him. He's retiring this month. Did I tell you about that?" I sat back with one leg crossed over the other at the knee.

"No, you didn't," Ruby said as she interlocked her fingers and relaxed her posture.

"Yeah, forty years. He got a job as a teenager when my mom got pregnant with Shannon. He has been with the same company longer than I've been alive. You want to know the craziest part?" I waited for her reply.

"What?" she asked, humoring me.

"He hated that job for all forty of those years." I raised my eyebrows and shrugged my shoulders. "This dude has the ability to put the entire world on his back and just chip away with his head down. He slowly carved out a life for us from scratch. He has been the only constant in my life. I don't want him to read this story because he will misunderstand. I battled my demons, and I'm in a better place. I thought I wrote this as a letter to him. I agonized about sharing it with him. I only recently realized I had to write this for myself, and I couldn't have done it alone. I had to write it to him because he is my rock. By writing it to him, I could feel safe exploring my trauma. He already did his part by raising me with unconditional support. This book has served its purpose without him having to read it. Now it's my turn to support him. I need to show my appreciation and let my kids fall in love with him as much as I have."

Ruby smiled, "I like that, Denver. How about your mom?"

"Nope. That ship has sailed."

"Would she be upset?" Ruby opened her notebook again.

"The only guarantee I've ever had from her is that she'll be upset." I shook my head and looked away. A small ceramic building on the bookshelf caught my eye. "Is that a David Winter cottage?

Confused, Ruby looked across the room and then answered, "Yes..."

"My mom collected those. They always remind me of her. They're so cute. I see them around Christmas every year. They're always displayed in a group like a nice, tiny little town. At first glance, they seem so charming, but when you get closer, you can see that the snow is fake and there's a hidden rat in each one." I looked back at Ruby,

"I can't trust her anymore. I think we're both better off without each other."

"I see." Ruby wrote a few more things on her pad. "I think we should keep working on those feelings. Are you ready to try regression again?"

"We can try," I said as I relaxed into the couch and grabbed my eye mask. Hypnosis felt impossible for me. On one of our first sessions together, we had established that I was basically hopeless. She told me to imagine walking down a hallway with several doors. Each door held a different memory from my childhood. I was supposed to be able to walk down the hallway in my mind. I could pick the rooms that stood out to me, and then we'd explore all the memories they potentially held.

I tried to imagine the hallway, but Ruby was asking for details I couldn't visualize. She would ask about the pattern on the carpet or the room numbers. I could tell she was getting frustrated with my inability to describe what I was supposed to be seeing.

"Ruby, I don't actually see anything. I'm not hypnotized yet," I said.

"You're not supposed to be hypnotized yet. I just want you to picture it in your mind." We had been over this several times.

"I see nothing but blackness. I know what a hallway looks like. I could draw one for you, but I don't actually see anything. It's hard for me to tell you what the carpet looks like without just making it up. Do you want me to make it up?" I asked.

"Denver! I think you might have Aphantasia." Ruby went on to explain that a small percentage of people are unable to picture images in their minds. We were both equally stunned. She couldn't wrap her mind around how I was able to paint and draw without seeing anything in my mind's eye. I was frustrated that my college classmates could see their notes in their heads. It felt like they were cheating.

Ruby had the ability to see my past lives for me and told me about my most recent lifetime. I found it entertaining, and I was curious to hear more, but I was too skeptical about it to find it helpful. I was fascinated by the concept that our purpose in this life is to learn. We are all returning to this world, life after life, in the pursuit of discovering the meaning of each of those lives. I found comfort in getting another chance to try it again in the event that we failed to reach that goal in this life. It was a guiding philosophy that inspired me to seek answers without the stress of running out of time in death. Ruby thought I might be holding onto stress from my childhood, but she also thought I might be holding onto something from a past life.

I was open-minded enough to try regression, but not because I believed in previous lives. I think Ruby just had an uncanny ability to reach the zone between wakeful consciousness and lucid dreaming. Everything she could access in that meditative state was nothing more than colorful interpretations of what her brain did while daydreaming. Still, she was able to perceive unexplainable things, and she seemed magical.

Her visions of my past lives said more about her than they did about me. I would always be skeptical until I could see it for myself. I wanted to analyze my visions like a weird dream, but I could never see anything. No matter how hard I tried. I briefly considered taking hallucinogens, but I was committed to maintaining my sobriety.

I was now lying on Ruby's couch again, focusing on my breathing while staring into the void that is my mind's eye. She took my inability to visualize as a challenge and brought a few new tools to try for today's session. We started by thinking about the most comfortable part of my body. My knees ached, and my hands felt awkward resting by my side, but my shoulders were relaxed. Ruby told me to concentrate on that level of comfort and to let the feeling spread across my body. Suddenly I heard the long droning tone of a single metallic note.

Ruby explained that she wanted me to forget about seeing with my eyes. My connection with music would be the path to hypnosis. I would instead visualize with my ears. She could produce a warm ringing sound by running a small mallet around the side of a large metal bowl. I focused my mind on the sound. Before long, I could sense the circular motion she was making. As I continued to relax, I felt my consciousness leave my head, and I was now on the other side of the room where the sound was coming from. I was also shocked to find that I could now "see" the bowl.

Instead of the low couch I had laid on, I felt like I was standing behind Ruby, watching her generate the sound. My mind was drawn to the sound, and I admired the decorative markings covering the outside of the bowl. I felt like I was dreaming, but I was wide awake and able to talk to Ruby from my body on the other end of the room. When I looked up from the bowl, she was gone, and I was no longer in her office.

I could see my younger self sitting on the floor of my childhood bedroom. I was crying, but I wasn't sure why. I didn't seem physically hurt. I had my head between my knees with my arms wrapped around my shins. I was about to call out to myself when the door suddenly opened, and my mother walked in. She was young and looked exactly how I remembered her from that time. Her hair smelled of excessive hairspray, and her bangs combined to make one long curl across her forehead. She walked over and sat on the floor next to my younger self. Without saying anything, she put one arm around my shoulders and rested her head against mine. She closed her eyes and squeezed me tight. We gently rocked from side to side together to the tempo of the singing bowl.

I slowly approached, not wanting to disturb them. I sat next to my mom and placed my hand on her shoulder. I was startled by her reaction to my touch. I had assumed they couldn't see or hear me. She put her right arm around me while still holding my inner child in her left. She squeezed us both tightly as we listened to the warm spinning sound that had brought us together again.